AF522554

DISASTER MANAGEMENT:
AN ANALYSIS

DISASTER MANAGEMENT : AN ANALYSIS

Dr. Virendra Singh Yadav

Associate

Indian Institute of Advanced Study

Rashtrapati Nivas, Shimla (H.P.)

OMEGA PUBLICATIONS

NEW DELHI 110002 (INDIA)

OMEGA PUBLICATIONS
4378/4B, G4, JMD House, Murari Lal Street,
Ansari Road, Daryaganj, New Delhi-110 002
Phone: 23278062, 65901906
e-mail: omega_publications@yahoo.com

Head Office :
79/23, Laxmi Garden,
Near Satya Jyoti School,
Gurgaon (Haryana)

Disaster Management : An Analysis

First Published, 2011

ISBN-978-81-8455-281-2

PRINTED IN INDIA

Printed at Tarun Offset Printers, Delhi - 110053

Dedicated to

Common Men of our Country

who are main

victims of Disasters

Editorial............

India has been badly affected from natural disasters such as flood, drought, cyclones, landslide, tsunami etc. due to its geographical diversity. The situations arising out of India's geo climatic patterns and population explosion make it the most disaster prone area of the world. More than sixty percent of its land is prone to landslides. Its forty million hectare area is prone to floods; sixty eight percent is prone to drought. According to Government of India's records, every year 750 million hectare land and two to ten thousand lives get affected from flood. Fifty nine percent land of India is prone to earth quake. More than twenty five thousand persons were died into earth quakes. Fire, floods, cloud burst, etc. are some other major natural disasters occurring in India, but sorry to say that the record of the deaths caused by these disasters has not been maintained till now.

We are living in a densely populated country. Natural disasters occur in a short span of time here. this is absolutely true that man can not stop the natural disasters, but if we get timely information about these disasters and skillfully manage it, we can only control the loss of lives and money as well. Every disaster gives some warning before it happens, but perhaps we don't give ears to it. We forget that precaution is the best cure. Government publicise this slogan all over India, but it is the government which don't follow it.

On 31st December, 2004 fifth world disaster training congress was organized in Delhi, in which commissioner of Zambia Dr. S.K. Balu Vita suggested that for better disaster management, there should be a traning programme for beaurocrats, scientists and teachers. Director General of Afro- Asian disaster control society Dr. Priyaranjan Trivedi presented a disaster awareness and control work plan for all 602 districts of India. This congress was jointly organized by Indian Institute of disaster control, World Institutional development programme and Sikkim Manipal University.

In India there are some rules and regulations to curb the menace of natural disasters. Indian government had started disaster management programme much earlier in 1954, but this programme was legalized in 2005. On 9th January, 2005 Government decided to form a National disaster management authority so that the affect of Tsunami type of disasters could be marginalised. It was also decided that indiamust know disasters of orechand to become the member of the International monitoring system. Union Agriculture minister Shri Sharad Pawar made 97 suggestions, of which 64 suggestions were accepted by the government. Disaster management bill was passed by the parliament on 9thJanuary, 2005. After this, National disaster management authority was duly formed. This authority is responsible for disaster management, reconstruction, rehabilitation after disaster takes place. It makes a central plan, implements this plan and coordinates and monitors it as well. Besides these duties, it develops new strategies to control the disasters, gives necessary training to the people, implements development programmes and tries to make the effect of disaters to its toe. This authority co-ordinates among various government departments, organizes training programmes for their employees and takes some concrete steps to overcome disasters. After occurring of disaster, it tries to go into the reasons for that disaster by a goroup of experts and takes some precautionary measures for the future.

Keeping in view of the above mentioned facts, an integrated national disaster management structure has been developed. Disaster management act 2005, which came into effect in 2006, suggests a detailed legitimate and institutional body for effective management of natural disasters. According to the provisions of the act, a national disaster management authority has been formed. Prime minister is the president of this body. It also has one Vice president and five mebers. According to this act state level state disaster management authorities had also been formed. This authority has been formed in 18 states and union territories till now. Chief Ministers of the states are the president of these authorities and persons nominated by chief Minister would be the member of these authorities. Main duty of state authority would be to make state level policies for effective management of disasters and to implement state plannings according to the instructions of national disaster management authority.

In India several steps has been taken for the effective management of disasters. Natural disaster area denoting maps have been prepared and micro area denoting maps for a specific area are also being prepared. For this, sensing and geological information technology based advanced technology is being used. Geological, climatic, hydrological, land use related and green belt as well as population related socio-economic data is being integrated with geo-information technology. Under this, flood and cyclones related research work has been carried out.Local level hazards are being calculated and on the basis of this data bank government is under taking some projects and some projects are being prepared. UNDP had organized national disaster loss management programme (2002-2007) in 169 districts of 17 states. This programme was meant for the socio-economical development of disaster hit people and to rehabilitate them from disaster affected area to a safer place. A similar drought relief management programme (1997-2002) was meant for 42 drought affected areas of five states, namely- Rajasthan, Chhattisgarh, Orissa, Gujarat and Andhra Pradesh. National earth quake relief programme, National cyclone relief programme, Landslide programme and National flood disaster management programme are some other major programmes organized by the union government of India.

It is imposasible to avoid natural disasters, but we can control and minimize the loss by systematic planning and management. In India, floods are the worst and frequently occurring natural disaster. Out of 329 million hectare, 40 million hectare area of India is flood prone. Home ministry of Government of India had launched a National disaster loss management Programme for flood prone states of the country. This programme has three phases. First phase is to be conducted in 2008-2010, second phase in 2010-2012 and third would be conducted in 2012-2015. When all these phases will be conducted successfully, it would be possible to manage flood control effectively. Under this programme, many work plans have been started at state, districts, tehsils, blocks and villages. In these plans a large number of people would be trained for flood management. At present, cabinet secretary, home ministry, chief ministers in states, national disaster management department and army are part of this work plan. They are co ordinating with each other to get the effective results, but besides all this exercise, the situation of disaster management is not satisfactory. Whenever natural disasters occur we could see the mismanagement and non co operation among various chains of the government. In terms of media, we can say it 'Administrative hang over' and in terms of judiciary we would call it 'criminal neglizance'

History of the country shows that disasters occur in India in regular intervals, but we don't learn lessons from these mishaps. Every time we only conduct relief work and after some time, we forget it and perhaps wait for another disaster. That is why we are the worst sufferer of natural disasters such as- floods, drought, cyclone, earthquake, landslide, tsunami etc. we also suffer from man generated disasters badly. A large number of our citizens die in these mishaps every year. But sorry to note that our disaster management system is not effective enough to co-up up with these disasters. If we make some systematic planning well before these disasters, we can save millions of lives of our valued citizens. If we look at the recent flood of eastern Uttar Pradesh, we find that according to government figures, 1122 persons loss their lives in this flood alone, crop sown in 42.5 million hectare of agriculture land was ruined and more than 375,000 houses were damaged severely. Preliminary calculation suggests the loss of 800crore rupees. These are the official records, the actual situation will certainly be worse. Floods of Bihar in June 2010 shows mirror to our policy makers. Though the exact loss of Bihar floods are yet not known, but we can easily assume it in between 500-1000 crore

Rupees. Out 0f 600 flood affected villages, about 350 villages had ruined completely. Administrative failure is so disheartening that officers of the flood affected areas were saying to the villagers that first of all we will try to servive ourselves then only we will think about your lives. The flood of Bihar has shown the cruel reality of the so called administrative set up of our society. Government system, Relief agencies and relief plans, all of them are a complete failure here. Mr. K.M. Singh asks, who the member of disaster management authority is, "Why you are expecting too much from us in just three years. Give us some time to act, we will provide an effective disaster management network." But the ground reality is alarming. Uttar Pradesh State disaster management Authority has yet not been operative. It was formed three years ago under the chief minister's leadership. There is no meeting at all since its inception. Recently U.P. has seen a severe flood in its eastern part, but government is in no mood to act. Floods of Punjab and Haryana in July 2010 has no effect on U.P. Government functioning. It has not learnt any lesson from past and recent examples. Neither emergency disaster management operation centre has yet not been established in the state, nor has disaster control room come in to effect. The whole disaster management system of the state is on God's mercy.

First requirement of an effective disaster management is awareness and second is the quick reach of relief material to the needful. If people are not aware of the disaster, the loss would be severe and there will be problems in relief. Loss occurring from the natural disasters can be marginalized if we organize training camps in disaster sensitive areas much before it occurs and inform the public about the precautionary measures to be taken at that time. Other important factors are perfect planning, proper communication system, honest and effective leadership, co ordination etc. The most disheartening fact in India is to blame others for our own blunders. According to a presumption, nation loses 5 to 10 thousand crores of rupees every year due to natural disasters where as our budget allocation for disaster management is 65 crore rupees only. A large chunk of this budget goes to the publicity for awareness. There is no planning for a nation wide training programme.

But there are some positive signals also. Gujrat has shown the country that by proper planning, we can get some good results. After Latur earthquake, Gujrat government's effective disaster management system put a glittering example for others. Gujrat model can be adopted by other states also. At present Gujrat disaster Management Deapartment is being presented as world class management organization. To effectively manage disasters and marginalize the loss, Gujrat type of policy is order of the day.

To control any disaster and to marginalize the loss occurring from this, pre disaster management system is the most important stage. All long time and short time preparations are included in this stage by which disaster can be controlled and put to the minimum. In second stage, disaster effected group or person is covered. Relief, First aid, temporary residence, food and water supply and basic requirement of life are covered. In third stage rehabilitation work, reemployment and proper supply of basic amenities are included.

The best way to overcome a natural disaster is to try to minimize human loss, to marginalize economic loss and to try to prepare an effective and result oriented management plan for attaining the above mentioned goal. There is no alternative of relief at the time of mishap. When disaster occurs, at first communication sevice goes off. That is why the disaster affected persons could not get relief immediately. This is the time when they need communication at once. When there is a forecast of natural disaster, government must take some urgent steps like to telecast warnings in that area, to arrange emergency rehabilitation centres, to store food, drinking water, and medicines for emergency requirement. If government constructs rehabilitation centres in disaster prone areas and a rapid transport system for transportation is assured then human and economic loss can be put on hold. General infrastructure facilities like schools, colleges, community centres can play important role in socio economic development of that region. International relief organizations, NGOs, defence services and different government departments can play an important role in reconstruction of infrastructure facilities, rehabilitation as well as repairing works. Government should ensure that there would be a disaster management topic in university, colleges and school level syllabus so that students canlearn about its consequences and they will become mentally well prepared and trained for the forthcoming mishaps. The geographical and climatic situations of India show that this part of the world is very sensitive for natural disasters. We can not stop any natural disaster, but we can control it effectively by scientific planning and positive and honest approach. This book is a small contribution in this regard. If a single person inspires with my efforts, I would consider it as my success for editing this book.

I extend my sincere thanks to my senior colleagues Dr. Aditya Kumar, Prof. Satchit Anand, Dr. Arun Kumar Srivastava, Dr. Anand Khare, Dr. Veena Srivastava for there valuable encouragement. I also want to extend my thanks to Dr. Alka Rani Purwar, Dr. Parmatma Sharan Gupta and Dr. Neeta Gupta for their generous support. I would specially like to thank my dearest friend Dr Ajay Singh and Dr. Puneet Bisaria for his keen interest in this project and for giving me some valuable suggestions and making some modifications in this book .Thanks to Mr. Mahendra Garg, Propwriter of Omega Publications, Daria Ganj, New Delhi,for his sincere co-operation.

Reader's suggestions are always welcome.

Dated-30/07/2010

Dr. Virendra Singh Yadav

Associate

Indian Institute of Advanced Study

Rashtrapati Nivas, Shimla (H.P.)

Contents

Nature of Disasters Management

1

Natural Hazards as Percieved Disaster : An Overview

Dr. Fatima Aashna
Asst, Professor
Department of English
D.B.S. (P.G.) College, Kanpur

A widely accepted definition characterizes natural hazards as "those elements of the physical environmnent, harmful to man and caused by forces extraneous to him."[1] More specifically, in this document, the term "natural hazards" refers to all atmospheric hydrologic, geologic (especially seismic and volcanic) and wildfire phenomenon that, because of their structures, as their activities adversely. The qualifier "natural" eliminates such exclusively manmade phenomena as war, pollution and chemical contamination. Hazards to human beings not necessarily related to the physical environment such as infectious disease are also excluded from consideration. In this paper I shall present a simplified list of natural hazard, and then the whole paper briefly summarize the nature of geologic hazards, flooding drought, Tsunamis, hurricanes and hazards in arid and semi-arid areas.

ATMOSPHERIC	–	Hailstorms, Hurricane, Lightning, Tornadoes, Tropical Storms
SEISMIC	–	Fault ruptures, Ground Shaking, Lateral Spreading, Liquefaction, Tsunamis, Seiches.

OTHER GEOLOGIC/ HYDROLOGIC	–	Debris avalanches, Expansive Soils, landslides, Rock falls, Submarine Slides, Subsidence.
HYDROLOGIC	–	Coastal flooding, Desertification, Salinization, Drought, Erosion and Sedimentation, River Flooding Storm Surges
VOLCANIC	–	Tephra (ash, cinders, lapilli) Gases, Lava flows, Mud flows, Projectiles and lateral blasts, Pyroclastic flows.
WILDFIRE	–	Brush, Forest, Grass, Savannah

Notwithstanding the term natural, a natural hazard has an element of human involvement. A physical event, such as volcanic eruption, that does not effect human beings in a natural phenomenon but not a natural hazard. A natural phenomenon that occurs in a populated area is a hazardous event. A hazardous event that causes unacceptably large numbers of fatalities and or overwhelming property change in a natural disaster. In areas where there are no human interests, natural phenomenon do not constitute hazards nor do they result in disasters. This definition is their at odds with the perception of natural hazards as unavoidable havoc wreaked by the unrestrained forces of nature. It shifts the burden of cause from purely natural processes to the concurrent presence of human activities and natural events.

Although human can do little or nothing to change the incidence or intensity of most natural phenomenon, they have an important role to play in insuring that natural events are not converted into disasters by their own actions. It is important to understand that human intervention can increase the frequency and severity of natural hazards. For example, when the toe of a landslide is removed to make room for a settlement, the earth can move again and bury the settlement. Human intervention may also cause natural hazards where none existed before. Volcanoes erupt periodically, but it is not until the rich soil formed on their ejecta are occupied by farms and human settlements that they are considered hazardous. Finally, human intervention reduces the mitigating effect of defense against ocean currents and storm surges, in a clear example of an intervention that diminishes the ability of an ecosystem to protect itself. An extreme case of destructive human intervention into an ecosystem is desertification, which, by its very definition, is a human-induced 'natural' hazard.

Earthquakes

Earthquakes are caused by the sudden release of slowly accumulated strain energy along a fault in the earth's crust. Earthquakes and volcanoes occur most commonly at the collision zone between tectonic plates. Earthquakes represent a particularly severe threat due to the irregular time intervals between events, lack of adequate forecasting, and the hazards associated with these :

- Ground sharing is a direct hazard to any structure located near the earthquake's centre. Structural failure takes many human lives in densely populated areas.
- Landslides occur because of ground shaking in areas having relatively steep topography and poor slope stability.
- Liquefaction of gently sloping unconsolidated material can be triggered by ground shaking. Flows and lateral spreads (liquefaction phenomenon) are among the most destructive geological hazards.
- Tsunamis or seismic sea waves, usually generated by seismic activity under the ocean floor, cause flooding in coastal areas thousands of kilometers from the earthquake centre.

Drought

Drought is the result of acute water shortages, causing severe and sometimes catastrophic economic and social consequences. Out of all the natural disasters common in the region, droughts affects more people and larger area than any other. The countries affected by droughts include, India, Pakistan, Bangladesh, Nepal, Afghanistan and Sri Lanka. But Bhutan and Maldives do not suffer from drought problem. In South Asian countries, agriculture production is highly dependent on rainfall. So drought has a number of short-term and long-term effects on the effected area. For example, 60 percent of rice area in India is rain fed. So food gain production is an important indicator of rainfall pattern. Prolonged drought has a direct impact on poverty. When the draught strikes, thousands of acres are left unsown and consequently wage earning drops, leaving thousand of people unemployed.

Volcanoes

Volcanoes are perforations in the earth's crust through which molten rock and gases escape to the surface. Volcanic hazards stem from two classes of eruption :

- Explosive Eruption which is originate in the rapid dissolution and expansion of gas from the molten rock as it nears the earth's surface. Explosion pose a risk by scattering rock blocks fragments, and lava at varying distances from the source.
- Effusive eruption where material flow rather than explosions is the major hazard. Flows vary in nature (mud, ash, lava) and quantity and may originate from multiple sources. Flows are governed by gravity, surrounding topography and material viscosity.
- Hazards associated with volcanic eruption include lava flows, falling ash land projectiles, mud flows and toxic gases. Volcanic activity may also trigger other natural hazardous events including local tsunamis, deformation of the landscape, floods when lakes are breached or when stream and rivers are dammed, and tremor-provoked landslides.

Landslides

The term landslides includes slides, falls and flows of unconsolidated materials. Landslides can be triggered by earthquakes, volcanic eruptions, soil saturated by heavy rains or ground water rise, and river under cutting. Earthquake shaking of saturated soils creates particularly dangerous conditions. Although landslides are highly localized, they can be particularly hazardous due to their frequency of occurrence.

The impact of events depends on the specific nature of the landslides. Rockfalls are obvious dangers to life and property but in general they pose only a localized threat due to their limited areal influence. In contrast, slides, avalanches, flows, and lateral spreads, often having great areal extent, can result in massive loss of lives and property. Mudflows, associated with volcanic eruption can travel at great speed from their point of origin and are of the most destructive volcanic hazards.

Flooding

Two types of flooding can be distinguished. (1) Land-borne floods, or river flooding, caused by excessive run-off brought on by heavy rains, and (2) Sea-borne floods, or coastal flooding, caused by storms surges, often exacerbated by storm him off from the upper watershed. Tsunamis are a special type of sea-borne flood.

Tsunamis

Tsunamis are long-period generated by disturbances seen as earthquakes, volcanic activity and under landslides. The crests of these waves can exceed height of 25 meters on searching shallow water. The unique characteristics of tsunamis (wave length commonly exceeding 100 km, deep ocean velocities of up to 700 km/hour, and smell crest heights in deep water) make their detection and monitoring difficult characteristics of coastal flooding caused by tsunamis are the same as those of storm surges.

Hurricanes

Hurricanes are tropical depression which develop into severe storms characterized by winds directed inward in a spiraling pattern toward the centre. They are generated over warns ocean water at low latitudes and are particularly dangerous due to their destruct the potential, large zone of influence, spontaneous generation, and erratic movement. Phenomena which are associated with hurricanes are :– Winds exceeding 64 knots (74 min/hr. or 119km/hr.), the definition of hurricane force. Damage results from the wind's direct impact on fixed structures and from wind-borne objects.

Heavy rainfall which commonly precedes and follows hurricanes for up to several days. The quantity of rainfall is dependent on the amount of moisture in the air, the speed of the hurricane's rainfall can saturate soils and cause flooding because of excess run off; it can cause landslides because of added weight and lubrication of surface material and it can damage crops by weakening support for the roots.

Management of Natural Hazards

The history of mankind is full of natural calamities and catastrophic events. These events are recurring phenomenon nature and inflict untold misery on vast number of people. In recent years the incidence of natural hazards are on rise because of un-scientific exploration of natural resources and undue interference of human being in the ecological balance – Climate change linked to human activity in underway and there is a rise in extreme weather events world over. According to a finding presented at UN climate change conference at New Delhi, only in the first nine months of the year 2002, more than 500 major natural disasters have occurred killing thousands, leaving lacs houseless and affecting millions and costing more than $ 70 billion.[3]

Disaster Management means a planned and systematic approach towards understanding and solving problems in the wake of disasters. The disaster plan outlines measures to facilitate effective rescue, relief and rehabilitation. It spells out what is to be done before, during and after a disaster by whom, when and how. Disaster Management plan includes following aspects in general:

1. **Disaster Zoning :** It is must an effective disaster management plan. The area must be divided into different zones as per type, intensity and frequency of disasters.
2. **Preparedness measures and warning system :** Preparedness may be described as measures to organize and facilitate timely and effective rescue relief and rehabilitation in case of disaster.

3. **Prevention :** Prevention may be described as means designed to prevent the natural phenomena from causing or resulting in disaster. Prevention efforts are meant to create better insight into the nature of neutral phenomena.

4. **Rescue operation and evacuation :** In the immediate wave the occurrence of the calamity, it is necessary to carry out large scale rescue operation to evacuate people to safer places and relief camps. If there are building collapses, it is necessary to have trained manpower and equipment to recover survivors/dead bodies from the debris and move them for treatment.

5. **Relief Operation :** This includes supply of essential commodities (food items, drugs, kerosene oil etc.) restoration of surface supply lines and prevention of disease turning into epidemics.

6. **Creation of strong buildings and structures at fairly elevated places :** To accommodate displaced population such as cyclone shelters, flood or earthquake relief camps etc. must be constructed. An important aspect of rehabilitation effort in repair/reconstruction of house damaged in the disaster.

7. Financial arrangement is a backbone of disaster management programmes. A certain amount of margin money should be earmarked in central and state budgets for unseen calamities.

8. In addition to central and state government agencies, the decentralized voluntary organization should also be made a party of disaster management programmes. These organizations are well acquinted with local requirements and situations.

The areas of common concern could be joint efforts for restoration of watersheds; engaging in joint projects for development of Himalayan resources and prevention of deforestation and soil erosion and mountain slopes; exchange of hydrological information on rainfall and water level discharge for flood forecasting; sharing of technical knowledge and grass root level information on the natural hazards management and their forecasting etc. In the 15th SAARC summit, the leaders of the member countries agreed that the greatest danger to the stability of the entire region was from the emerging trend of terrorism and extremism. There should be joint efforts to protect the values of pluralism, peaceful co-existence and law and order in the region. It was advised to fight this problem collectively and to adopt an integrated legal system for the entire region to fight this menace.[4]

A survey of environmental constraints, whether focused on urban, rural, or wild land ecosystems, includes the nature and severity of resource degradation; the underlying causes of degradation, which include the impact of both natural phenomena and human use; and the range of feasible economic, social, institutional, policy and financial interventions designed to retard or alleviate degradation. In this sense, too, natural hazards must be considered an integral aspect of development planning process.

Recent development literature sometimes makes a distinction between environmental projects and development projects. Environmental projects include objectives such as sanitation, reforestation and flood control, while development projects may focus on potable water supplies, forestry, and irrigation. But the project by project approach is clearly an ineffective means of promoting socio-economic well being. Development projects, if they are to be sustainable, must incorporate sound environmental management. By definition, this means that they must be designed to improve the qualities of life and to protect or restore environmental quality at the same time and must also ensure that resources will not be degraded and that the threat of natural hazards will not be exacerbated. In short, good natural hazard management is good development project management.

Indeed in high-risk area, sustainable development is only possible to the degree that development planning decisions, in both the public and private sectors, address the destructive potential of natural hazards. This approach is particularly relevant in post-disaster situations, when tremendous pressure are brought to bear on local, national and international agencies to replace, frequently on the same site, destroyed facilities. It is at such times that the pressing need for natural hazard and risk assessment information and its incorporation into the development planning process become most evident.

Finally to address hazard management, specific action must be incorporated into the various stages of the integrated development planning study : First, an assessment of the presence and effect of natural events on the goods and services provided by natural resources in the plan area; second, estimates of the potential impact of natural events on development activities, and third, the inclusion of measures to reduce vulnerability in the proposed development activities. Within this frame work, "lifeline" networks should be identified : components or critical segments of production facilities, infrastructure, and support systems for human settlements, which should be as nearly invulnerable as possible and be recognized as priority elements for rehabilitation following a disaster.

REFERENCES

1. Burton Robert, W. Kafes Gilbert F. White. The Environment As Hazard (New York : Oxford University Press, 1978).
2. S.S. Acharya, Draught and Response of Rural Families, Economic and Political Weekly, 27 (30), 5 Sep. 1992, p. 1895.
3. Natural disaster can cost more than $ 70 billion. The Times of India, New Delhi, 31.10.2002.
4. Yojana (Hindi), Sep. 2008, N-9, p. 13.

2

Disaster Management 2009

Dr. Ranjana Srivastava
HOD of Geog. Department
DBS Degree College, Kanpur

Sushma. D. Parihar
TGT (Social studies),
KVONGC, Dehradun

Introduction

Disaster literally means 'Catastrophe', 'Calamity', or 'Aapada'. The Second Wednesday of every October during the Decade was observed as "World Disaster Reduction Day". National Day for Disaster Reduction was observed on 11th October. Theme for the year 2000 was "Community Participation and Public Awareness". The United Nations observed the Nineties as the "International Decade For Natural Disaster Reduction" (IDNDR), in order to focus on International Initiatives for minimizing the adverse impact of natural calamities particularly in the developed countries like India.

Man Made Disasters as a result of Toxic Chemicals; Explosions, Fire Incidents; High Rising Building's Collapse; And Hazardous Waste etc. have been the cause of many deaths and casualties. The increase in Chemical Processes and Manufacturing Industry inevitably carries the risk of accidents. Enrico Fermi and his associates in the year 1944 at the University of Chicago developed the First Atomic Reactor and when proved that chain reaction was in fact a reality the world was introduced to new and terrifying dimensions, in the cause and scope of disasters. The Nuclear Bomb was dropped in Hiroshima and Nagasaki in1945, since then the threat of Nuclear War is ever increasing (Mass Casualties Management, 1983).

One of the worst Industrial Disaster in the World "Bhopal Gas Tragedy" in the Night of 3rd –4th December, 1984 which killed 2500 victims and 17500 victims were hospitalized, besides, incapacitating thousands. The 'Chemical Disaster Prevention Day' being observed all over India on 4th December every year is a grim reminder of the worst recorded accident in the history of Chemical Industry.

A powerful Earthquake on 26th December 2003 strikes Bam (an Ancient Silk Road City) in South- Eastern Iran, killing some 40000 people and injuring some 30000 others.

Thus, disaster management plan is a must for every hospital as a disaster can happen anywhere anytime. No one can claim that, "It cannot happen here". The fact is that it can happen here, anywhere, not necessarily a nuclear bomb but it could be a riot, road traffic accident, fire incident, building collapse, or any of natural disasters or an act of man that can suddenly bring about a localized or widespread state of disaster.

Aims and Objectives

To create a medical community, which is adequately knowledgeable about the disasters, natural or otherwise, it is likely to face and the safe ways of surviving community affected. The ultimate aim of disaster management plan is to save as many lives as possible by providing best possible medical care under those circumtances.

What is Disaster?

The *Oxford Dictionary* describes disaster as "A sudden Calamitous Event bringing great damage, loss or destruction".

WHO Definition: "A situation, which implies unforeseen serious and immediate threat to public health".

Colin Grant's Definition: "Catastrophe causing injury or illness simultaneously to at least thirty people who will require hospital emergency treatment"-*(Colin Grant's-1973).*

Rutherford's Definition: "An emergency of such magnitude as to require extraordinary mobilization of emergency service"- (*Rutherford-1974*).

Jenkins A's Definition: "Disaster needs declaration when immediate patient load in the emergency medical services system is greater than normal, operator can care for" (Jenkins An-1978).

No definition seems to be complete which is suited to every **Hospital / Institution.**

What is my perception?

A disaster involves following Ingredients:

- Unforeseen, Serious and Immediate Threat to Public Health i.e. Suddenness in terms of time;
- An Emergency, Calamity, Catastrophe, Misadventure, Tragedy, Epidemic, Cataclysm etc.;
- Where number of casualties far exceeds medical facilities in normal situation that disrupts the normal routine of life i.e. Magnitude in terms of severity of damage or deaths.

In other words declaration of disaster depends on gravity or magnitude of situation, number of victims involved, time factor i.e. Suddenness of an event, availability of medical care in terms of space, equipments, medical and paramedical staff, medicines and other basic human needs i.e. food, shelter and clothing, weather conditions in the locality of incident etc. Thus, enhancing human sufferings and create human.

DISASTER MANAGEMENT PLAN

Aim of Disaster Management

The ultimate aim of disaster management is basically the prevention and minimization of death, disability, sufferings and losses.

There are certain fundamental principles, which should be thoroughly understood by everyone who may have responsibility for helping the victim of a disaster. Furthermore, it is important that these principles be applied in the proper sequence; otherwise they loose effectiveness or cause even more deaths and injuries.

Principles

Disaster management means a planned and systemic approach towards understanding and solving problems in the wake of disasters. Some general principals of disaster planning are:

- It should be a continuous process.
- It should reduce the unknown in a problematic situation.
- Plan must evoke appropriate action.
- Plan must foresee what is likely to happen.
- Plan must be based on valid knowledge.
- Plan must focus on general principles.
- Plan should serve as an educational activity.
- Plan for overcoming resistance.
- Plan must be tested.

Adjust planning to people rather than expecting people to change their behavior in order to conform to the planning.

These principles include following steps:

- "Prevent" the occurrence of the disaster whenever possible.
- "Minimize The Number Of Casualties" if the disaster cannot be prevented.
- "Prevent Further Casualties".
- "Rescue The Victims".
- "Provide First Aid To The Injured".
- "Evacuate The Injured To Medical Installation".
- "Provide The Definite Medical Care".

"Promote The Reconstruction Of The Lives Of Victims"

Disaster Prevention:

Described as measures to prevent natural phenomena from causing or resulting in disaster or other related emergency situations.

Prevention concerns the following:

- To prevent or eliminate the occurrence of disaster, need for Formulation and Implementation of long-term policies and programmes,
- On the basis of vulnerability analysis of all risks, prevention includes legislation and regulatory measures, principally in the field of physical and urban planning, public works and building.

Disaster Preparedness:

Described as action designed to minimize loss of life and damage and to organize and facilitate timely effective rescue relief and rehabilitation in case of disaster:

- Preparedness is supported by the necessary legislation and means a readiness to cope with disaster or similar emergencies, which could not be avoided.
- Preparedness is concerned with forecasting and working, the education and training of population, staff, organization for and management of disaster, including preparation of operational plan, training of relief group, the stock piling of supplies and the earmarking of the necessary funds.

Continuous preparedness to provide quick and effective relief, together with the adoption of such preventive measures as are possible to save life, lessens personal suffering and loss when a calamity strikes.

Disaster Mitigation:

Mitigation means reducing the actual or probable effects of an extreme hazard on man and his environment.

Role of Forensic Expert

Role of Forensic Expert is of immense value due to medico-legal nature of all the cases especially in 'Man Made Disasters' like terrorist attack etc., and when MCI Recommendations are that emergency services to be brought under the supervision of Forensic Medicine Department and posting of Inters for two weeks in the casualty under the supervision of Forensic Experts.

Triage

Need for Emphasis on 'Triage' and plan for allocation or extension of emergency department space.The concept of 'Triage' or 'Sorting' was originally developed for Mass Casualty Disaster or Battle Field Situations in which decision had to be made about the allocation of resources and Medicare. This concept was being expanded to emergency department in which unscheduled patients arrive by ambulance or other means seeking urgent care. Triage is a core process in the emergency department.

The origin of Modern Triage is attributed to Baron Dominique Jean Larry in the Napoleonic Wars who created a system for sorting the thousands of French causalities into groups with different priorities for evacuation and treatment, not based on soldiers rank, but on the nature of their injuries.

Aims and Objectives

An effective 'triage' system will achieve the following:

- To ensure immediate medical intervention in life threatening situation.
- To expedite the care of patients through an accurate initial assessment of urgency.
- To ensure that patients are prioritized for treatment in accordance with the severity of their medical condition.
- To reduce the morbidity associated with medical conditions through early intervention.
- To assist patient requiring treatment in another hospital, department, or community health services.

- To improve public relations by communicating accurate information to friends and relatives who accompany patients.
  - To improve patients flow within Emergency Department.
  - To provide supervised learning for appropriate personnel's (like Interns, J.R.'s etc.).
  - To assist with all aspects, in performance measurement in Emergency

•Sorting of dead from injured.

- Fixing of identity is a great challenge for Forensic Expert, and in almost all cases autopsy is to be performed as unknown, unclaimed dead bodies.
- Post mortem examination of all the casualties is must to confirm the cause of death.
- Fixing Identity and confirmation of event by Preservation and collection of evidences for Forensic Examination (DNA Evidence, Blood Grouping etc.).
- Almost all wounded patients need Casualty Services.
- For Post Mortem Examination, Demarcation of additional staff & space and rapid disposal of cases is the need of hour in cases of Mass Casualties.
- For creating Temporary Mortuary, use of tents, folding tables & adequate quantity of equipments may be needed.
- Mobile vans may be used for 'On the Site Post Mortem Examination'.
- Facility of 'Cold Storage Cabinets' or arrangement of Ice Cubes (blocks) for keeping the dead bodies till waiting for relatives or final disposition of dead bodies may be available.
- Provision for adequate water supply, arrangement of

lights must be ensured before performing 'On the Site Post Mortem Examination'.

- Another important point needs emphasis here is to ask for adequate security arrangements to avoid 'Secondary Disaster' due to Law and Order problems.

Role as a Leader

Forensic Expert being an expert of medico legal nature of cases and also having administrative e knowledge and experience of working with law enforcement persons, must come forward and play a role as a Leaderin such disastrous situations.

Role as a doctor

The primary role of doctors should be to function as a doctor and they should not be diverted, to other functions, and keeping in mind the directions of S.C. regarding treatment offered to a patient in emergency situation. No patient left unattended & treatment must not be delayed in the name of medico-legal nature of the cases.

Role as a Coordinator

Forensic Expert must act as a Coordinator of following's activities:

- Nursing staff,
- NGO's (like Red Cross for ambulance services, setting up first aid team, help in providing food, drink, and temporary shelters for victims and rescuers, supply of drugs and equipments, help in rehabilitation, supply of cloths blankets etc.)
- Volunteers (like NCC, NSS etc.) for rescue, first aid, evacuation etc. the volunteer's should act in coordination with professionally trained persons. The volunteer's help should correspond as closely as possible to his training and experience- (Grab & Eng.-1969).

Public Health Work Personnel

- To perform any work that would lessen the chance of a 'Secondary Disaster' and then take other activity to support the rescue operation.

The usual task to be performed includes:

- Removing traffic jams or road blocks so that clear passage may be available for relief vehicles, ambulance, and fire brigade vehicles etc.
- Prevention of any untoward effects like break down of electric, water, and gas supply.
- To assist Fireman in obtaining adequate water for Fire Fighting.
- Rescue operations particularly of removing victims from under debris etc.

Prevention of Health Problems

Prevention of 'Secondary Disaster': 'Secondary Disaster' means 'Disaster After Disaster' or 'Disaster Over Disaster' due to law and order problems during treatment or at nay stage of disaster management, like public outrage, conflicts between hospital staff and attendants of patient's or so called self made local leaders, creating strike like situation.

Need for Change of Attitude

"Delusion Of Personal Invulnerability": Most people believe that a disaster is something that happens to someone else not to themselves or their families. This is called the "Delusion Of Personal Invulnerability". As a result they are likely to ignore or minimize warning and refrain from taking preventive measures-(Grab. & Eng.-1969).

Students can be trained in 'first aid' and remain in a constant state of preparedness. The idea that assumes the supreme importance is –the elimination of the critical difference between 'runaway' to 'run-in', in case of any disaster.

Future Trends in Disaster Management

The disaster management has come a long way from disgraceful history. The scientific development in many discipline have made significant breakthrough in better prediction, preparedness and mitigation (Stephan et al, 1985).

The use of satellite, computers, electronics, better communication facilities are going to make significant difference in disaster management. The data processing and computers are providing a useful tool in decision making in disaster.

Summary and Conclusions

When the disaster strikes, power goes out, all modes of communication (Telephone etc.) becomes inoperable, lifts stop functioning, when drinking water becomes contaminated, when normal modes of transportation suddenly becomes impossible, when casualties start coming in groups that is not the time for planning but that is the time of acting. This fact makes it imperative for community disaster preparedness and particularly health care system with its critical component "the hospital" which are to be prepared consistently to mobilize all their facilities for maximum use.

Creating public awareness about safety from disasters by organizing workshops, symposium, seminars etc. There is need for amending, enacting & effectively enforcing legislations for safety from disasters like Protection of habitations from adverse impacts of disasters, constructing new buildings safe from disasters and retrofitting existing buildings for improving disaster resistance.

Need for change of strategy from 'post-disaster reactive approach' to 'pre-disaster pro-active approach' to reduce the damage, losses to the property, and human sufferings along with prevention of human lives on one hand and reduce the cost of relief, rehabilitation and reconstruction on the other hand.

No master plan can be evolved to fit every emergency situation but a general schedule of emergency activity could prove extremely helpful in times of disaster, if executed in a coordinated and disciplined fashion.

The better awareness for disaster preparedness and mitigation is expected to result in coordinated extensive efforts to ensure better disaster management (Stephen et al, 1985).

Adequate procedures to deal with disaster should be formulating in every country of the world as no country is completely immune from both natural and man made catastrophe -(Skeet, 1979).

REFERENCES

1. Employment News; 10th – 16th January, 2004: 8.
2. Satendra, Gupta A. Managing Disaster Must For Sustainable Development. Employment News, Vol. XXVIII NO.30, 25th – 31st Oct. 2003: 1,
3. Anandan S. Manic Monday Revives '9's Memories. Hindustan Times, 26th August 2003: 9.
4. Mhasawade SC,Unnikrishanan C. Mahyem in Mumbai"; Hindustan Times; 26th August 2003: 01.
5. "9 Climbers Killed In Avalanche"; Hindustan Times; 23rd September 2003: 01.
6. "41 Feared Killed In Himanchal Cloud Burst"; Hindustan Times; 9th, August 2003: 1.
7. "NHRC Calls For Restructuring Emergency Medicare Facilities" Daily Excelsior, 6th September 2003: 8.
8. "Vajpayee to Convene C.M.'s Meeting on Disaster Management"; Hindustan Times; 5th June 2003: 7.
9. Tikoo A. CBSE Chairman Asks Jammu Schools To Make Effective Changes In Education System. 6th May 2003: 4.
10. Zuthsi M. The agony doesn't end with Death. Hindustan Times, 17th May 2003:11.
11. Express Disaster. Hindustan Times, 16th May 2003: 1.

3

Earthquakes - Disasters And Displacements Role of Community in Managing Disasters

Dr. Priya Srivastava
Associate Professor
Department of English
D.A-V. College, Kanpur

Dr. Sudhanshu Chamanji
Associate Professor,
Department of Commerce
D.A-V. College, Kanpur.

Every year various natural hazards such as earthquakes, landslides, volcanic eruptions, cyclones, floods and fires kill, destroy and displace thousands of people all over the world and forces the government officials at both International and National levels to think about the immediate requirements to be made available to the disaster victims. It is essential to firstly understand the meaning of the word disaster. As mentioned in the Oxford dictionary disaster means- "a sudden accident or natural event that causes great damage or loss of life". Section 2(d) of Indian Disaster Management Act, 2005 also defines disaster as, "a catastrophe, mishap, calamity or grave occurrence in any area, arising from natural or man made cause, or by accident or negligence which results in substantial loss of life or human suffering or damage to, and destruction of, property, or damage to, or degradation of, environment, and is of such a nature or magnitude as to be beyond the coping capacity of the community of the affected area". So on the basis of the above definitions, it is visualized that the word disaster itself is "sudden" causing extensive damage to human life.

Normally disasters are not limited to any particular area of the world like Pacific region is earthquake prone area, coastal areas prone to cyclones, some nations prone to activities related to terrorism and some to floods etc. In the past few decades a rapid growth is visible in the severity of natural disasters as well as man-made disasters. It is observed that developing countries are severely at a major loss due to the unstable climatic conditions, deforestation and unplanned constructions without implying any safety measures towards disasters of any kind. The frequent rise in the number of natural disasters compelled the General Assembly of the United Nations to pass a resolution 44/236 0f 22nd December, 1989 declaring 1990s as the year of IDNDR i.e. International Decade for Natural Disaster Reduction. Despite of IDNDR, the whole decade and then after, the world is coming across major disasters of and on. Visualizing globally all the continents, Asia is the most vulnerable amongst all for the occurrence of natural disasters and especially affecting a large part of Indian sub-continent. It is very natural that disasters either geophysical or climatic are beyond the control of human beings. But important measures can be applied to avoid disasters and therefore bringing forth lesser calamities on human lives as well as property and infrastructure.

Talking about natural disasters, earthquakes are undoubtedly the most dangerous of all. The earth comprises of four layers – deep below in the centre is the *inner core*, above is the *outer core*, followed by the *mantle* and the outer most layers is the *crust*. The earth is hot and molten right and deep inside the centre. Because of the rotation and other energy factors there is a constant move in the rock layers. The pieces called tectonic plates are in a continuous moving mode sliding and at times bumping into each other. The seismic waves reading from 1-10 on the Richter scale shake the earth reaching the surface and causing the ground to shake. The sudden slip in the earth between the two block into one another causes earthquake. Those earthquakes reading 03 or less magnitude are almost unnoticeable whereas reaching a magnitude of 07 cause severe damage and destruction over large areas.

Earthquakes often begin with small tremors called *foreshocks*, followed by the *main shock*- the bigger and main earthquake. The experience of the foreshock and the main shock is felt in the same place followed by *aftershocks* – smaller earthquakes occurring for weeks and months. Occurring without any prior warning, earthquakes cause disasters of all kinds including the loss of precious human lives. Not only the intensity but other factors also determine damage and death like local geologic conditions, the density and types of building construction, population densities, earthquake depth, distance from the epicenter, how long the shaking continues and the degree of earthquake preparedness in the region. Recognized by the shaking and movement of the ground earthquake also triggers landslide, tsunamis and volcanic activities. Along with this, they are also a big cause in the breakdown of the communication and transportation system, disruptions of gas lines and power lines, water supply, sewerage system etc. Not only the villages, towns and cities are destroyed but the aftermath destabilizes the social and economic structure of the nation also.

Disasters whether natural or man-made come without any prior information and force a large number of people to evacuate their homes for a period not known. Immense human sufferings are seen all over and especially those who are actually a part of the disaster event. After shocks brings a lot of damage to human settlements, structures, buildings and various infrastructures such as – bridges, railways, utility lines, electrical facilities and water supply. The already weak structures are thoroughly damaged in the aftershocks. The breakdown of communication facilities and destruction of property further leads to a complete collapse in the affected area. The people of affected community are left displaced and homeless due to the aftermath of an earthquake.

The tremors of earthquake even leads to a very high causality rate especially in densely populated areas particularly where there are narrow roads with non earthquake resistant buildings. It is also analyzed from the past earthquake disasters that the causality rate is very high during the night time as the tremors are not felt while sleeping and people are also not tuned to various media warnings. The rate of causality is very low in the areas far away from the epicenter and those having light weight constructed houses especially made of wood. Though this may also cause some deaths and injuries due to the spread of fire.

Another widespread problem is related to the public health with multiple fractures injuries and with poor sanitation facilities leading towards a fear of epidemic causing high rise in the death rate. People are shifted to high density relief camps where the provisions in the relief camps heighten their anxiety level making them anxious of the fact of the water borne diseases due to disrupted and contaminated water supply. Along with this there is a failure in the electricity and communication system too. All the modes of transport network are also severely affected giving rise to disrupted food supply and its marketing system.

Having a long history of earthquakes, the Indian sub – continent is susceptible to seismic damage. The intensity of threat of earthquake is almost 59 percent of Indian geographical area including the capital city of the country. A seismic zone map is prepared to follow the damage caused by earthquakes in different parts of the country and to design the required structures and buildings to posses the capacity to bear different levels of ground shaking. India is divided into four seismic zones – II, III, IV &V. The North- East region, Northern part of Bihar, Jammu & Kashmir, Himanchal Pradesh and parts of Kutch are vulnerable to seismic disturbances and falls in the fifth category of seismic zone in India whereas parts of Rajasthan and the entire Gangetic area is placed in seismic zone four. An observation is made that in the span of the past one and a half decade our country has witnessed almost six moderate intensity earthquakes causing immense loss and damage to life and property. The extreme damage caused in the year 1993 by the Lattur earthquake and the earthquake in Bhuj in 2001 highlighted and focused on the requirement of the long term preparation and remedy to reduce the heavy human and economic losses due to earthquakes. The Bhuj earthquake was one of the devastating one in the last five decades and the first major earthquake to hit an urban area of the country where more than thirteen thousand people lost their lives and over a lakh and a half were injured. The tremors were experienced at far away places like Shillong in East, Quetta in the West, Kashmir in the North and Chennai in the South. The location of the Himalayas and the sub Himalayan regions, Kutch and the Andaman and Nicobar Islands are current earthquake prone areas. Various intense earthquakes were experienced in this region causing a great threat to environment and life. Seismic studies reveal that the entire Himalayan region measures earthquake of more than 08 magnitudes and they occur after every 200-300 years all along the Himalayan range.

It is truly observed that animals have a sense to detect earthquakes before it occurs. But the change in their behavior cannot be used as a recognized pattern to predict an earthquake. However, an unsolved mystery, scientists are still in a fix as to search that what makes animals sense the occurrence of an earthquake. But in the advancement in technology earthquakes detected instruments are created using amplifiers and electronic sensors covering a broad frequency range. Teleseismometers using digital technology is the latest instrument used in detecting earthquakes and helping us in giving a warning of a possibility of an earthquake.

A tremendous amount of energy is released by earthquakes causing immense destruction. Individuals experiencing major losses affect them for a longer period of time. In the quake affected area, number of multi - story buildings are collapsed completely during the primary jolt while with multiple after shocks cause a complete destruction of numerous partially destroyed buildings. It is observed that if earthquake occurs during the very early hours of the day when most of the inhabitants are indoors the disaster is very high. People become homeless because homes are partially or wholly destroyed. Due to destruction and disorganization of various essential facilities it is impossible to provide immediate aid at least during the first two days.

The loss of their loved ones, material loss, medical injuries and displacement are psychologically more devastating to the victims. The trauma and flashback of tragedy disturbs the mental state of the victims to the extent of more suffering in remembering and missing their friends, neighbors and even their family members who were burned or trapped under collapsed buildings.

Along with the terrible destruction all over, the weather conditions still worsen the condition of the survivors who are exposed to extreme heat during the day and chill and rain during the night. Therefore, lack of adequate shelter is the major concern of all the victims. Unsuitable shelters and less provision of tents leave the survivors as well as the patients in a state of dilemma and confusion and are at times forced to live outside their homes in the open air day and night. The most vulnerable of all the surviving victims are the children below five who face problems of hunger due the shortage of food supply. Water and sanitation facilities are also questioned in the earthquake affected areas as most of the household toilets are destroyed and availability of the fresh water in the wells is also limited. In case of earthquake, though the chances of outbreak of diseases are very low, yet the concern remains very high for the sick, young and old. Earthquake disaster leads to major loss during the actual event but the losses are multiplied due to the mismanagement of the situation afterwards. Due to the prevailing confused and chaotic situations, the loss is extensive in the absence of required resources.

It is essential to visualize displacement after the shock and the trauma of helplessness, dislocation, deprivation and economic disability which lasts long in the mind of the victims of all the age groups. The displaced aspect is not the only feature of their worry but they are permanently diminished with the feeling of having no hope of getting in return what they have actually lost? At a family level and essentially those below the poverty line with the sudden illness or death of the bread winner is undoubtedly a disaster within the family. Not being able to cope with the economic and emotional situation the surviving members of the family are ruined completely.

But important measures can be applied to avoid disasters and therefore bringing forth lesser calamities on human lives as well as property and infrastructure. To reduce the impact of disaster and displacements, it is essential to spread public awareness and establish strategies related to managing disaster. Early warning methods, predictions, communication, rehabilitation centre, tele-medicinal services and relief management are various steps which can be adopted in minimizing the impact of disaster and helping in controlling and reducing the destruction.

Though, after the tremors are felt, a lot of activities are seen from the side of rescue operators focusing on immediate needs. Various rescue teams from medical and military, recognized NGOs and the residents from the near by areas volunteer personally and rush to the earthquake affected area saving victims and survivors. Immediately provisions are made to supply food packets etc. for the displaced. Helping with bear minimum needs rescue camps are setup with medical aid in order to provide some sort of relief to the sufferings of the people.

Reaching for the relief of earthquake victims various International organizations like World Health Organization (WHO), Red Cross, United Nations, International Medical Corps, etc.also come forward to provide required help to earthquake victims. These organizations being a part of a crisis management immediately supply medical aid, food, shelter and clothing. As earthquakes are more prone to certain areas of the world than other areas they can occur anywhere and should be a matter of concern to everyone. Therefore, individuals, business, governments and schools should formulate and adopt certain measures towards the preparedness of earthquakes in order to minimize the risk. Training should be given to all adults in basic medical first aid and using fire extinguishers when required. As there are news updates on emergency conditions knowledge to close the gas and water supply valves and using fluorescent bulbs instead of halogen helps in minimizing the risk of fire. Heavy weight items like bookshelves, furniture and other dangerous objects should be shifted to lower areas. Above all, the most important is to setup an emergency exit plan in homes and offices to evacuate and reduce the risk of life.

Along with the above preparedness some important safety measures should be implemented during an earthquake. The first and the foremost action within the building are to hold on a table strongly or get under the table or desk and close your eyes. One can also sit close to a wall away from windows or anything that can fall and cause injury and remain in that position until the tremors are over, inclusive of after shocks. After the tremors are over, one is advised to check oneself and others injuries, watch out for fires and always use stairs instead of elevators to reach a safer place. Those outside the buildings in the open area should bend down and cover their heads and eyes and maintain a proper distance from trees, power lines, and high-rise buildings.

In India, the data presented at the government level indicates that earthquakes of various intensities hit almost about 60% of the Indian landmass causing damage in terms of economic losses, agriculture productivity, human sufferings and above all loss of life. It is the basic responsibility of the state governments to undertake measures related to rescue, relief and rehabilitation in the event of disaster with the extended financial support of the centre. A National Disaster Framework is formed by the government comprising of disaster mitigation, disaster prevention strategy, early warning system and preparedness. For an efficient and long term strategy to manage natural disasters, a National Crisis Management Committee and Crisis Management Group is also setup by the government. The state governments have also setup a Calamity Relief Fund for each state towards which 75% is contributed by the central government and the rest by the various state governments. The government in the disaster management policy laid stress on using advanced technologies in forecasting and warning, contingency to ensure the availability of food grains and preparedness through specific programmes.

Despite the government efforts in establishing a Crisis Management Group to provide better rescue operations we are far behind the western countries due to lack of coordination amongst the relief operations and the varying rescue agencies resulting in high casualties in the earthquake areas.

Besides the efforts made by the various government agencies and non – government organizations students also have a major role to play in managing disasters. The most vital aspect of disaster management is preparedness. NSS and NCC students can provide the service and aid with minimal training and support by professionals. Other students should also work and help in spreading awareness related to disasters and how to handle them during and after the disaster. Training should be given to the students to organize camps in the earthquake prone areas and to help the community to cope up and bare the danger like earthquake shocks and tremors in order to lessen the panic and pain and sufferings of the surviving class. This shall also help in reducing the death toll when people are well acquainted with the strategies and training given to them in basic medical and first aid by the student's community.

To prevent earthquakes there is no known way, but its impact can be minimized. The destruction caused by earthquakes can be softened greatly by using earthquake resistant design building structures, making safe building interiors so to avoid damage by falling objects and educating community about earthquake safety. An earthquake can only give painful and damaging results in case of ignorance. Education about disaster like earthquake is vital so as to protect against all dangers. As earthquakes are not glamorous natural disasters like volcanoes or tornadoes and even don't receive names like hurricanes but they can do the same or more danger. It's the need of the society to wake up and inform about the danger and precautions related to earthquakes. Therefore, people require understanding about what makes an earthquake and how can its impact be minimized.

A recent earthquake in Chile is a great example that preparedness is a key to survival. An earthquake measuring 8.8 magnitude was one of the most powerful earthquake ever recorded and could have been proved to be worse in terms of destruction and death. But yet when comparing with Haiti's earthquake in January this year which measured 7.0 magnitudes killed and displaced million of people more than Chile. Through International aid agencies it is notified that the death rate was less in Chile due to being a more developed country with better disaster preparedness along with more quake resistant buildings. Chile's preparedness is categorized in the list-A with the employment and management of planning, response, recovery and mitigation. Though they may not help completely in putting an end to natural disasters but the survival rate is comparatively high. The Chile quake was 500 times stronger than Haiti and dominated the agricultural area whereas in Haiti it was much closer to the populated area. The poorly and weak constructed edifices were already shattered and damaged in the past number of quakes in Chile. Therefore, for the last 20 years the government worked and focused on the survival rate and established a foundation named PTWC (Pacific Tsunami Warning Centre) in1968 which immediately sent a warning to the countries in the Pacific Rim when on February 27th, 8.8 magnitude quake hit Chile. With the result as almost with no signs of Tsunami, still with evacuation which happened for the first time gave more lives than destruction. For almost past three decades children were trained in Chilean schools following the instructions, "Drop, cover, hold on" when an earthquake hits until the shaking stops. Implementing these simple emergency techniques, it ensured protection of life and property and unfortunately with all most nil preparations and lack of education, training and awareness, Haiti suffered in lives, property, government and infrastructure.

It can be better understood that emergencies in calamities and disasters do happen and bring pains, sufferings and damage of all kinds. However, the preparedness, response, recovers and mitigation on the country level can very well determine the survival rate and here both Chili and Haiti are lessons to be learned and understood. After all, it is impossible for anyone to control Mother Nature.

REFERENCES

1. Managing Disasters and Displacements, Vombatkere S. G., Mainstream, Vol XLVII, No.48, Nov. 14, 2009.
2. Earthquake Forecasting, Marian K, 2009.
3. Earthquake Detected, Manali Oak, 2008.
4. Interesting Facts about Earthquake, Maya Pillai, 2008.

5. Earthquake Emergency Preparedness, Streeter L. 2008

6. Chili Earthquake, Nguyem Katie, March 2010.

Websites:

1. www.buzzle.com

2. http://alternet.org

4

Interrelated Perspectives of Climate Change and Natural Disasters

Dr. Rashmi Dubey
Department of English
D.B.S. (P.G.) College,
Kanpur

The impending climate crisis has assumed the dimensions of a true planetary emergency that foretells the destruction of order of the present day world. The rapid advancement of civilization led to the unprecedented development of science and technology leading to indiscriminate industrialization resulting in conversion of land use and ruthless exploitation of the natural resources. The faith in anthropocentrism has created immitigable problems which have begun to threaten the very existence of survival of mankind. Realizing the magnitude of the ensuing danger emanating from human-induced actions which have accelerated climate changes, altered atmospheric composition and increased the temperature of the Earth, the academic community is endeavouring to make mankind aware and conscious of the perils of the planet.

A recent report of the Secretary General of the United Nations underlined that the threat posed by climate change is the greatest environmental and development challenges in the twenty-first century. Pantagon commissioned analyst to consider the implications of abrupt climate change for international security who labeled climate change as the 'mother of all security problems'.

In 2004, the British government's chief scientist, Sir David King, suggested that 'climate change is a far greater threat to the world's stability than international terrorism'. These changes are very dangerous to our human race as well as for the whole planet. Most scientists believe that climate change is being taking place and is human induced, and that it will lead to more extreme weather patterns and will cause many hazards or disasters. A larger part of Indian Sub-continent is prone to various kinds of natural disasters and India has suffered a lot in terms of life and properties.

A disaster can be said to be that sudden calamity which brings misfortunes and miseries to humanity. It is the result of an immediate situation or the result of a long set process which disrupts normal human life in its established social, traditional, economic and physical system. The term 'Disaster' can be interpreted as 'dis' means bad or evil and 'astrum' means star. Thus the word disaster suggests that mostly all happenings on earth are attributed to different celestial bodies. The definition of disaster keeps on changing from time to time. We can define disaster as an occurrence that causes damage, ecological disruption, loss of human life, deterioration of health and health services on a scale sufficient to warrant an extraordinary response from outside the affected community. Disasters are so powerful as they can easily shatter normal human life and compel men to think that 'it is nature that is the master and not the man.'[1]

And as we all know that man and nature both are interdependent on each other and if we are disturbing the calmness of our life source nature, it is bound to react. This disturbance may lead to various hazards such as hurricanes and drought, longer spells of dry heat or intense rain and seriously affect the world's ecosystems as well as humanity. In the present paper we will discuss harmful impacts of climate change as they work like a catalyst to various disasters. They can be said to be direct or indirect stimulators to miseries in human life as a report released by American scholars in April 2007 argued that climate change will act as a 'threat multiplier' that makes existing concerns, such as water scarcity and food insecurity, more complex and intractable and presents a tangible threat to security interests of the nations. Security analysts have warned that climate change threatens water and food security, the allocation of resources, which in turn could increase forced migration, raise tensions and trigger conflict and destabilization. The climate change is likely to alter the variability of precipitation and the quantity of available water and food security could also worsen in some regions as climate change increases the risk of harvest failure, especially in developing countries. Climate change is also likely to result in further sea-level rise and more intensive storms and heavy precipitation. This

DISASTER INTERFACE, HAZARDS AND VULNERABILITY

HAZARDS>	VULNERABLE CONDITIONS ——>>>	RESULT	<<<PRESSURES	ROOT CAUSES
NATURAL	MACRO– AND MICRO-FORCES CAUSE POOR BASIC INDICATORS ——>>>	INTO	<<<—— RAPID URBANISATION	<<<– UNDER
METEOROLOGICAL			<<<—— DEFORSTATION	
-DROUGHT/FAMINE> STORMS/FLOODS> HEAT/COLD WAVES>			<<<—— LANDLESS	
TOPOGRAPHICAL/ EARTH MOVEMENTS	POVERTY ——>>>	DISASTER	<<<—— WARS	DEVELOPMENT
EARTHQUAKES/ ERUPTION> – LANDSLIDES>	POPULATION PRESSURE		<<<—— ILLITERACY	
			<<<—— NO LAW ENFORECEMNT/ MIS-ADMINISTRATION/ MIS-DIRECTED RESOURCES/UNPOPULAR POLICIES	
BIOLOGICAL – EPIDEMICS> – INFESTATIONS>	UNSAFE SETTLEMENTS ——>>>			
MAN–MADE	LACK OF OR INADEQUATE BASIC SERVICES ——>>>	IMPACT	<<<—— LITTLE OR UNWISE INVESTMENT	&
– WARS/CIVIL STRIFE> – ARGE ACCIDENTS> – ENVIRONMENT			<<<—— UNWISE EXPENDITURES	BAD
	LACK OF DISASTER PLANS AND AWARENESS ——>>>			GOVERNANCE

will greatly increase the risks of natural disasters occurring in many cities and industrial regions in coastal zones. These impacts could overburden weak states in particular and, in extreme cases, encourage their collapse. We will look at various natural and man-made hazards; their vulnerable conditions; their results and their various causes with the help of a chart.

Disaster may be seen as the interface between (whether natural or man-made) and the Adapted from reference : Ian Davis, safe shelter within unsafe cities, Disaster Vulnerability and Rapid Urbanisation Open Home Internationa, 1997 : 12(5); p.

The concentration of the green house gases such as CO2, CO, CH, Nitrogen dioxide and chlorofluorocarbons, is increasing steadily. They absorb long wave radiation and reemit to warm the surface of the planet earth and raise the temperature. Scientific evidence indicates that a growing concentration of greenhouse gases in the earth's atmosphere is having an effect on climate. The Intergovernmental Panel on Climate Change (IPCC) has been publishing periodic assessment reports on atmospheric carbon concentrations and their likely effect on the environment. In its contribution to the Fourth Assessment Report of the IPCC on the Physical Science Basis (2007), the working group observed that the "understanding of anthropogenic warming and cooling influences on climate has improved since the Third Assessment Report (TAR), leading to very high confidence that the globally averaged net effect of human activities since 1750 has been one of the warming."2 This triggers a cascade of impact throughout the entire ecosystem. These impacts can Include expansion of species into new areas, intermingling of formerly non overlapping species, and even species extinctions. Scientists expect that the average global surface temperature could rise 1 – 4.5°F (0.6–2.5°C) in the next fifty years, and 2.2–10°F (1.4–5.8°C) in the next century, with significant regional variation evaporation will increase as the climate warms, which will increase average global precipitation soil moisture is likely to decline in many regions and intense rainstorms are likely to become more frequent. Sea level is likely to rise two feet along most the U.S. coast. Rising sea level is already affecting many small islands. The World Watch Institute reports that the Earth's ice cover is melting in more places and at higher rates than at any time since record keeping began. Rising sea level will impact many coastlines, and a large mass of humanity lives near the coasts or by major rivers.

According to the expectation of scientists the biggest impact of climate changes would be on water resources and it will increase the rate of disasters related to water. Water resources will be impacted by their occurrence, distribution and circulation. As mountain glaciers shrink, large regions that rely on glacial run-off water supply could experience severe shortage. Rising temperatures will diminish snow pack and increase evaporation, affecting seasonal availability of water. Higher demand from economic development agriculture and population growth will further limit surface and ground water availability. It will result in the change of coastal area and large population migration.

As water supply become scarce, the importance of this life sustaining resource is felt now more than eves. "Climate change debates highlight the threat to the world's dwindling freshwater sources, which range from mountain glaciers and mighty rivers to the lakes, tiny inland wet lands and reservoirs. AT the same time, intensifying drought and rising average temperature stalk many regions." The World Bank report India's Water Economy makes the point that India is fast running out of water and by 2020 will be under severe stress and forecasts that by 2050, demand will have outstripped supply. Due to this lack of water epidemics would spread. Disasters like Drought and desertification have started to spread and intensified in some parts of the world already. The Guardian summarizes a United Nations warming that, "one in six countries in the world face food shortages this year because of severe droughts that could become semi-permanent under climate change.

An increase in pests and disease is also feared. A report in the Journal Science in June 2002 described the alarming increase in the outbreaks and epidemics of diseases throughout the land and ocean based wildlife due to climate changes. Thus climate change is disrupting natural ecosystem in a way that is making life better for infectious diseases. Increased temperatures will also lead to an increase in pest populations and resultant crop loss. New diseases, mutations and movements of virus, pests etc. will cause to death of human beings. Vector-born diseases, such as malaria, are likely to invade new areas, including the highlands, as temperatures increase in these regions, making for more conductive conditions for vector populations to thrive.

Besides, weather is directly related to our health. If the overall climate becomes warmer, there will be an increase in the number of deaths due to greater frequency and severity of heat waves and other extreme weather events. The high intense rays cause skin problems in man. The ultra-violet rays of the sun can cause skin cancer also. The elderly, the very young and those suffering from respiratory and cardiovascular disorders will probably be affected by such weather extremes as they have lesser coping capacity. Climate change would also increase air pollution levels by accelerating the atmospheric chemical reactions that produce photochemical oxidants due to a rise in the temperature. Increased temperature would increase sea level and the direct impact of this rise would include deaths and injury caused by the intense flood disaster. The natural disasters are proving to be more and more hazardous and acute because we are becoming short in medicinal and aromatic plants. The environmental changes have significantly affected the universal flora i.e. various plants and fauna i.e., the animal content and scientists are continuously warning us for the hazardous impacts on the environment in future. With the help of a diagram we will understand the inter-relationship between a disaster and its effect on health.

These natural and man-made hazards affect not only physical health, but are harmful for mental health also. A disaster is the result of an immediate situation or the result of a long set process which disrupts normal human life in its established social, traditional, economics and physical systems. It brings about sudden and immense miseries to humanity. Besides, with the increase in world temperature the psychology of man is also changing. They

Relationship between onset of disaster and its effects on health

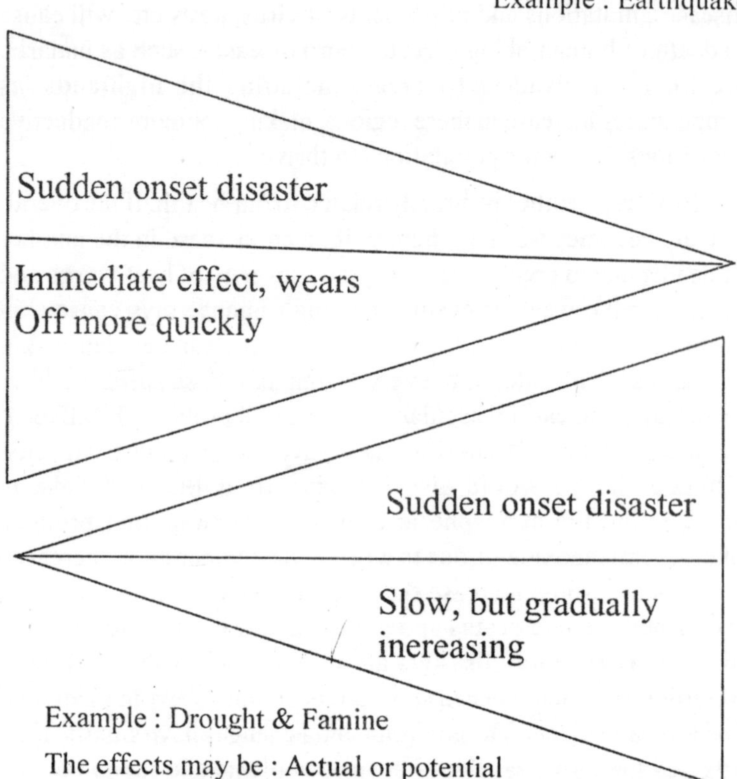

are unable to adjust with their conditions and consequently there is a rapid increase in the number of mental patients. Without a strong will power and weak mental health when they are exposed to disasters and terrifying experiences, they shows psychological 'shock' reactions. The nature of 'disaster syndrome' may vary for different people and for different stages i.e. 'shock stage', 'the suggestable stag' and the 'recovery stage' and responses of an individual varies from heroism to pest, traumatic stress disorder (PSID) depending on one's personality. The feeling of fear, guilt, anxiety, depression etc. become prominent in vulnerable persons. One may feel betrayed up life. Suppressed anger can take a bad shape and can be repressed. In such situations ego becomes shaky and support system damaged and emotional reactions blow up. A sense of loneliness, helplessness, vacuum and emptiness are common and all these conditions become more severe when human beings are not supported by their environment also as nature itself is struggling and facing several disasters due to continuous changes in the climate.

Biodiversity boosts ecosystem productivity, where every species no matter how small all have at important role to play. Climate change affect both individual species and their ecosystems. With the change in climatic conditions, we can have unexpected results. Each species will respond in an individual fashion, according to its climate tolerances and its ability to disperse into a new location, alter its phenology (e.g. breeding date) or adapt to shifting food sources."[4] It will affect marine ecosystems not only by an increase insea temperature and changes in ocean circulation, but also by ocean acidification, as the concentration of dissolved carbon dioxide (carbonic acid) rises. Polar ecosystems are especially vulnerable to climate change, with effects such as thawing permafrost, decreased snow cover and changes in ocean temperatures. A Biosafety Protocol melting was hosted in Montreal, Canada and there was an somewhat successful treaty "to regulate the international transport and release of genetically modified organisms to protect natural biological diversity."[5]

Thus we can say that the impact of climate change on international security is not a problem of the future but already of today and one which will stay with us. Even if progress is made in reducing the emission of greenhouse gases, weather pattern have already changed, global temperatures have already risen and, above all climate change is already felt around the globe. As says Caldwell "At the advent of the 21st century approaches a crisis. Our customary ways of thinking and governing are maladapted to the new environmental relationships that human ingenuity has created through applied science and technology. Our survival as a civilization perhaps as a species – requires a better adaptive response to the problems that we as a species have created."[6]

REFERENCES

1. Arun Bapat, 'Natural Disaster – Man : Slove of Master, Nagpur, Maharashtra State Council of Educational Research and Training, 1992., p. 32.
2. Climate Change 2007 : Impacts, Adaptation and Vulnerability. IPCC Summary for Policymaker (2007).
3. The Hindu Survey of The Environment, 2009, p. 53.
4. Climate Change and Biodiversity, Yale University Press(2006).
5. Proceedings of The Ninety Fourth Session of the Indian Science Congress, Annamalainagr, 2007.
6. Caldwell, L.K. 1998. Governance or the environment in the 21st Century Environmental Awareness, 21 : 5–10.

5

Technique of Disaster Management

Sandeep Kumar Singh
Research Scholar
Lect. Sociology.
A.S.R.R.B.S.D.C Gaura, Unnao.

Dr. Virendra Singh Yadav
Senior Lecturer in Hindi
D.V. (P.G.) College,
Orai (Jalaun)

Introduction

Disasters are as old as human history. They have been mostly dealt with from a merely humanitarian angle, while natural hazards such as cyclones, floods, droughts,and earthquakes have been analyzed technically and scientifically with in scientific disciplines.

Disasters can no longer be seen as 'Acts of God ' or 'Act of Nature' over which we have little control nor can we leave disasters to de understood by Natural, scientists. It is high time that we as responsible knowing about risk that lead to disasters, understanding now they affect our livelihoods and environment and dedicating collective efforts to manage those conditions.

Defining Search and Rescue

Search and rescue is a technical activity rendered by an individual or a group of specially trained personnel, who rescue and attend to the casualties under adverse conditions, where life is at threat.

Search and rescue is organized in close cooperation with the community and in a team approach. The search and rescue activities are undertaken in two manners:

* Community as Local Rescuers:

  With adequate safety measures, rescue activities are taken up immediately by the community after any disaster.

* Outside Community Resources:

  Circumstances where the situation is grave and the local rescuers do not have required skills and equipments then specialist assistance from outside the community is required.

  The main Objectives of a Search and Rescue Team are to:

* Rescue the survivors trapped under the debris, from the damaged building or from a cyclonic storm surge.
* Provide First Aid services to the trapped survivors and to dispatch them for medical care.
* Take immediate necessary actions, as for temporary support and protection to endangered collapsed buildings to structures.

Hand- over, recover and dispose-off the bodies of the deceased.

Train, demonstrate and raise awareness on how to use the local materials for rescuing the community people.

1.1 Team Composition

Honest, emotionally sound, professionally decisive, volunteers male and female, having good physical condition, with demonstrate capacity and willingness to work in an emergency could constitute a rescue team.

Volunteers, of both sex, above the age of 18 years with a minimum education level (reading and writing the local language) can be a part of the search and rescue team.

Preference would be given to ex-military or army personnel's.

What are the duties of a Rescuer?

The first job of a rescuer is to assess the area so as to save time, which would help.

Search and Rescue Skills-

Whenever and where ever disasters strike the first responder for search and rescue always begins at the local levels: individual and neighborhood. It is a daunting task for the locals to rescue the victims due to lack of skilled human resources. Disasters or emergencies disrupt normal life. We cannot stop hazards from happening but preparedness can make all the difference between life and death. People habituating in highly vulnerable pocket scope up with frequent disasters on the basis of their acumen, accumulated knowledge, accumulated skills ad resources of the community and they have managed to survive the fury of the nature through centuries.

In a post disaster scenario Search and Rescue has always played a major role in disaster management. It is on the strength, capability and effectiveness of the search and rescue team that more of human lives could be saved.

What are the duties of a rescuer?

The first job of a rescuer is to assess the area so as to save time, which would help in effective response. It is very important for rescuer to collect information on the extent of damage, approach to the damage and understand if any further damage is likely to occur the local leaders or the people residing in that particular locality provide all this information. Follow three key principles during the surrey:

(a) Look: See physically the incidents and make a thorough visual inspection.

(b) Listen: Listen to all the sources of information-from the community, Government records and media reports.

(c) Feel: feel convinced regarding the fact, the gravity of the dangers and our own capacity to respond.

Plan

Rescue is a team effort that needs coordination and planning amongst the members for an optimum response operation. After the assessment, the rescue Team would be in a position to adequately plan the Rescue operation based on the following specifications:

(a) Manpower (b) Equipment (c) Method

(a) Manpower- The Rescuers can use the skilled manpower if available and also take the help of the local community if required.

(b) Equipment: Ropes, ladders, bamboos, or stick, stretchers, boats etc. are essential to rescue the affected victims. Sometimes these rescue materials are not available to the rescue team at the site of emergency. Therefore the rescuers use locally available resources like barrels tinned cans, tubes etc.

(c) Method: There are various other methods, which would-be useful for rescuing the victims. The adequate method of rescue is to be determined depending upon the nature of the casualty, the nature of the injuries and the position in which the casualty is found.

DISASTERS

1. Earthquakes

On December 23, 1972, a series of earthquakes shook the Central American nation of Nicaragua. The largest earthquake registered 6.2 on the Richter scale. The earthquake's epicenter was located precisely at the capital city of Managua. The earthquake resulted in the destruction of the heavily populated central zone and damage to a total area of about 27 square kilometers (10 square miles). Subsequent fires blazed throughout the city, compounding the damages. In the wake of the disaster, at least 8,000 of Managua's total population of 430000 had died, 20,000 were injured, over 260,000 had fled the city, 50 percent of the employed were jobless, and 70 percent were left temporarily homeless. At least 10 percent of the nation's industrial capacity, 50 percent of commercial property, and 70 percent of government facilities were rendered inoperative. Overall; the damage estimated in US dollars was $845 million.

Ground Movements

The ground movements caused by earthquakes can have several types of damaging effects. Some of the major affects are:

1. Ground shaking, i.e. bake-and-forth motion of the ground, caused by the passing vibratory waves through the ground.
2. Soil failures, such as liquefaction and landslides, caused by shaking;
3. Surface fault ruptures, such as cracks, vertical shifts, etc.
4. Tidal waves (tsunamis), i.e. large waves on the surface of bodies of water that can cause major damage to shoreline areas.

2. Landslides

Landslides are among the major natural disasters or calamities in the world. In hilly terrains of India, including Himalayan mountains landslides have been a major and widely spread natural disasters that strike life and property almost perennially and occupy a position of major concern. These landslides, to transportation and communication network.

Landslides, debris fall, debris slide, debris flow rock toppling etc. cause destruction of slope and ground surface, initiating the change of uncontrolled erosion in the mountain terrains.

On 21st August, 2002, heavy monsoon in eastern Nepal triggered landslides and flash floods which killed 419 people and injuring105 people. More than53, 152 families were affected and about 19,485 houses were destroyed. A total of 47 districts were affected.

FACTORS THAT CAUSE LANDSLIDES

Landslides occur because of the interplay of several factors.

Natural factors-

* Intensity of rainfall
* Steep slopes
* Stiffness of slopes

* Highly weathered rock layers
* Soil layers formed under gravity
* Seismic activity
* Poor drainage
* Deforestation leading to soil erosion
* Non-engineered excavation
* Mining and quarrying
* Non-engineered construction
* Land use pattern

3. Floods

Bangladesh is a reverie country where recurrent flooding is both common and necessary. Every year large areas are submerged during the monsoon season and fertilized by deposits of fresh alluvium, i.e., the soil deposited by moving water. However, if the waters remain stagnant for too long, these beneficial floods become major disasters. Such was the case in the summer and fall of 1974 when flooding extended over nearly one-half of the country and stagnated for more than a month. At least 1200 people died in the floods and another 27,500 died from subsequent disease and starvation. Approximately 425,000 houses were destroyed or severely damaged. A total of 36 million people suffered severe hardship and losses due to the disaster.

Water is a source for all life forms. Without water no life is sustainable. How tragic it is, when water in the form of floods takes away thousand of human and cattle lives. More than one million huts and poor houses are lost every year in floods in India. Can we prevent this loss?

4. Cyclones

Cyclones pose a major threat to life and property in many parts of the world. Every year these sudden, violent cyclones bring widespread devastation to coastlines and islands lying in their erratic paths. A windstorm's destructive work is done by the high wind; flood producing rains and associated storm surges.

On November19, 1977, a cyclone, which had been expected to hit Tamil Nadu, instead struck the central coast of Andhra Pradesh State in the Krishna Godavari Delta. Many people perished because advance warning was either too slowly or too narrowly disseminated. Damage in Andhra Pradesh was caused primarily by a storm surge that devastated some 65 villages, about 21of which were completely washed away. The storm surge was reported to have been 5.7 meters (19feet) high, 80 kilometers (50 miles) long, 16 kilometers (10 miles) wide, with a speed of 190 kilometers per hour (120 miles per hour). Many of the victims of the Andhra Pradesh cyclone were migrant laborers. This made identification of the dead difficult.

Sharing Responsibility Role of Local And State Bodies

At the time of disaster various agencies both government and non-government organizations play a crucial role in preparing the society. Home Guards, Civil Defense, Volunteers of National Service Scheme, Nehru Yuva Kendra Sangathan too play a major a major role at the functions and role of these agencies in disaster management, who make the society a better place to lives.

READ THE FOLLOWING

26th January 2001, Earthquake of an intensity of 6.9 occurs in Bhuj.

26th January 2001, reports of the State Government state that, more than 13,000 people have been declared dead and about 1.67 lakh people have been injured. About 1.97 core population spread over 21 districts have been affected. About 3.20 lakh, permanent and semi permanent (pucca / kucha) houses and 14,000huts have been fully destroyed and about 7.33 lakh permanent and semi (pucca / kucha) houses and 31,000 huts have been partially damaged....What went wrong? Did the houses have faulty structural design?

28th January 2001, relief teams started reaching Ahmadabad and Bhuj. Individuals, Voluntary organizations, Professionals, Aid agencies have started approaching materials for providing assistance.

Mr Khan is a driver in the town of Bhuj. Thankfully none in his family was injured during the quake; they lost all their valuables, cash, and their house. More than 100 organizations, private, government and non-government, were providing relief materials after the earthquake, but Mr. Khan could not get a single tent for his family, who were living on the street.... who will coordinate?

It is not only Mr. Khan a poor driver who was suffering. Think about it..... When disasters occur they teach us lessons at a very high cost usually to life and property. This indicates how important and how crucial planning for a disaster is. So are we prepared to face another jolt like the Bhuj? Isn't it time for us to learn from our past experiences?

Managing of Disasters

Disasters can be managed effectively through close coordination's with various government and non-government agencies..... Do you know the agencies that work for our safety?

Let's understand the various agencies which play a key role in Disaster Management.

How is Disasters Managed?

The flow chart given below would give you a better understanding about the management of disasters at various levels in our country.

National	:	Nodal Ministries
State	:	Relief and Rehabilitation Department/ Department of Disaster management
District	:	Office of the District Magistrate
Block	:	Office of the Panchay at Samiti
Village	:	Village Disaster Management Committee

India with its federal system of Government has specific roles for the Central and the State Governments. The country has integrated administrative machinery for management of disasters at the National, State, District and sub-District levels. The basic responsibility of undertaking rescue, relief and rehabilitation measures in the even of natural disasters is with the concerned State Government by providing financial and logistic support.

NATIONAL LEVEL

The response from the Central Government is based keeping in view the following factors:

1. The gravity of the disaster
2. The scale of the relief operations
3. The requirements of the Central assistance for augmenting financial recourses and logistics support at the disposal of the State Government.

The Ministry of Home Affairs is the Nodal Ministry at the centre for coordinating disaster management activities for all natural hazards except drought which is taken care by Ministry of Agriculture under the Department of Agriculture and cooperation. Other Ministries are assigned the responsibility of providing emergency support in case of disasters that fall within their preview.

Sl.No.	*Disasters*	*Nodal Ministry*
1	Natural Disasters	(other than drought) Minister of Home Affairs
2	Drought	Minister of Agriculture
3	Air Accidents	Minister of Civil Aviation
4	Railway Accidents	Minister of Railways
5	Chemical Disasters	Minister of Home Affairs
6	Biology Disasters	Minister of Home Affairs
7		Nuclear Minister of Home Affairs
8	Epidemics	Minister of Health and Family Welfare

State

The responsibility to cope up with natural disasters is essentially that of the State Government. The role of the Central Government is to support in terms of physical and financial resources. The chief Minister or the Chief Secretary of the State heads a state level committee which is in overall charge of the relief operations at the State and the Relief Commissioner who is in charge of the relief and rehabilitation measures in the wake of natural disasters. In many of the states, Secretary, Department of Revenue is also in charge of relief operations. The states have the relief manual called as the 'State Relief Code' and the State Contingency Plan which guides them to manage disaster scenarios.

District

The district administration is the focal point for implementation of all government plans and activities. The actual day-to-day function of administering relief is the responsibility of the District Magistrate/District collector/ Deputy Commissioner who exercises coordinating and supervising powers over all the departments at the district level.

The 73rd and the 74th constitutional amendments recognize Panchayati Raj Institutions as 'Institutions of self-government'. These local bodies can be effective instruments in tackling disasters through early warning system, relief distribution, providing shelter to the victims, medical assistance etc.

A Disaster Management Committee has been set up at the district level headed by the District Magistrate and officials from the health department, irrigation Department, Veterinary Department, Department of Water and Sanitation, Police, Fire services, representatives from National and International NGOs, etc. The Disaster management Committee which is basically the decision making body takes the help of the Disaster Management Teams, like the Fire Services, police, Health practioners etc. are:

Block

The Block Development Officer/ Taluka Development Officer is the nodal officer at the Block level for all the disaster management activities. The Disaster Management Committee at the Block/ Taluka level for, is headed by this Nodal Officer. The other members of the committee are officers from the Social Welfare department, Health department, Rural water supply and Sanitaion Department, Police, Fire Services, representatives from youth Organizations, Community Based Organizations, Nongovernmental, Organizations, eminent senior citizens, elected representatives etc. The main functions of Block Disaster Management Committee are:

- Helping the Block administration in preparation of the Block Disaster Management Plan.
- Coordinating training for the members of the Disaster Management Teams.
- Carry out mock drills.

Village

At the village level, the Village Disaster Management Committee geared by the Sarpanch/Village headman is responsible for preparing the Village Disaster Management Plans and also coordinating with various agencies for providing training to the Disaster Management Teams. The members should see to it that mock drills are carried out by the villagers at regular intervals by the villagers for various hazards.

It is accepted that the Government alone cannot take on the entire responsibility of Disaster Management. Apart from national, state, district and local levels there are various institutions who are involved in disaster management at various levels in the country. This includes the police and Para-military forces, Civil Defense and Home Guards, fire services, National Cadet Corps (NCC), Youth organizations, UN agencies, International and National voluntary groups, public and private sector enterprises, media etc. play a major role in managening disaster. Functions of some of the organizations have been mentioned below.

1. UN Disaster Management Team (UNDMT) India

UN Office for Coordination of Humanitarian Affairs (UN

OCHA), has been made responsible by the UN General Assembly mandate for all International disaster response. In India, UNDMT represents various Un agencies to implement disaster preparedness and mitigation efforts and strengthen Government's capacities on disaster risk management. The UNDMT has representation from various UN Agencies such as FAO, ILO, UNFPA, UNICEF, WFP and WHO which act together whenever there is a disaster. The primary purpose of the UNDMT is to ensure prompt, effective and concerted country level disaster preparedness by the UN system, and the response when appropriate.

Indian Armed Forces

The Armed Forces are the core of the Government's response capacity. They intervene and take on specific takes only when the situation is beyond the capacity of civil administration. Due to their ability to organize action in averse ground circumstances, speed go operational response and the resources an capacities at their disposal, the armed forces have historically played a major role in emergency support functions such as communications, search and rescue operations, health and medical facilities, transportation, power food and civil supplies, public works and engineering, especially in the immediate aftermath of disaster.

National Cadet Corps (NCC)

The National Cadet Corps, a body formed in 1948 aims at:

- Developing qualities of character, courage, comradeship, discipline, leadership, secular out look, spirit of adventure and sportsmanship and the ideals of selfless service among the youth to make them useful citizens.
- This it done by creating a human resource of organized, trained and activated youth.
- Providing leadership in all walks of life including the Armed Forces and making themselves available for the service of the nation.

Civil Defence

Civil Defense aims at saving life, minimizing damage to the

property and maintaining continuity of industrial production in the event of a hostile attack. The two war emergencies faced by the country in 1962 and 1965 compelled the Government of India to reorient its emergency training activities from natural disasters to those concerning protection of life and property against enemy action. The National Civil Defense College was founded on 29th April 1957 at Nagpur as the Central Emergency Relief Training Institute (CERTI) to function as the training wing of the Emergency Relief Organization of the Government of India. This Central Institute focuses on advanced and specialist training to the leaders of relief services, which was essential for efficient conduct of relief operations during natural disasters. Today there are around 500,000 Civil Defense volunteers throughout the country.

National Service Scheme (NSS)

Ever since independence there has been growing awareness of the desirability of involving students in national services. The first Education Commission (1950) recommended the introduction of national service by students on a voluntary basis. Ministry of Education introduced the National Service Scheme during 1969-70. The motto of NSS is "NOT ME BUT YOU". It underlines that the welfare of an individual is ultimately dependent on the welfare of the society as a whole. The NSS system is based on the "Rath Wheel" of the Konark Sun Temple of Orissa.

It Stand for dynamism and progressive out look of youth. Any enrolled as a NSS volunteer, as per NSS Manual should put in at least 240 hours of useful social work in a continuous period of two years (i.e. 120 hours per year). A work dairy is to be maintained by each NSS volunteer, which will help him/her in the assessment in his/her performance. Such volunteer is eligible to get NSS service Certificate from the colleges. The Service Certificate given in the NSS Manual should be strictly adhered. Each NSS unit in the college is expected to adopt a near by village/slum and work for its all-round development. Regular activities and special corpus should preferably be organized in the adopted village/ rural unit / slum for this purpose.

Nehru Yuva Kendras

The Nehru Yuva Kendras were launched in the year 1972 as part of the Silver Jubilee celebration of India's Independence. This was on the recommendation of the National Advisory Board on Youth with the objective of providing the non-student rural youth avenues to take part in nation building activities and also to provide opportunity for the development of their own personality and skills. As volunteers the members have helped the community at times of crisis. Today, it functions under the Ministry of Youth Affairs & Sports. NYKS is a registered society and is governors headed by the Minister of Youth Affairs & sports.

Home Guard

Home Guard is a voluntary force, first raised in India in December 1946, to assist the police in controlling civil disturbance and communal riots. Subsequently, the concept of a voluntary citizen's force was adopted by several States. In the wake of Chinese aggression in 1962, the Centre advised the States and Union territories to merge their existing voluntary organization into one uniform voluntary foreknown as 'Home guards'. The function of Home Guards is to.

- Serve as an auxiliary to the police in maintenance of internal security.
- Help the community in any kind of emergency such as air raid, fire, cyclone, earthquake, epidemic etc.
- Help in maintenance of essential services.
- Promote communal harmony and assist the administration in protecting weaker sections.
- Participate in socio-economic and welfare activities and perform Civil Defense duties.

MAIN STREAMING DISASTER MANAGEMENT IN EDUCATION:

In order to make available a competent force, training right from the School to the Technical colleges and Higher education courses about disaster management is being introduced. Courses have been designed with a purpose to sensitize students in all the aspects of Disaster Management.

Various leading institutes of the country like the Indian Institute of Technology (IITs) and The National Institute of Disaster Management (NIDM) intend to upgrade. The skilled human resources for the country by providing training to various government level functionaries of various departments. All India council of Technical Education (AICTE) has introduced Disaster Management courses in Engineering. Similar efforts drew being made to introduce Disaster Management in Architecture course and urban planning, Medical courses etc. Disaster Management has also been made a part of the foundation course for All India Services like the Indian Administrative Services (IAS), Indian police Services (IPS) and Indian Forest Services (IFS) etc.

6

Consequence Assessment in Earthquake Risk Management/ Disaster Management (Different aspects)

Dr.Mridula shukla
Head Deptt of Sociology
Kanpur Vidya Mandir P.G.College
Kanpur

Varun Shukla
(B.Tech, PGDBA)
Lecturer
PSIT, Kanpur

Introduction

The developments in earthquake engineering research during the last 2-3 decades provide, within acceptable limits, reliable design of new structures against earthquake loads. In the more developed part of the world, such methods are presently implemented in the best practice design of new structures. However, the existing older building stock still represents a significant risk in regard to the safety of people as well as to the economical assets of the society. In less developed countries, both the new building stock and the existing building stock exhibit a significant vulnerability, mainly due to inadequate design, missing supervision during construction, insufficient quality of construction materials and inadequate ground investigation/interpretation.

The recent series of earthquakes, Turkey (1999), Taiwan (1999), India (2001) and Iran (2003) not only lead to an improved awareness with regard to seismic hazards, but also highlights the difficulties involved in an efficient decision making process in such situations, especially in less developed countries. Consistent and quantitative risk assessment tools for buildings and infrastructure in seismic active areas are urgently needed to ensure an efficient decision making process that facilitates the optimal allocation of available economical resources for the management of risks before, during and after an earthquake.

General Frameworks for the Earthquake Risk Management

An important feature of the earthquake risk management framework is that it provides cost efficient decision support on how to optimize investments into risk reducing measures in three situations, namely, prior, during and after an earthquake, see **Figure 1**. It should be noted that the "during" period corresponds to the period between the occurrence of the first ground motions till the end of the last after shocks, i.e. in the order of 4-6 weeks.

A key element in the pursued approach is the quantification of the effect of various types of determinable (e.g. by observation or calculation) information (indicators) on the risks. These risk indicators may have very different characteristics and necessitate that different expertises are integrated into the project, see **Figure 2**.

An example of such a risk indicator is the information about the structural design codes applied for the design of a group of structures. Another indicator could be the characteristics of the soil implicitly describing how the energy from a given earthquake will be transferred from the bedrock to the structures. In addition, more traditional indicators of accumulated damage in structures, such as deflections and cracks, will be utilized in the formulation of the framework. Many indicators are based on the availability of spatial data, describing the terrain, building structures and traffic networks.

As a first step, the consequences are categorized; see

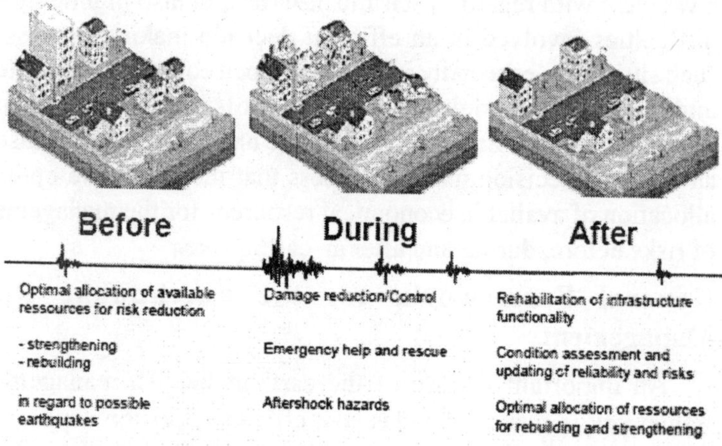

Fig. 1 : Illustration of the different decision problems in earthquake risk management.

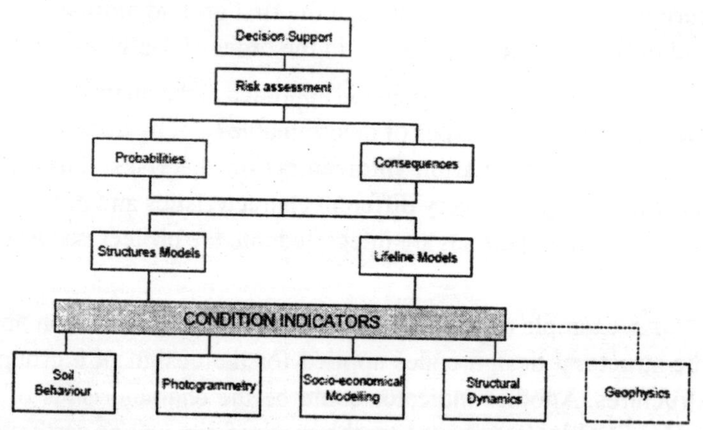

Fig.2 : Illustration of the interrelationships between the research groups and the tasks of the project.

Figure 4, and the characteristics of each are identified. Also the related indicators in each case are discussed.

3.2.1 Structural and Lifeline Consequences

Loss-estimation methods currently exist to project direct damage to buildings from ground motion. In determining and quantifying the consequences regarding the lifelines and structures

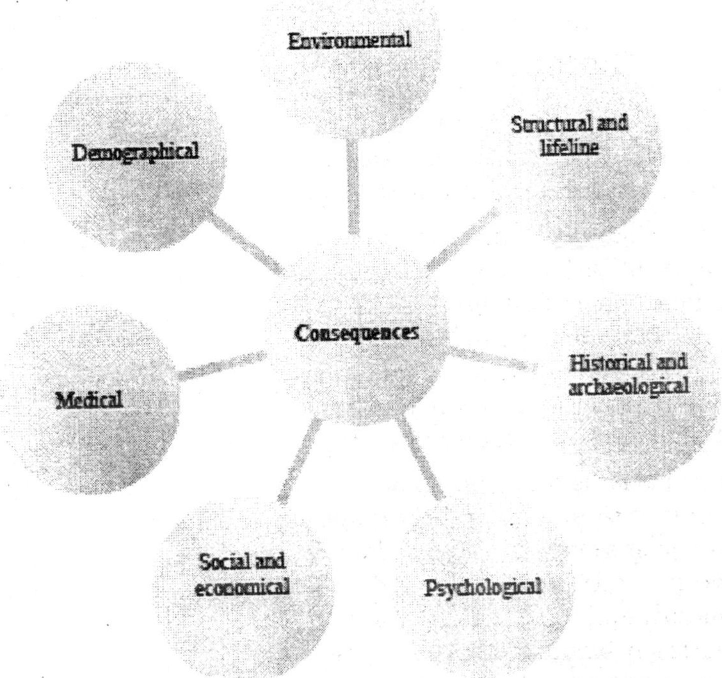

Fig.4 : Categorization of Consequences in Earthquake risk management

two important issues should be considered: description and damage. The important factors defining these two are shown in **Figure 5**.

In this category only the direct physical losses resulting from the damage or failure of the structures and lifelines are considered and no indirect consequences are taken into account for this purpose the vulnerability curves play an important role, which themselves are an outcome of Earthquake intensity, distance from the center, structural type, age and height of the structure, soil profile and etc. also, for assessing the loss of inventory the occupancy classes are needed. At the end the costs of debris removal should be added to the whole calculations of structural and lifeline's monetary

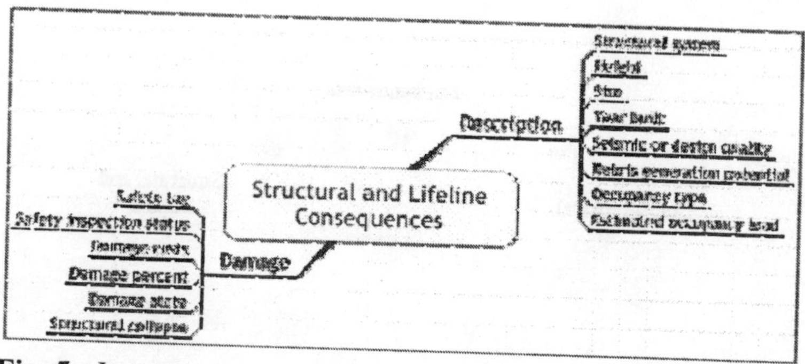

Fig. 5 : Important Factors in Structural and Lifeline Consequences

consequences.

The primary type of information needed is inventory of existing buildings and structures. Such an inventory might include: ages of the structures, construction types (e.g., configuration, height, and materials), usage patterns, and number of inhabitants. From this structural inventory, response to ground motion estimates, and hazard characterizations, projected damage estimates could be made, including economic costs for replacement and repair of the structures, following earthquakes of various magnitudes for specific communities. Without good inventory data, however, these damage estimates are, at best, educated guesses.

3.2.2 Medical consequences

The medical consequences are considered to be the costs related to injuries, evacuation and reallocation of the people. The main factor determining the size of sanitary losses (SL) and the share of injuries with different degree of severity is intensity of earthquake, which is resulted in severity of damage. At the same time number of people at risk and number of injured allow substantiating the common medical-and-evacuation indices of the casualties for the given intensity of earthquake. The important factors identifying the costs can be summarized as: Cause of injury (EQ-relatedness, Structural relatedness, Secondary hazards, Injury mechanism), Severity, Treatment (Level, Immediacy), Costs (Direct medical care costs, Indirect costs), Diagnosis and Location of individual when injury occurred.

3.2.3 Psychological Consequences

These findings summarized as; fear, helplessness, distress, depression and suicides, can suggest that the psychological consequences of earthquake exposure are long lasting and seem to be related to the consequences of the earthquakes in terms of damage/loss. All these aspects are indirect consequences which are rarely assessed in risk management area, but are of great importance and can cause less efficiency afterwards.

3.2.4 Social/Economical Consequences

The economic consequences of seismic events are becoming greater every year. The accumulation of investments in buildings, equipment, and infrastructure such as highways, bridges, gas, water and sewer pipelines, electricity, telephone and cable wires are mounting at enormous rates. The growth of the economy means that business disruption is more costly. Urbanization is occurring throughout the world, and there are more extremely large metropolitan agglomerations than ever before. Potential losses are becoming greater than ever before at an enormous rate.

The major economic consequences of earthquakes result from damage to elements of the built environment that are essential to the operation of the economic activities in the impacted region. Some economic sectors are by their nature more vulnerable than others. Some sectors will even find an increase in their activity because of demands placed on them by the disaster. Some activities will be winners while others will be losers. From the perspective of the market analyst, impact is gauged by product line, the specific good or service a business offers. Statistical and economic analysis deals with sectors of economic activity that group a number of products together. There may be both winners and losers in a particular sector. Factors that will cause businesses to lose include the direct damage they entail to their facilities because of their location in the area that was stricken. Other factors include their dependency on damaged or destroyed support systems of transport and communication for workers, customers, supplies, shipments, water, electricity, gas, telephone, and other services. Businesses that may benefit are ones for which there is an increased demand for their products or services for relief, clearing and removing debris, repair and restoration, and reconstruction.

In total, to an extent depending on flows of external assistance from other regions and local accumulation of resources, the regional economy may experience an increase rather than a decrease in income. However, regardless of the level of specificity of analysis, whether product or sector or region, there is agreement that the funds that are spent will be diverted from other uses for which they were intended. Whether or not a business lose will be greatly influenced in addition to its sector, by the extent to which the managers have planned, taken precautionary preparations, and necessary measures to mitigate the impact of a seismic event.

The number of casualties is considered to be the direct consequence and the rest, indirect consequences of an earthquake. For all these consequences, the indicator in charge is the number of people at risk, occupancy class and the damage state of the building, as discussed earlier.

3.2.5 Historical and Archeological Consequences

The history of humankind is partially represented in the historical monuments and sites around the globe and thus for sure need preservation. The vulnerability of the cultural heritage is growing every day, due to age, deterioration of materials by geophysical and environmental conditions as well as by human interaction. Cultural heritage is found in most of the countries and thus constitutes a growing concern among the governments and the population alike.

- Destruction of entire or particular elements of past cultures or phases of human activity, particularly the earliest or less monumental manifestations.
- Damage to the integrity of cultural landscapes by removing cultural features that are important archaeological evidence of the relationship between sites.

- Potential damage to sub-surface remains by changes to the surrounding environment as a result of development.

The loss of these heritages would be a great consequence of a natural disaster and because of that the decrease in the number of tourists in the area and the stagnancy in tourist industry, can have a great influence on the economical situation of the area. But it is possible that the loss of normal tourist income will be replaced, if not exceeded, by income from visitors involved in the reconstruction.

The historical consequences regarding the heritage itself are considered to be direct and the rest taking into account the tourist industry and loss of heritage is considered to be indirect consequences, both in relation with the age, material deterioration as discussed above.

3.2.6 Demographical Consequences

The analysis of the previous information after earthquakes shows that during the years after disaster a sharp birth rate reduction and an increase of the death rate is seen, and that the median age of the population grows. This affects the process of achieving the pre-quake number of the people. The population of the area will reach its pre-quake level in ten to fifteen years at best. Restoration of the natural annual increase levels will take several years.

Delays in the arrangements of living conditions and employment of the refugees are also critical. So is procrastination in returning of data on the evacuated, mainly children and youth who have aspirations to remain where they were evacuated. So there is always an urgent need of a new demographic program for the survivors to normalize the demographic situation in affected areas and to stop the migration of people to other places.

The important demographical issues are categorized as:

- Age
- Gender
- Race/Ethnicity

- Level of education
- Occupation
- Income
- Disabilities and pre-existing conditions
- Dependency

The most important indicators for assessing the demographical consequences therefore are the number of people evacuated from the area (a function of number of people at risk), duration of reconstruction and the age of evacuated people.

3.2.7 Environmental Consequences

Environmental consequences may have effects on plants, animals, and not least persons. The damage of water and sewer pipelines can cause the water and waste flow to the environment. Also considerable amounts of oil and chemical can be released into the underground waters and the ground surface. Moreover, the debris from the collapsed buildings and enterprises are sometimes of a problem to the environment. The probability of chemicals in the debris is another major environmental concern.

The consequences of damage to structures housing intrinsically dangerous goods or processes is another category of consideration, and concerns the potential hazards of fire, explosion, toxicity or pollution represented by installation such as liquid petroleum gas storage facilities or nuclear power or weapon plants. These types of consequences often become difficult to consider objectively, as strong emotions are provoked by the thought of them.

CONCLUSIONS

In this paper, different consequences (direct and indirect) of an earthquake are briefly presented and the possible indicators for each consequence have been discussed.

Therefore, to be able to reach the target, it has been decided to focus on only two categories, namely; Structural and Lifeline consequences, and, Social/Economical consequences.

NEW STRATEGY FOR EARTHQUAKE RISK MANAGEMENT

HOW TO MOTIVATE PEOPLE FOR SAFETY

SUMMARY

In earthquake disasters, most of deaths are attributed to collapse of vulnerable buildings, particularly houses. Governments are forced to invest a huge amount of resources for aid of the evacuees, demolition of debris, construction of temporary houses and permanent houses, due to collapse of houses. Vulnerable houses with adobe, stone, or brick, which are commonly seen throughout the developing world, exist in a huge number and are being reproduced. The Kobe Earthquake in 1995 revealed that the Japanese common wooden houses are also vulnerable against earthquakes. It is therefore indispensable to make existing houses safer by retrofitting for effective earthquake disaster management. However, it is difficult to motivate people for retrofitting as people tend to choose future uncertain loss rather than the current loss, i.e. investment for retrofitting. This paper discusses how people can be motivated for retrofitting and then proposes new directions to be incorporated into earthquake disaster management.

The earthquake is the most deadly natural disaster in our modern society while the flood, another deadly disaster, is less deadly recently thanks to development of science and technology. Table 1 shows the most deadly natural disasters in the past 30 years in the world.

More than a half of these deadly disasters are induced by earthquakes. While the twentieth century saw huge progress in seismology and earthquake engineering, it does not seem that such progress has reduced the damage caused by earthquakes.

Vernacular houses with adobes, bricks, blocks, and woods, which are commonly seen throughout the world, are vulnerable to earthquakes. Strong earthquakes destroy these houses, killing thousands of people almost every year. It is ironic that the shelters which are supposed to protect people from various hazards often

Table 1: Ten most deadly disasters in the past 30 years in the world

Nation	Disaster	Year	Death
China	Earthquake	1976	290,000
Colombia	Volcano	1985	21,000
Armenia	Earthquake	1988	25,000
Iran	Earthquake	1990	35,000
Bangladesh	Cyc/flood	1991	140,000
Venezuela	Flood	1999	30,000
India	Earthquake	2001	20,000
Iran	Earthquake	2003	27,000
Indonesia, others	Eq/tsunami	2004	over 300,000
Pakistan	Earthquake	2005	over 80,000

end up killing them.

These vulnerable vernacular houses may be characterized as follows;

- Houses made of locally available and cheaper materials.
- Relatively low quality of construction work
- No building regulation or no conformity to the regulation and thereby no check from the formal sector
- Use of intuitive knowledge (non-engineered)

In Japan, wooden houses are traditional and still common now, many of which are also vulnerable against earthquakes. In the case of 1995 Kobe Earthquake, which claimed more than 6,000 lives, 80% of the total death toll was caused by crushing or suffocation mainly due to collapse of the wooden houses. In the central area of Kobe City, where a detailed research on damage was conducted, 95 % of collapsed houses, mainly wooden, were built before 1981, when the seismic requirements of the Japanese Building Codes were revised.

Due to rapid urbanization and rapid spread of modern life style, it appears that earthquake disasters are becoming more complicated and deadly. As the cities are growing and more crowded than ever, they are becoming more vulnerable. The urban poor who have no choice but to live in hazardous areas are particularly vulnerable. Substantial rapid urbanization took place worldwide in the last 50 years while the return period of a big earthquake would be more than 50 years. A medium size earthquake could even devastate a city if it takes place beneath or near the city.

As earthquakes cannot be predicted precisely even by applying the most advanced science and technology, it is indispensable to make existing houses safer in order to reduce the number of victims and severe damage. No matter how effectively emergency management and relief activities are conducted, the lost lives can never be regained. The more resilient the existing houses are against earthquakes, the lower the death rate would be, and the less would be the disruptions to economic and social activities in the affected areas. It is one of the most important lessons from the past earthquake disasters.

Although mankind has the technologies to reduce the impact of disasters and knows what kind of regulations are necessary, vernacular houses still remain vulnerable. A big challenge here is that the house owners are hardly motivated to invest for retrofitting to secure safety required. The vulnerable houses can be retrofitted only by the homeowners themselves, not by the authorities. It is thus essential to motivate them for retrofitting. This paper discusses the decision making mechanism regarding retrofitting and what would be incentives for retrofitting, then proposes new directions to motivate people effectively for retrofitting.

2. EFFORTS FOR SAFER HOUSES

In Japan, the houses constructed before 1981 may not be safe enough as they do not meet the current safety requirements. The total number of housing units in Japan is 47 million, of which it is officially estimated 11.5 million houses or 25% were built before 1981 and therefore may not be safe enough. It should be pointed out, however, a number of houses constructed after 1981 may not meet the current seismic safety requirements either, due to poor consideration on seismic safety, poor construction work, or degradation. In fact, it turned out in 2005 in Japan that the structural calculation of some condominium-type RC buildings had been false, terrifying many residents there. Aging of houses also imposes a serious problem in seismic safety as the common structure of houses is wooden, which is susceptible to degradation due to bad or lack of maintenance.

It is broadly understood that securing safety of newly constructed houses and retrofitting of existing vulnerable houses is essential to reduce seismic damage. To deal with the new construction of vernacular houses, development and enforcement of the building codes and strict inspection system would suffice, though it is a difficult task. In order to deal with already existing vulnerable vernacular houses, which would be by far a bigger challenge, retrofitting is critical, if demolition or reconstruction is not feasible.

Practical technologies for retrofitting of vernacular houses are available. 10-15% of the construction cost would be sufficient for retrofitting. The Japanese governments enforced, immediately after the 1995 Kobe Earthquake, Act for Promotion of Retrofitting, aiming to promote retrofitting of important facilities and existing vulnerable houses, based on the lessons learnt from the Kobe Earthquake. It stipulates that the owners of buildings which many people use must make their efforts toward seismic diagnosis and retrofitting, and that some technical requirements other than earthquake-resistant related provisions may be exempted.

In order to promote retrofitting of vulnerable houses in addition to the Act, the governments started financial assistance for seismic diagnosis and retrofitting, opened local consultation desks, encouraged technical development for retrofitting, and developed "Simplified Seismic Diagnosis Tools" for wooden houses. The inspection system at construction sites was strengthened. The Housing Quality Assurance Act was also enforced in 1999 to secure quality, including safety, of houses and to protect the interest of house purchasers.

3. CHOICE UNDER UNCERTAINTY

It can be simplified that the choice on retrofitting is made based on comparison between the current loss (CL), i.e. the loss caused by retrofitting, and the future probable loss (FL), i.e. the expected loss caused by probable future earthquakes. As far as retrofitting is concerned, the life cycle cost is not considered like building management, as the cost for purchase can be regarded as the sunk cost, i.e. cost to be neglected because it cannot be recovered anyhow, and as the cost for retrofitting would not bring about any visible benefit immediately. The benefit of retrofitting may be recognized when a big earthquake will have occurred some time in future, and may be never recognized if there will be no big earthquake during the lifespan of a given house. Thus, the cost for retrofitting would be "the current loss," while the cost for not retrofitting would be the future probable loss, i.e. loss of the house and loss caused by collapse of the house.

Therefore, the choice is made as follows.

- If a person conceives CL < FL, retrofitting is reasonable. (He/she may be motivated for retrofitting)
- If a person conceives CL > FL, retrofitting is not reasonable. (He/she may not be motivated for retrofitting)

4. INCENTIVES FOR RETROFITTING

In order to motivate people for retrofitting, it is most effective to enhance understanding what will be lost due to the unsafe houses. However, as far as the loss due to the unsafe house lies in future with uncertainty, many people would not be motivated for retrofitting yet. Thus, it is logically proposed, to promote retrofitting, that the future uncertain risk should be transformed into the current certain loss. In other words, if those who keep their house unsafe should pay a certain amount at present every year, not in future, while those who keep their house safe would not pay it, then they would be motivated for retrofitting. The more they would have to pay, the more they would be willing to invest for retrofitting rather than continuing the payment for keeping the unsafe house.

The same effect could be attained if the owners of the safe house would gain some interest every year.

It is therefore proposed that any earthquake disaster management policies should be restructured so that they should be in favor of those who keep their house safe ("safe people") and not in favor of those who keep their house unsafe ("unsafe people"). For example, "safe people" may pay less property tax while "unsafe people" must pay more property tax. "Safe people" may pay fewer premiums for earthquake insurance while "unsafe people" must pay full premium. Such incentives could be given through taxation, subsidy, penalty, insurance policy, and so on. If the difference in payment would be approaching the cost of retrofitting, people would obviously be motivated for retrofitting.

Are such policies justifiable and acceptable? First, it should be noted that under any building codes, the minimum safety should be secured and the owners have the responsibility to maintain the safety. In case of earthquake disasters, however, the governments are forced to burden a huge amount of expenditure for relief, recovery, and reconstruction activities, most of which were caused by the unsafe houses. Figure 1 shows the expenditure of the Japanese central governments, directly attributed to collapse of houses, such as immediate aid for rebuilding livelihood, disposal of debris, construction of temporary and permanent rental houses publicly operated, and redevelopment of the damaged areas. The total expenditure is approximately $12 billion, in the form of the subsidy to the local governments. Such enormous expenditure was mainly caused by the totally damaged 100,000 houses and severely damaged 140,000 houses (approx. $50,000 per a damaged house). Yet, people who lost their house had to bear the total cost of $15,000 - 20,000 for reconstruction of their house, with a new housing loan in addition to the remaining loan for the lost house, as the governmental aid should not be used for private property in principle.

5. COMMUNITY BASED DISASTER MANEGEMENT

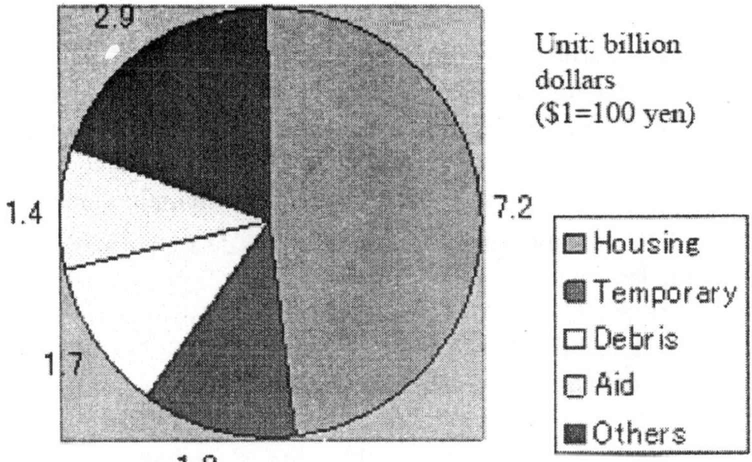

Fig. 1: Expenditure of the Japanese central governments attributed to collapse of houses in 1995Kobe Earthquake

As discussed, the highroads to motivate people for safer houses would be to enhance understanding of the individual risk among people, particularly as to what will be lost by the unsafe houses. Such awareness rising would be achieved through appropriate risk communication among the stakeholders as the risk differs from person to person, from house to house, and community to community. This risk communication should not be one way-education from experts to people, but rather multi-ways communication between experts and people. Such activities may be called "co-learning" through which the stakeholders can better understand their risk and role, and how to deal with the risk.

Since disasters greatly reflect the local conditions, such co-learning should be promoted at community level as Community Based Disaster Management (CBDM). CBDM is essential for disaster risk management because the local people are potential victims and assume responsibility in managing the risk. They respond first to a disaster and are the last remaining to rebuild safer communities. Local population has local knowledge regarding vulnerability and capacity conditions. CBDM would strengthen confidence, social cohesion, and cooperation within the community and society. Participatory decision making process of CBDM would lead to ownership of risk and actions. CBDM should involve not only the people living in a certain location, but also the local government, local business sectors, local academic bodies and NGOs, which could play crucial roles for disaster mitigation.

CBDM activities should be sustainable as disaster management is a long lasting process. The United Nations Centre for Regional Development (UNCRD) has been focusing on CBDM, particularly on its sustainability, and has developed a simplified and general set of guidelines and tools for sustainable CBDM as "A User's Guide". It provides complete discussion of the factors, best practices and examples that will enhance sustainability of CBDM and provides guidelines and tools for different users, namely, policymakers, national disaster managers, local disaster managers, trainers, and community workers.

Fig. 2 : Improvised Shake Table Demonstration in Kabul, Afghanistan, 2003.

7

Disaster : A Tragedy of Natural or Human-made Hazard

Sangeeta Aroora
Head of the Department of English
SRDA Girls PG College
Navipur Road, Hathras
(Affiliated to Dr. B.R Ambedkar University Agra)

A disaster is the tragedy of a natural or human-made hazard (a hazard is a situation which poses a level of threat to life, health, property, or environment) that negatively affects society or environment.

Disasters are consequence of inappropriately managed risk. Developing countries suffer most – more than 95 % of all the deaths caused by disasters occur in developing countries. Developing countries suffer 20 times more losses due to natural disasters than industrialized countries. A disaster can be defined as any tragic event with great loss stemming from events such as earthquakes, floods, catastrophic accidents, fires, or explosions.

The word derives from Middle French *désastre* and that from Old Italian *disastro*, which in turn comes from the Greek pejorative prefix *äõó*. The root of the word *disaster* ("bad star" in Greek) comes from an astrological theme in which the ancients used to refer to the destruction or deconstruction of a star as a disaster. A disaster may have the following main features:-

- Unpredictability
- Unfamiliarity
- Speed
- Urgency
- Uncertainty
- Threat

Risk:

Risk is a measure of the expected losses due to a hazardous event of a particular magnitude occurring in a given area over a specific time period. Risk is a function of the probability of particular occurrences and the losses each would cause. The level of risk depends on:

- Nature of the Hazard
- Vulnerability of the elements which are affected
- Economic value of those elements

Vulnerability

It is defined as *"the extent to which a community, structure, service, and/or geographic area is likely to be damaged or disrupted by the impact of particular hazard, on account of their nature, construction and proximity to hazardous terrain or a disaster prone area"*

Hazards

Hazards are defined as *"Phenomena that pose a threat to people, structures, or economic assets and which may cause a disaster. They could be either manmade or naturally occurring in our environment."*

The extent of damage in a disaster depends on:

(1) The impact, intensity and characteristics of the phenomenon and

(2) How people, environment and infrastructures are affected by that phenomenon

This relationship can be written as an equation:

Disaster Risk = Hazard + Vulnerability

Disasters can be classified as follows:

1. Natural
2. Manmade Disaster

Natural Disaster: A natural disaster is a consequence when a natural hazard (e.g., volcanic eruption or earthquake) affects humans and/or the built environment. Human vulnerability, caused by the lack of appropriate emergency management, leads to financial, environmental, or human impact. Major natural disasters are flood, cyclone, earthquake and drought whereas minor natural disasters are cold and heat waves, thunderstorms, mud slides.

Manmade Disaster: Disasters caused by human action, negligence, error, or involving the failure of a system are called man-made disasters. Man-made disasters are in turn categorized as technological or sociological. Technological disasters are the results of failure of technology, such as engineering failures, transport disasters, or environmental disasters. Sociological disasters have a strong human motive, such as criminal acts, stampedes, riots and war. Major manmade disasters are setting of fires, deforestation, pollution due to prawn cultivation, chemical pollution whereas minor manmade disasters are road/ train accidents, industrial disaster.

India is the most vulnerable developing country which suffers from natural disasters like drought, flood, earthquake, landslides, forest fire etc. All these have a devastating impact on human life, economy and environment. Although it is impossible to recoup the damage caused by the disasters, it is possible to (i) minimize the potential risks by developing early warning strategies (ii) prepare and implement developmental plans to provide resilience to such disasters (iii) mobilize resources (iv) to help in rehabilitation and post-disaster reconstruction.

Space Technology Plays a Crucial Role in Mitigation of Disasters

Communication satellites help in disaster warning provide required database for pre-disaster preparedness programmes, disaster response, post-disaster damage assessment, and reconstruction, and rehabilitation.

Role of Space Technology for Disaster Management

There are certain space technology and GIS technique in monitoring and management for sustainable development in places that are more prone to disasters. This is mainly for the places that are more prone to disasters and calamities eg. Bangladesh. For monitoring and measuring disaster management it is very important to keep the sequential information on nature and environment. Space technology with integration with GIS has emerged as a useful tool in monitoring the environment and hence helps in taking appropriate measures in pre and post disaster management.

The Geographical Information System (GIS) is another versatile tool added to the new technology which makes the data acquired either through remote sensing satellites, aerial photographs or through physical surveys carried out for a purpose to be more useful to the decision makers and the planners. These technological provisions have made planning and development activities more handy towards achieving sustainable development and successful disaster management.

Disasters like earthquake, landslides, volcanic eruptions, flood and cyclones are natural hazards that kill thousands of people and destroy a lot of property each year. The increase of the world's population has escalated both the frequency and severity of natural disasters. The tropical climate and unstable land forms, with deforestation, non-engineered constructions, make the disaster-prone areas more vulnerable. Developing countries suffer more or less chronically by natural disasters.

Earthquakes, landslides, floods and cyclones are the major disasters affecting very large areas and population in the Indian sub-continent. Earthquakes, volcanic eruptions, landslides are natural disaster of geophysical origin whereas drought, flood, cyclone, locust, forest fire are disasters of climatic origin. Though it may not be possible to control nature but the efforts could be made to avoid disasters. Rising frequency, amplitude and number of natural disasters and attendant problem coupled with loss of human lives prompted the General Assembly of the United Nations to proclaim 1990s as the International Decade for Natural Disaster Reduction (IDNDR) through a resolution 44/236 of December 22, 1989 to focus on all issues related to natural disaster reduction. Although It is impossible to prevent the occurrence of natural disasters and their damages, but it is possible to reduce the impact of disasters by adopting suitable disaster mitigation strategies like:

1. minimize the potential risks by developing disaster early warning strategies
2. prepare and implement developmental plans to provide resilience to such disasters,
3. mobilize resources including communication and tele-medicinal services
4. to help in rehabilitation and post-disaster reduction

Disaster reduction involves different professions and different scientific fields, and has become an important measure for human, society and nature. First Aid group, Health group, Welfare group are well trained by some local community members to help local community that is suffering from a disaster. They move the people from the area affected from disaster to safe regions. Affected people are given shelter and every possible facility by local management communities. Government is also making effort to provide good facilities during the disaster.

Emergency Management

Emergency management or disaster management is the discipline of dealing with and avoiding risks. It is mainly a management that prepares us for the disasters that can affect us very badly before it occurs and also help us to overcome the natural disaster and rebuild the society. In other words emergency management is a continuous process by which an individual put their efforts in order to ameliorate the impact of disaster. The actions that are taken in the emergency management depend upon the perception of risk in a particular area. To make an emergency management effective it should rely on thorough integration of all emergency plans at all levels(as each level is interconnected) government and non-government involvement. Emergency management starts from the lower level and increases to the next higher organizational level after the resources of the current level got exhausted.

Phases of Emergency Management

The emergency management nature depends upon local, economic and social conditions prevailing in a particular area. There are mainly four phases of emergency management:

1. Mitigation
2. Preparedness
3. Response
4. Recovery

Mitigation

Mitigation mainly focuses to prevent the developing hazard to convert into a disaster or if it has already occur then to reduce its effects and taking an appropriate action. Mitigation is totally different from all other phases as it mainly focuses on taking long term measures to reduce or eliminate the risk. If strategy of mitigation is implemented after the occurrence of disaster then it is considered as a recovery phase. There are mainly two measures of Mitigation:

a. Structural

b. Non Structural

Structural measures use technological solutions like flood levees (Levee is an artificial slope or wall to regulate water levels) whereas nonstructural measures use legislation, insurance and land use plans (designation of unused area like parks as flood zones).

Mitigation mainly starts from identifying the risk. Hazard specific risk (R_h) combines both probability and level of impact of risk. The equation for the same is shown below:

$$R_h = H * V_h$$

This equation shows that if the risk is higher than the hazard vulnerability is targeted as early as possible. If there is no risk there is no vulnerability e.g. Earthquake occurring in a desert where nobody lives.

Preparedness

Preparedness is a continuous cycle of planning, organizing, training, equipping, exercising, evaluation and improvement activities to ensure effective coordination and the enhancement of capabilities to prevent, protect against, respond to, recover from, and mitigate against natural disasters, acts of terrorism, and other man-made disasters. In this phase action are taken to manage the risk take action to develop necessary capabilities to overcome the risk.

Another aspect of preparedness is casualty prediction that means the study of number of injuries and deaths in a particular event. It should always be kept in mind that preparedness planning should be flexible.

Response

Response phase mainly states for the first responders in the disaster area. This mainly include first wave of emergency services like fire fighters, police, first aid (ambulance). The well developed preparedness plan enables efficient coordination of rescue. Whenever required, rescue is decided at an early stage only.

Recovery

This stage mainly focuses on converting the hazard area or disaster area to its previous state. It is different from the response as response is the immediate effect or trying to focus on the immediate need of the affected area whereas recovery phase are concerned with the issues and decisions that must be made after the addressing of the immediate needs. Recovery phase make effort to "build back better", and aims to reduce the predicated risk.

In the United States, the National Response Plan dictates how the resources provided by the Homeland Security Act of 2002 will be used in recovery efforts.[1] It is the Federal government that often provides the most technical and financial assistance for recovery efforts in the United States.

To make all these phases work effectively emergency managers are trained in a very well manner to deal with all the phases in an efficient as well as an effective manner. They focus on both government and non government (private) preparedness.

To overcome the disaster and return to the previous stage there are few principles of emergency management that are as follows:

1. **Comprehensive:** that means managers have taken into account all hazards, all phases and all impacts to disaster into consideration.
2. **Progressive**: emergency manager should anticipate future disaster and preventive and preparatory measures to build the disaster relief community.
3. **Risk Driven**: emergency managers use hazard identification, risk analysis, and impact analysis) in assigning priorities and resources.
4. **Integrated:** emergency managers ensure unity of effort among all levels of community.
5. **Collaborative**: emergency managers create and sustain broad and sincere relationships among individuals and organizations to encourage trust, advocate a team atmosphere, build consensus, and facilitate communication.
6. **Coordinated** – emergency managers synchronize the activities of all relevant stakeholders to achieve a common purpose.
7. **Flexible** – emergency managers use creative and innovative approaches in solving disaster challenges.

8. **Professional** – emergency managers value a science and knowledge-based approach; based on education, training, experience, ethical practice, public stewardship and continuous improvement.

Some Recent Examples of Disaster:

Bhopal Disaster:

Bhopal Disaster, one of the major hazard taken place in the chilling month of December. On 2nd December night the pesticide plant that is owned and operated by union carbide released methyl isocyanate (MIC) gas and other toxins, resulting in the exposure of over 500,000 people. Approximate number of deaths are 15,000 and around 8,000 people died within a week due to gas related diseases.

Some 25 years after the gas leak, 390 tones of toxic chemicals abandoned at the UCIL plant continue to leak and pollute the groundwater in the region and affect thousands of Bhopal residents who depend on it though there is some dispute as to whether the chemicals still stored at the site pose any continuing health hazard.

Factors leading to the gas leak include:

- The use of hazardous chemicals (MIC) instead of less dangerous ones
- Storing these chemicals in large tanks instead of over 200 steel drums.
- Possible corroding material in pipelines
- Poor maintenance after the plant ceased production in the early 1980s
- Failure of several safety systems (due to poor maintenance and regulations).
- Safety systems being switched off to save money—including the MIC tank refrigeration system which alone would have prevented the disaster.

The problem got worse as the plant is located in densely populated area, shortcomings in health care and socio-economic rehabilitation.

Contributing Factors

- The deficiencies in the Bhopal plant design can be summarized as: choosing a dangerous method of manufacturing pesticides; large-scale storage of MIC before processing; location close to a densely populated area; under-dimensioning of the safety features; dependence on manual operations.
- Deficiencies in the management of UCIL can be summarized: lack of skilled operators due to the staffing policy; reduction of safety management due to reducing the staff; insufficient maintenance of the plant; lack of emergency response plans.

Cyclone Laila: Community Based Disaster

As cyclone Laila put entire east coast on alert, community-based disaster taskforce groups swung in to action too. In Vishakhapatnam as soon as cyclone arrived community task force members wasted no time in putting their efforts to action. The task force groups leading the way shifted boats and nets to safer locations to minimize potential damage to be caused by cyclone Laila. Immediately the fishers were also alerted about the cyclone. They were also shifted the health centers in villages to deal with possible injuries and medical needs. In Krishna district 300 task forces were engaged for evacuation and shelter management purpose. Rice, dal and packets of cooking oil were being handed over to village task force groups and were pre-positioned for distribution..

Airplane Overshot the Runway

This is the very recent disaster that has directly affected hundreds of people and their lives. There was a plane coming from Dubai to Mangalore having around 165 passengers with 6 crew members. The plane overshot the runway after landing at the Mangalore airport on 22nd May and caught fire as it crashed into forest gorge. In this disaster only 8 people survived and out of which 1 person died on the way to hospital. The airport at Bajpe, about 30 km from Mangalore, is in a hilly area and considered one of the most difficult airports to take off and land. The area had been experiencing heavy rains for the last two days. This incident took place t 6:30am in few minutes only 25 ambulances and 20 fire tenders have got involved into frantic operation. After such a fast operation and everything they are able to save only 7 lives. That's why it is said that if disaster is unplanned or natural then it is more dangerous.

Conclusion

Disaster cannot be prevented totally. However, timely warning and planning can minimize the effect of a disaster. An accurate disaster management plan needs to be prepared. The use of modern technology like GIS and RS can be of vital importance in the preparation of plans. Keeping records of vulnerable areas, monitoring of rescue and relief operations deciding response, managing the data base etc. Mutual aid schemes shall be of great help in mobilization of resources while mock drills shall ensure the efficiency and affectivity of response. Training of the various functionaries, and an effective public awareness and education campaign involving the communities will ensure that the plans are disseminated to the lowest levels.

8

Hurricane: A Natural Disaster

Dr. Alka Dwivedi
Sr. Lecturer, Hindi Deptt.
Juhari Devi Girls P. G. College
Canal Road, Kanpur-208004

Dr. Meenakshi Bajpai
Lecturer, Psychology Deptt.
Juhari Devi Girls P. G. College
Canal Road. Kanpur-208004

A natural disaster is the effect of a natural hazard (e.g. flood, tornado, hurricane, volcanic eruption, earthquake or landslide) that affects the environment, and leads to financial environmental and/ or human losses. The resulting loss depends on the capacity of the population to support or resist the disaster, and their resilience . This understanding is concentrated in the formulation: "disasters occur when hazards meet vulnerability." A natural hazard will hence never result in a natural disaster in areas without vulnerability, e.g. strong earthquakes in uninhabited areas. The term natural has consequently been disputed because the events simply are not hazards or disasters without human involvement.

The Basics

Easier- A hurricane is a very powerful, sometimes violent storm with strong winds and heavy rains.

Harder - A hurricane is a powerful, spiraling storm that begins over a warm sea, near the equator. When a hurricane hits land, it can do great damage through its fierce winds, torrential rains, inland flooding, and huge waves crashing ashore. A powerful hurricane can kill more people and destroy more property than any other natural disaster.

As the storm builds from thunderstorm to hurricane, it passes through three distinct stages based on wind speed.

- **Tropical depression-** wind speeds of less than 38 miles per hour (61.15 kilometers per hour)
- **Tropical storm-** wind speed of 39 mph to 73 mph (62.76 kph to 117.48 kph).
- **Hurricane-** wind speeds greater than 74 mph (119.09 kph)

Hurricanes are given a different label, depending on where they occur. It they begin over the North Atlantic Ocean, the Caribbean Sea, the Gulf of Mexico, or the Northeast Pacific Ocean, they are called hurricanes. Like storms that occur in the Northwest Pacific Ocean west of the imaginary International Date Line are called typhoons. Near Australia and in the Indian Ocean, they are referred to as tropical cyclones.

Hurricane intensity is based upon the highest sustained (1 minute average) wind speed the hurricane is producing. The "Saffir-Simpson" scale rates hurricane strength in this way from Category 1 to Category 5. These categories were chosen based upon the amount of damage that each category can produce.

Intensity	*Wind Speed*	*Damage*
Category-1	74-95 mph	**Minimal:** tree branches, shrubs, unanchored mobile homes
Category-2	96-110mph	**Moderate:** mobile homes, poorly constructed buildings, some trees down
Category-3	111-130 mph	**Extensive:** small buildings damaged, large trees down, mobile homes destroyed
Category-4	131-155 mph	**Extreme:** outer walls damaged, roof failure on small buildings, extensive damage to and windows, mobile homes destroyed

Category-5	>155 mph	**Catastrophic:** complete roof failure on many buildings, some buildings destroyed, window and door damage, mobile homes destroyed.

Types Of Hurricanes

Tropical Storm

Winds 39-73 mph

Category 1 Hurricane

winds 74-95 mph (64-82 kt)

No real damage to buildings. Damage to unanchored mobile homes. Some damage to poorly constructed signs. Also, some coastal flooding and minor pier damage. Examples: Irene 1999 and Allison 1995.

Category 2 Hurricane

winds 96-110 mph (83-95 kt)

Some damage to building roofs, doors and windows. Considerable damage to mobile homes. Flooding damages piers and small craft in unprotected moorings may break their moorings. Some trees blown down. Examples: Bonnie 1998, Georges (FL & LA) 1998 and Gloria 1985.

Category 3 Hurricane

winds 111-130 mph (96—113 kt)

some structural damage to small residences and utility buildings. Large trees blown down. Mobile homes and poorly built signs destroyed. Flooding near the coast destroys smaller structures with larger structures damaged by floating debris. Terrain may be flooded well inland. Examples: Keith 2000, Fran 1996, Opal 1995, Alicia 1983 and Betsy 1965.

Category 4 Hurricane

winds 131-155 mph (114-135 kt)

More extensive curtain wall failures with some complete roof structure failure on small residences. Major erosion of beach areas. Terrain may be flooded well inland. Examples: Hugo 1989 and Donna 1960.

Category 5 Hurricane

winds 156 mph and up (135+ kt)

Complete roof failure on many residences and industrial buildings. Some complete building failures with small utility buildings blown over or away. Flooding causes major damage to lower floors of all structures near the shoreline. Massive evacuation of residential areas.

Causes and Effects of Hurricanes:

Hurricanes are the most destructive natural disaster; they are very powerful and violent storms, often associated with strong winds and heavy rains. A storm is classified as a hurricane when the speed of wind reaches 74 miles (119 kilometers) per hour, Hurricane storms usually start over warm sea (near the equator) and are accompanied by fierce winds, flash floods, mudslides and huge waves.

Causes of Hurricanes:

There are two main factors that are responsible for causing hurricane storms, viz. warm water and moist, warm air. Hurricanes occur when the moist, warm air form the surface of the ocean rises and meets the cooler air. In such a situation, the moist, warm air condenses and forms storm clouds and raindrops. There is also release of latent heat due to condensation process, which increases the temperature of the cooler air above. In the cycle, more warm, humid air from the ocean surface rises and joins the developing storm, Hence, there is a transfer of heat from the surface of the ocean to the atmosphere above.

As the cycle of exchanging heat continues, a wind pattern is created that moves in a spiral fashion around a calm center, which is referred to as the hurricane eye. Converging winds near the ocean surface collide with the developing storm, resulting in an increased circulation of warm, humid air and also enhancing the speed of wind. Presence of strong winds at high altitude pull the rising warm air away from the center, causing the storm to swirl in the typical cyclone pattern.

Another factor that increases the speed of wind is high-pressure air at high altitude. This high-pressure air draws the heat away from the center of the storm. As this high- pressure air moves to the center and meets the low-pressure air, the wind speed again increases.

Effects of Hurricanes

When a powerful hurricane hits land, it can cause more damage to life and property than any other natural disaster. The effects of hurricanes include storm surge, strong wind, inland flooding and tornadoes.

- Storm surge is the most devastating effect that accounts for 90 percent of the hurricane deaths. It refers to the rapid rise in the level of water that comes ashore, as the hurricane hits land
- The overall effect of a hurricane depends on speed of the wind. It helps to determine the force of the hurricane storm, the storm surge and the damage that the storm can cause.
- It is a fact that inland flooding causes more deaths than the actual hurricane storms. On an average, 5-10 inch rainfall is common. However, rainfall may increase depending upon the storm.
- Hurricane storms may also result in tornadoes. However, the frequency and occurrence vary from one hurricane storm to another. Very often, such tornadoes are of minimal strength.

An example of powerful storms is the Hurricane Katrina on August 29, 2005, which struck the United States, causing death of more than 1,800 people and property damage worth $81 billion. It was the costliest hurricane in the history of US. Though, heavy rainfall may prove to be beneficial at times of drought, the overall effects of hurricanes are more devastating. Some researchers are of the opinion that hurricanes are caused due to climate change and/or global warming. However, studies are ongoing to study the relation between climate change and hurricanes.

Ten Worst Hurricanes

Date	*Location*	*Dead*
1970, November 13	East Pakistan (Bangladesh)	500,000 to 1 million
1737, October 7	Bengal, India	Over 300,000
1881	Haiphong, Vietnam	300,000
1876	Bengal, India	200,000
1882, June 6	Bombay, India	Over 100,000
1864, October 5	Calcutta, India	50,000 to 70,000
1965, May and June	East-Pakistan (Bangladesh)	35,000 to 40,000
1942, October 16	Bengal, India	Over 35,000
1963, May 28-29	East Pakistan (Bangladesh)	22,000
1780, October 10-12	Caribbean Islands	20,000 to 30,000

Seasons why frequency and severity of Hurricanes are increasing:

- Air and water temperatures are rising worldwide.
- Human activities such as deforestation and greenhouse gas emissions from a wide range of industrial and at those temperature changes at a greater rate today than in the past.
- Failure to take action now to lower atmospheric levels of greenhouse gases is likely to lead to more frequent.

When a hurricane watch is issued, you should:

- Fill your automobile's gas tank.
- If no vehicle is available, make arrangements with friends or family for transportation.

- Fill your clean water containers.
- Review your emergency plans and supplies, checking to see if any items are missing.
- Tune in the radio or television for weather updates.
- Listen for disaster sirens and warning signals.
- Prepare an emergency kit for your car with food, flares, booster cables, maps, tools, a first aid kit, fire extinguisher, sleeping bags, etc.
- Secure any items outside which may damage property in a storm. such as bicycles, grills, propane tanks, etc.
- Cover windows and doors which plywood or boards or place large strips of masking tape or adhesive tape on the windows to reduce the risk of breakage and flying glass.
- Put livestock and family pets in a safe area. Due to food and sanitation requirements, emergency shelters cannot accept animals.
- Place vehicles under cover, if at all possible.
- Fill sinks and bathtubs with water as an extra supply for washing.
- Adjust the thermostat on refrigerators and freezers to the coolest possible temperature.

If You are Ordered to Evacuate

Because of the destructive power of a hurricane, you should never ignore an evacuation order. Authorities will be most likely to direct you to leave if you are in a low-lying area, or within the greatest potential path of the storm. Be aware that most shelters and some hotels do not accept pets. If a hurricane warning is issued for your area or you are directed by authorities to evacuate the area:

- Take only essential items with you.
- If you have time, turn off the gas, electricity, and water.
- Disconnect appliances to reduce the likelihood of electrical shock when power is restored.

- Make sure your automobile's emergency kit is ready.
- Follow the designated evacuation routes- others may be blocked- and expect heavy traffic.

If You Are Ordered Not to Evacuate

The great majority of injuries during a hurricane are cuts caused by flying glass or other debris. Other injuries include puncture wounds resulting from exposed nails, metal, or glass, and bone fractures

To get through the storm in the safest possible manner:

- Monitor the radio or television for weather conditions, if possible.
- Stay indoors until the authorities declare the storm is over.
- Do not go outside, even if the weather appears to have calmed- the calm "eye" of the storm can pass quickly, leaving you outside when strong winds resume.
- Stay away from all windows and exterior doors, seeking shelter in a bathroom or basement. Bathtubs can provide some shelter if you cover yourself with plywood or other materials.
- Prepare to evacuate to a shelter or to a neighbor's home if your home is damaged, or if you are instructed to do so by emergency personnel.

MANAGING TRAUMATIC STRESS: AFTER THE HURRICANES:

What Happens to People when there is a Hurricane

Shock and denial are typical responses to traumatic events and disasters especially shortly after the event. Both shock and denial are normal protective reaction.

Shock is a sudden and often intense disturbance of your emotional state that may leave you feeling stunned or dazed. Denial involves your not acknowledging that something very stressful has happened, or not experiencing fully the intensity of the event.

You may temporarily feel numb or disconnected from life. Both are normal responses.

As the initial shock subsides, reactions will vary from one person to another. The following, however, are normal responses to a traumatic event:

- Feelings become intense and sometimes unpredictable. You may become more irritable than usual, and your mood may change back and forth dramatically. You might be especially anxious or nervous, or even become depressed.
- Thoughts and behavior patterns may be affected by the trauma. You might have repeated and vivid memories of the event. These are called flashbacks and they may occur for no apparent reason and may lead to physical reactions such as rapid heart beat or sweating. You may find it difficult to concentrate or make decisions, or become more easily confused. Sleeping and eating patterns also may be disrupted.
- Recurring emotional reactions are common. Reactions can be prompted by sights and smells that remind you of preparing for or responding to the hurricane. These sensory perceptions can trigger fear that the hurricane or its damage may reoccur.
- Interpersonal relationships often become strained. Greater conflict, such as more frequent arguments with family members and peers, is common. On the other hand, you might become withdrawn and isolated and avoid your usual activities.
- Physical symptoms may accompany the extreme stress. For example, headaches, nausea and chest pain may result and may require medical attention. Pre-existing medical conditions may worsen due to the stress.

How do People Respond Differently over Time?

It is important to realize that there is not one standard pattern of reaction to the extreme stress of traumatic experiences. Some people respond immediately, while others have delayed reactions sometimes months or even years later. Some have adverse effects for a long period of time, while others recover rather quickly.

And reactions can change over time. Some who have suffered from trauma are energized initially by the event to help them with the challenge of coping, only to later become discouraged or depressed.

A number of factors tend to affect the length of time people need to recover from the storm, including:

- The degree of intensity and loss. Events that last longer and pose a greater threat, and where loss of life or substantial loss of property is involved, often take longer to resolve.
- The duration of exposure to the events and damage of the events can have an impact on those involved.
- A person's general ability to cope with emotionally challenging situations. Individuals who have handled other difficult, stressful circumstances well may find it easier to cope with the trauma.
- Other stressful events preceding the traumatic experience. Individuals faced with other emotionally challenging situations, such as serious health problems or family-related difficulties, may have more intense reactions to the new stressful event and need more time to recover.

How can I help myself and my family?

There are a number of steps you can take to help restore emotional well being and a sense of control in the wake of the hurricane or other traumatic experience, including the following:

- Allow yourself to mourn the losses you have experienced. Try to be patient with changes in your emotional state.
- Take a news break. Watching replays of footage from the hurricane can make your stress even greater. Often, the media tries to interest viewers by presenting worst case

scenarios. These may not be representative of your home or community.

- Ask for support from people who care about you and who will listen and empathize with your situation. But keep in mind that your typical support system may be weakened if those who are close to you also have experienced or witnessed the hurricane.
- Communicate your experience in whatever ways feel comfortable to you such as by talking with family or close friends or keeping a diary.
- Find out about local support groups led by appropriately trained and experienced professionals. Support groups are often available in communities following large-scale disasters. People can experience relief and comfort connecting with other hurricane survivors who have had similar reactions and emotions. These can be especially helpful for people with limited personal support systems.
- Engage in healthy behaviors to enhance your ability to cope with excessive stress. Eat well-balanced meals and get plenty of rest. If you experience difficulties sleeping, you may be able to find some relief through relaxation techniques. Avoid alcohol and drugs since these can increase a sense of depression and/or impede you from doing what is necessary to be resilient and cope with events.
- Establish or reestablish routines such as eating meals at regular times and following an exercise program. Take some time off from the demands of daily life by pursuing hobbies or other enjoyable activities.
- If possible, avoid major life decisions such as switching jobs because these activities tend to be highly stressful.

When should I Seek Professional Help?

Some people are able to cope effectively with the emotional and physical demands of the hurricane by using their own support systems. It is not unusual, however, to find that serious problems persist and continue to interfere with daily living. For example, some may feel overwhelming nervousness or lingering sadness that adversely affects interpersonal relationships and job performance.

- Individuals with prolonged reactions that disrupt their daily functioning should consult with a trained and experienced mental health professional.
- Psychologists and other appropriate mental health providers help educate people about normal responses to extreme stress. These professionals work with individuals affected by trauma to help them find constructive ways of dealing with the emotional impact. Psychologists and other crisis counselors are deployed to the affected areas. Ask the various organizations providing assistance to direct you to those individuals.

With children, continual and aggressive emotional outbursts, serious problems at school, preoccupation with the hurricane, continued and extreme withdrawal and other signs of intense anxiety or emotional difficulties all point to the need for professional assistance. A qualified mental health professional can help such children and their parents understand and deal with thoughts, feelings and behaviors that result from the storm.

REFERENCES

1. G. Bankoff, G. Frerks, D. Hilhorst (*eds.*) (2003). *Mapping vulnerability: Disasters, Development and People.* ISBN ISBN 1-85383-964-7.
2. B. Wisner, P. Blaikie, T. Cannon, and I. Davis (2004). *At Risk-Natural hazards, people's vulnerability and disaster. Wiltshire: Rout ledge* ISBN ISBN 0-415-25216-4.
3. D. Alexander (2002).Principles of Emergency planning and Management. Harpended: Terra publishing. ISBN ISBN 1-903544 -10 - 6.
4. Weather Encyclopedia, The Weather Channel, Accessed on June 2, 2009, http://www.theweatherchannelkids.com.
5. BBC: Oxfam warns of climate disasters.
6. III. (2008). 2008 Natural Catastrophe Review.

Disasters Management and Community

9

Disaster: A Serious Disruption of The Functioning of Society

Dr. Sudhir Kumar
Lecturer, Geography
Handia P.G. College. Handia, Allahabad

Dr. Ajay Singh
Reader, Political Science
Handia P.G. College, Handia, Allahabad

Disaster is a sudden, calamitous event bringing great damage, loss and destruction and devastation to life and property. The damage caused by disasters is immeasurable and varies with the geographical location, climate and the type of the earth surface/ degree of vulnerability. This influences the mental, socio-economic, political and cultural state of the affected area. Generally, disaster has the following effects in the concerned areas.

1. It completely disrupts the normal day to day life.
2. It negatively influences the emergency systems
3. Normal needs and processes like food, shelter, health, etc are affected and affected and deteriorate depending on the intensity and severity of the disaster

It may also be termed as "a serious disruption of the functioning of society, causing widespread human materials or environmental losses which exceed the ability of the affected society to cope using its own resources."

Unpredictability, Unfamiliarity, Speed, Urgency, Uncertainty, Threat

Thus, in simple terms we can define disaster as 3 hazard causing heavy loss to life, property and livelihood.

TYPES OF DISASTER

Generally, disasters are of two types – Natural and Manmade, Based on the devastation, these are further classified into major/ minor natural disaster and major/minor manmade disasters. Some of the disasters are listed below.

Major natural disasters:	Minor natural disasters:
• Flood	• Could wave
• Cyclone	• Thunderstorms
• Drought	• Heat waves
• Earthquake	• Mud slides
	• Storm
Major manmade disaster:	**Major manmade disaster:**
• Setting of fires	• Road/train accidents, riots
• Epidemic	• Food poisoning
• Deforestation	• Industrial disaster
• Pollution due to prawn cultivation	• Crisis Environmental pollution
• Chemical pollution	• Wars

From Management to Mitigation of disasters

Various disasters like earthquake, landslides, volcanic eruptions, fires, flood and cyclones are natural hazards that kill thousands of people and destroy billions of dollars of habitat and property each year. The rapid growth of the world's population and its increased concentration often in hazardous environment has escalated both the frequency and severity of natural disasters. With the tropical climate and unstable land forms. Coupled with deforestation, unplanned growth proliferation non-engineered constructions, which make the disaster- prone areas mere vulnerable, tardy communication, poor or no budgetary allocation

DISATER MANAGEMENT CYCLE

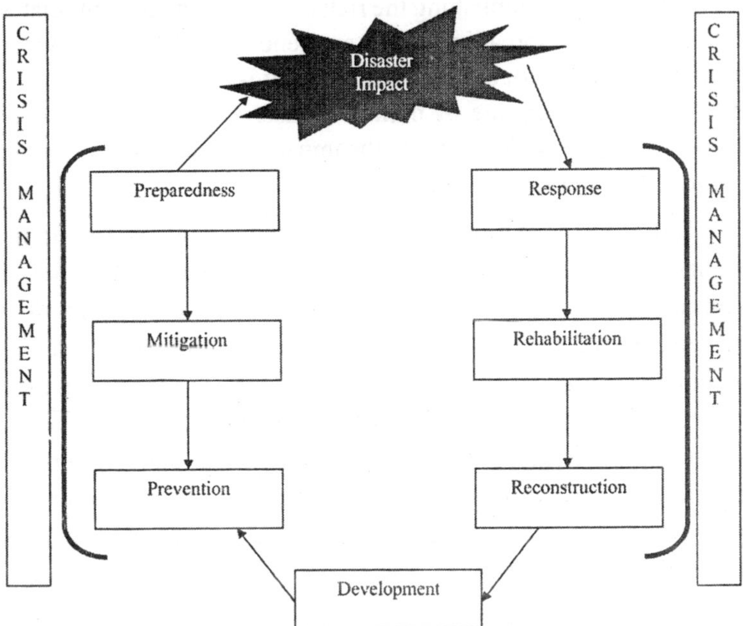

for disaster prevention, developing countries suffer more or less chronically by natural disasters. Asia tops the list of casualties due to natural disaster, Among various natural hazards, earthquakes, landslides, floods and cyclones are the major disasters adversely affecting very large areas and population in the Indian sub-continent, These natural disasters are of (I) geophysical origin such as earthquakes, volcanic eruptions, land slides and (ii) climatic origin such as drought, flood, cyclone, locust, forest fire. Though it may not be feasible to control nature and to stop the development of natural phenomena but the efforts could be made to avoid disasters and alleviate their effects on human lives, infrastructure and property, Rising frequency, amplitude and number of natural disasters and attendant problem coupled with loss of human lives prompted the General Assembly of the United Nations to proclaim 1990s as the International Decade for Natural Disaster Reduction (IDNDR) through resolution 44/236 of December 22, 1989 to focus on all issues related to natural disaster reduction in spite of IDNDR. There had been a string of major disaster throughout the decade, Nevertheless, by establishing the rich disaster management related traditions and by spreading public awareness the IDNDR provided required stimulus for disaster reduction. It is almost impossible to prevent the occurrence of natural disasters and their damages. However it is possible to reduce the impact of disasters by adopting suitable disaster mitigation strategies.

Today, we have a range of early warning systems for a range of natural hazards, although they are more accurate than before and can help in prediction, it is not enough to ensure communities are safe from disasters. This is where disaster mitigation can play an important role, 'Mitigation' means lessening the negative impact of the natural hazards, it is defined as sustained action taken to reduce long- term vulnerability of human life and property to natural hazards, while the preparatory, response and the recovery phases of emergency management relate to specific events, mitigation activities have the potential to produce repetitive benefits over time.

Certain guidelines, if followed correctly, can result in an effective mitigation program.

- Pre-disaster mitigation can help in ensuring faster recovery from the impacts of disasters.
- Mitigation measures must ensure protection of the natural and cultural assets of the community.
- Hazard reduction methods must take into account the various hazards faced by the affected community and their desires and priorities.
- Any mitigation program must also ensure an effective partnership between the Government, scientific, private sector, NGOs and the community.

The main elements of a mitigation strategy are as follows:

Risk assessment and vulnerability analysis

This involves the identification of hotspot areas of prime concern, collection of information on past natural hazards, information of the natural ecosystems and information on the population and infrastructure, Once this information in collected, a risk assessments should be done to determine the frequency, intensity, impact and the time taken to return to normalcy after the disaster. The assessment of risk and vulnerabilities will need to be revised periodically. A regular mechanism will therefore have to be established for this. The use of Geographical Information Systems (GIS), a computer program, can be a valuable tool in this process as the primary data can be easily updated and the corresponding assessments can be made.

Applied Research and Technology Transfer

There is a need to establish or upgrade observation equipment and networks, monitor the hazards property, improve the quality of forecasting and warning, disseminate information quickly through the warning systems and undertake disaster simulation exercises.

Thus, space technologies such as remote sensing, satellite communications and Global positioning Systems (GPSs) have a very important role to play. Government organization like the ISRO (Indian Space Research Organization) can play a vital role. Similarly, other government organizations like the National Building Research Organization, the Meteorological Department, Irrigation Department, etc., can undertake applied research for devising local- specific mitigation strategies in collaboration with educational institutions or universities.

Such steps could lead to the formulation of locale- specific mitigation measures. A combination of scientific knowledge and expertise with the community based mitigation measures would not only enhance the database but would also form the basis of a successful mitigation strategy.

Public awareness and training : One of the most critical components of a mitigation strategy is the training to be imparted to the officials and staff of the various departments involved at the state and the district level. Will depend to a large extent on the inter- sectional, inter- departmental coordination and efficient teamwork, thus, a well- designed training program taking into account the gaps in knowledge, skills and attitude, with respect to the various that need to be undertaken, is a vital component.

Institutional mechanisms : The most important need at the national level is to strengthen or develop the capacity to undertake disaster – mitigation strategies. There is a need to emphasize on proactive and pre- disaster measures rather than post – disaster response. It is, thus essential to have a permanent administrative structure which can monitor the developmental activities across departments Center (NDMC) can perform such a task. Professionals like architects, structural engineers, doctors, and chemical engineers who are involved with management of hazardous chemicals, can be asked to form groups that can design specific mitigation measures.

Incentives and resources for mitigation : To a very large extent, the success of mitigation programs will depend upon the availability of continued funding. So there is a need to develop mechanisms to provide stable sources of funding for all mitigation programs. This will include incentives for the relocation of commercial and residential activities outside the disaster- prone areas. Housing finance companies should make it mandatory for structures to such hazard – prone areas to follow special building specifications. The introduction of disaster- linked insurance should be explored and should cover not only life but also household goods, cattle, structures and crops.

Landuse planning and regulations : Long – term disaster reduction efforts should aim at promoting appropriate landuse in the disaster prone areas. The separation of industrial areas from residential areas, maintenance of wetlands as buffer zones for floods, creation of public awareness of proper land practices and formation of land use policies for long – term sustainable development are all imperative.

Hazard- resistant design and construction: In areas that are prone to disasters, protection can be enhanced by the careful selection of sites and building technologies. Thus, it is essential to promote the knowledge of disaster- resistant construction materials, techniques and practices among engineers, architects and technical personnel.

Structural and constructional reinforcement of existing buildings

It is also possible to reduce the vulnerability of existing buildings through minor adaptations or alterations, thereby ensuring their safety. This can be done by the insertion of walls on the outside of the building, buttresses, walls in the interior of the building, portico fill-in walls, specially anchored frames, covering of columns and beams, construction of new frame system, placing residential electrical equipment above flood level, designing water storage tanks to be able to withstand cyclonic winds, earthquakes and floods, etc.

Floods and mitigation measures : The lower plain regions of India, in particular Bihar, Uttar Pradesh and West Bengal with respect to the River Ganga, and Assam with respect to the Brahmaputra, suffer from the adverse effects of floods every year. The Ganga- Brahmaputra basin receives the maximum run – off within the three monsoon months. Based on hydrological studies carried out, it is estimated that only 18% of the rainwater can be stored in dams, reservoirs, etc., while 32% of the rainwater flows through rivers ultimately into the sea. Floods will, therefore, be a recurring phenomenon in our country.

Floods can be caused by natural, ecological or anthropogenic factors, either individually or as a combined result. Anthropogenic activities, such as deforestation and shifting cultivation, can also contribute to floods. Forests on the hill- slopes normally exert a sponge effect', soaking up the abundant rainfall and storing it before releasing it in small amounts over a period of time, However, when the forests are cleared the rivers turn muddy and swollen during the wet monsoon season and run dry later on in the year during the drier periods. An increasing proportion of the rainfall is, therefore, released shortly after precipitation in the form of floods.

The mitigation measures for floods include both structural and non – structural measures. The structural include :

- Reservoirs for impounding monsoon flows to be released in a regulated manner after the peak flood flow passes.
- Prevention of over- bank spilling by the construction of embankments and floodwalls
- Improvement of flow conditions in the channel and anti – erosion measures
- Improved drainage

The non – structural measures include :

- Flood – plain management such as flood plain zoning and flood proofing, including disaster preparedness.
- Maintaining wetlands
- Flood forecasting and warning services.
- Disaster relief, flood fighting and public health measures
- Flood insurance.

Earthquakes and mitigation measures: It has been several years since the earthquake struck Gujarat on January 26, 2001. In these years, rehabilitation has been done on a massive scale. Gujarat's experience has taught that building shelters with less vulnerability to earthquakes should also take into consideration the specific needs of the victims instead of being a top – down approach. The role of NGOs in this is very important. Their strength lies in their manpower, informality in operations and valuable human resources. Their ability to reach out to the community and sensitivity to local traditions is an asset in such situations. A report on the various initiatives in Gujarat, in Down to Earth (Vol 12, No.2) by Mihir Bhatt, throws throws light on the various developments that have taken place after the earthquake. According to the report, the initiatives of the international fund for Agriculture Development in supporting the Self- Employed Women's

Association (SEWA) and the Government's initiative in community based livelihood security for earthquakes and drought victims have the potential to shape future disaster response and development projects in Gujarat, Similarly, the Gujarat Woman's Economic Development Corporation (GWEDC) initiative in reviving women's businesses after the calamity also provides many practical lessons in regenerating local economies and artisan markets. This project, supported by the Asian Development Bank, puts a premium on investments in income generation and asset building after a natural disaster. The farming kits provided to affected farmers by Gujarat's agriculture ministry is also showing promising results after two seasons. The author however states that coordination between Government, local NGOs and local community initiatives, both for rescue as well as rehabilitation, needs to be strengthened as this can cause delays, overlaps and waste of relief material and efforts.

Cyclones and mitigation Measures : Tropical cyclones are the worst natural hazards in the tropics. They are large revolving vortices in the atmosphere extending horizontally from 150-1000 km and vertically from the surface from 12-14 km, These are intense low-pressure areas. Strong winds spiraling anti-clockwise in the Northern Hemisphere blow around the cyclone center at the lower level. At the higher levels, the sense of rotation is just opposite to that at the lower level. They generally move 300-5000 km per day over the ocean. While moving over the ocean, they pick up energy, from the warm water of ocean and some of them grow in to a devastating intensity. On the average about 5-6 tropical cyclones from in the bay of Bengal and the Arabian Sea every year out of which 2-3 may be sever. More cyclones form in the Bay of Bengal than in the Arabian Sea. The main dangers from cyclones are very strong winds, torrential rains and high storm tides. Most of the causalities are caused by coastal inundation by storm tides. This is often followed by heavy rainfall and floods. Storm surges cause the greatest destruction.

Although one cannot control cyclones, the effects of cyclones can be mitigated through effective and efficient mitigation policies and strategies. A brief description of the same is given below.

Installation of early warning systems: Such system fitted along the coastlines can greatly assist forecasting techniques, thus helping in early evacuation of people in the storm surge areas.

Developing communication infrastructure: Communication plays a vital role in cyclone disaster mitigation and yet this is one of the first services that get disrupted during cyclones. Amateur Radio has today emerged as a second line unconventional communications systems and is an important tool for disaster mitigation.

Development shelter belts: Shelter belts with plantations of trees can act as effective wind and tide-breakers. Apart from acting as effective windbreakers and protecting soil crops being damaged, they also prevent soil erosion.

Developing community cyclone shelters: Cyclone shelters at strategic locations can help in minimizing the loss of human life. In the normal course of life, these shelters can be used as public utility buildings.

Construction of permanent houses: There is a need to build appropriately designed concrete houses that can withstand high winds and tidal waves.

Training and education: Public awareness programs that inform the population about their response to cyclone warning and preparedness can go a long way in reducing causalities.

Land use control and settlement planning: Ideally, no residential and industrial units should be permitted in the coastal belt of 5 km from the sea, as it is the most vulnerable belt. No further growth of settlements in this region should be permitted. Major settlements and other important establishments should be located beyond 10 km from the sea.

Landslides and mitigation measures : Landslides are recurring phenomena in the Himalayan region. In recent years, however, intensive construction activity and the destabilizing forces of nature have aggravated the problem. Landslides occur as a result of changes on a slope, sudden or gradual, either in its composition, structure, hydrology or vegetation. The changes can be due to geology, climate, weathering, changing landuse and earthquakes.

A significant reduction in the hazards caused by landslides can be achieved by preventing the exposure of population and facilities to landslides and by physically controlling the landslides. Developmental programs that involve modification of the topography, exploitation of natural resources and change in the balance load on the ground should not be permitted. Some critical measures that could be undertaken to prevent further landslides are drainage measures, erosion- control measures such bamboo check-dams, terracing, jute and coir netting and rock fall control measures such as grass plantation, vegetated dry masonry walls, retaining walls and, most importantly, preventing deforestation and improving afforestation.

Disasters cannot be totally prevented. However, early warning systems, careful planning and preparedness on part of the vulnerable community would help in minimizing the loss of life and property due to these disasters.

OVERVIEW OF THE DISASTER RISK MANAGEMENT PROGRAMME [2001-2007]

Government of India (GoI), Ministry of Home Affairs (MHA) and United Nations Development Programme (UNOP) have signed an agreement on August 2002 for implementation of "Disaster Risk Management" Programme to reduce the vulnerability of the communities to natural disasters, in identified multi- hazard disaster prone areas.

Goal : "sustainable Reduction In Natural Disaster Risk" in some of the most hazard prone districts in selected states of India".

The four main objectives of this programme are

1. National capacity building support to the Ministry of Home Affairs.

2. Environment building, education, awareness programme and strengthening the capacity at all levels in natural disaster risk management and sustainable recovery.
3. Multi- hazard preparedness, response and mitigation plans for the programme at state, district, block and village/ward levels in select programme states and districts.
4. Networking knowledge on effective approaches, methods and tools for natural disaster risk management developing and promoting policy frameworks.

Programme Phases

The programme has been divided into two phases over a period of six years. Phase I [2002-2004] would provide support to carry out the activities in 28 select districts in the states in the states of Bihar, Gujarat and Orissa, In phase II [2003-2007] the programme would cover 141 districts in the states of Assam, Maghalaya, Sikkim, West Bengal, Uttaranchal, Uttar Pradesh, Delhi, Maharashtra, Tamilnadu, Manipur, Mizoram, Tripura, Arunachal Pradesh and Nagaland.

REFERENCE

1. Harsh K. Gupta, Disaster management University Press, Hyderabad.
2. Erach Bharucha 2005 Environmental studies, University Press, Hyderabad.
3. White, G.F. (1994) Natural Hazards : Local National global Oxford University Press, London.
4. Mandal, G.S. 1993 National Disaster Reduction, Reliance Publication, New Delhi.
5. Rao, D.P. 1998, Disaster Management, Hyderabad.
6. Green stephen 1980: International Disaster Relief's : towards a Publishers Newyork.

10

Disaster as a Social Crisis Situation

Dr. Sharda Agarwal	Dr. Shweta Garg	Dr. Satyadev Garg
HOD	Asst. Professor	Professor
D.V.C., Orai	RKGEC, Ghaziabad	LKCE, Ghaziabad

Dictionary meaning of "disaster" may be taken as: "a sudden accident or natural event that causes great damage or loss of life" - Oxford Dictionary. So, as can be seen, disaster by definition itself is "sudden" and causes immense damage to property and/or life.

The term 'disaster', meaning 'bad star' in Latin, is defined as an impact of a natural or man-made hazard that causes human suffering or creates human needs that the victims cannot alleviate without assistance. The word's root is from astrology and implies that when the stars are in a bad position, a bad event is about to happen. In a recent document published by the United Nations Development Programme (UNDP) in the Americas, a disaster is defined as 'a social crisis situation occurring when a physical phenomenon of natural, socio-natural or anthropogenic origin negatively impacts vulnerable populations ... causing intense, serious and widespread disruption of the normal functioning of the affected social unit. According to another widespread definition, disasters occur when hazards strike in vulnerable areas.

Disaster is a sudden, calamitous event bringing great damage, loss, and destruction and devastation to life and property. The damage caused by disasters is immeasurable and varies with the geographical location, climate and the type of the earth surface/

degree of vulnerability. This influences the mental, socio-economic, political and cultural state of the affected area. Generally, disaster has the following effects in the concerned areas,

1. It completely disrupts the normal day to day life
2. It negatively influences the emergency systems
3. Normal needs and processes like food, shelter, health, etc. are affected and deteriorate depending on the intensity and severity of the disaster.

It may also be termed as "a serious disruption of the functioning of society, causing widespread human, material or environmental losses which exceed the ability of the affected society to cope using its own resources." Thus, in simple terms we can define disaster as a hazard causing heavy loss to life, property and livelihood.***e.g. a cyclone killing 10,000 lives and a crop loss of one crore can be termed as disaster.***

Features of Disaster

Disaster may have the following main features:-

- Unpredictability
- Unfamiliarity
- Speed
- Urgency
- Uncertainty
- Threat

Types of Disaster

Generally, disasters are of two types – **Natural and Manmade**. Based on the devastation, these are further classified into major/minor natural disaster and major/minor manmade disasters. Some of the disasters are listed below,

Major natural disasters:	Minor natural disasters:
• Flood	• Cold wave
• Cyclone	• Thunderstorms
• Drought	• Heat waves
• Earthquake	• Mud slides
• Storm	
Major manmade disaster :	**Minor manmade disaster:?**
• Setting of fires	• Road / train accidents, riots
• Epidemic	• Food poisoning
• Deforestation	• Industrial disaster/ crisis
• Pollution due to prawn cultivation	• Environmental pollution
• Chemical pollution	
• Wars	

Disaster Risk

Risk is a measure of the expected losses due to a hazardous event of a particular magnitude occurring in a given area over a specific time period. Risk is a function of the probability of particular occurrences and the losses each would cause. The level of risk depends on:

- Nature of the Hazard
- Vulnerability of the elements which are affected
- Economic value of those elements

Vulnerability

It is defined as "the extent to which a community, structure, service, and/or geographic area is likely to be damaged or disrupted by the impact of particular hazard, on account of their nature, construction and proximity to hazardous terrain or a disaster prone area"

Hazards are defined as "Phenomena that pose a threat to people, structures, or economic assets and which may cause a disaster. They could be either manmade or naturally occurring in our environment."

The extent of damage in a disaster depends on:

(1) The impact, intensity and characteristics of the phenomenon and

(2) How people, environment and infrastructures are affected by that phenomenon

This relationship can be written as an equation:

Disaster Risk = Hazard +Vulnerability

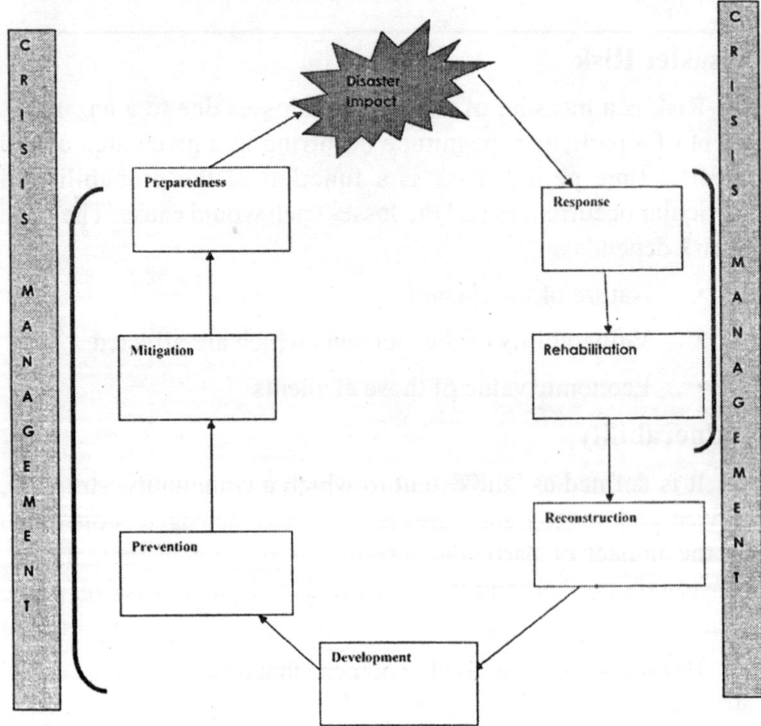

Disaster Management

Various disasters like earthquake, landslides, volcanic eruptions, fires, flood and cyclones are natural hazards that kill thousands of people and destroy billions of dollars of habitat and property each year. The rapid growth of the world's population and its increased concentration often in hazardous environment has escalated both the frequency and severity of natural disasters. With the tropical climate and unstable land forms, coupled with deforestation, unplanned growth proliferation non-engineered constructions which make the disaster-prone areas mere vulnerable, tardy communication, poor or no budgetary allocation for disaster prevention, developing countries suffer more or less chronically by natural disasters. Asia tops the list of casualties due to natural disaster. Among various natural hazards, earthquakes, landslides, floods and cyclones are the major disasters adversely affecting very large areas and population in the Indian sub-continent. These natural disasters are of (i) geophysical origin such as earthquakes, volcanic eruptions, land slides and (ii) climatic origin such as drought, flood, cyclone, locust, forest fire. Though it may not be feasible to control nature and to stop the development of natural phenomena but the efforts could be made to avoid disasters and alleviate their effects on human lives, infrastructure and property. It is almost impossible to prevent the occurrence of natural disasters and their damages. However it is possible to reduce the impact of disasters by adopting suitable disaster mitigation strategies. The disaster mitigation works mainly address the following: (i) minimise the potential risks by developing disaster early warning strategies, (ii) prepare and implement developmental plans to provide resilience to such disasters, (iii) mobilise resources including communication and tele-medicinal services and (iv) to help in rehabilitation and post-disaster reduction. Disaster management on the other hand involves: (i) pre-disaster planning, preparedness, monitoring including relief management capability. (ii) prediction and early warning. (iii) damage assessment and relief management. Disaster reduction is a systematic work which involves with different regions, different professions and different scientific fields, and has become an important measure for human, society and nature sustainable development.

Various Disaster Management

Almost all of us can think of several disasters that have occurred in the recent past. Earthquakes, Cyclone, Flood, Fires, Landslides, industrial accidents etc are some of the more commonly encountered disasters.

Safety Tips for Earthquakes

Earthquakes usually give no warning at all.

Prepare your Family

Before the Earthquake

Now is the time to formulate a safety plan for you and your family. If you wait until the earth starts to shake, it may be too late. Consider the following safety measures:

- Always keep the following in a designated place: bottled drinking water, non-perishable food (chura, gur, etc), first-aid kit, torchlight and battery-operated radio with extra batteries.
- Teach family members how to turn off electricity, gas, etc.
- Identify places in the house that can provide cover during an earthquake.
- It may be easier to make long distance calls during an earthquake. Identify an out-of-town relative or friend as your family's emergency contact. If the family members get separated after the earthquake and are not able to contact each other, they should contact the designated relative/friend. The address and phone number of the contact person/relative should be with all the family members.

Safeguard Your House

- Consider retrofitting your house with earthquake-safety measures. Reinforcing the foundation and frame could make your house quake resistant. You may consult a reputable contractor and follow building codes.

8 Kutchha buildings can also be retrofitted and strengthened.

During Quake

Earthquakes give no warning at all. Sometimes, a loud rumbling sound might signal its arrival a few seconds ahead of time. Those few seconds could give you a chance to move to a safer location. Here are some tips for keeping safe during a quake.

- Take cover. Go under a table or other sturdy furniture; kneel, sit, or stay close to the floor. Hold on to furniture legs for balance. Be prepared to move if your cover moves.
- If no sturdy cover is nearby, kneel or sit close to the floor next to a structurally sound interior wall. Place your hands on the floor for balance.
- Do not stand in doorways. Violent motion could cause doors to slam and cause serious injuries. You may also be hit be flying objects.
- Move away from windows, mirrors, bookcases and other unsecured heavy objects.
- If you are in bed, stay there and cover yourself with pillows and blankets
- Do not run outside if you are inside. Never use the lift.
- If you are living in a kutcha house, the best thing to do is to move to an open area where there are no trees, electric or telephone wires.

If Outdoors

- Move into the open, away from buildings, streetlights, and utility wires. Once in the open, stay there until the shaking stops.
- If your home is badly damaged, you will have to leave. Collect water, food, medicine, other essential items and important documents before leaving.

- Avoid places where there are loose electrical wires and do not touch metal objects that are in touch with the loose wires.
- Do not re-enter damaged buildings and stay away from badly damaged structures.

If in a Moving Vehicle

Move to a clear area away from buildings, trees, overpasses, or utility wires, stop, and stay in the vehicle. Once the shaking has stopped, proceed with caution. Avoid bridges or ramps that might have been damaged by the quake.

After the Quake

Here are a few things to keep in mind after an earthquake. The caution you display in the aftermath can be essential for your personal safety.

- Wear shoes/chappals to protect your feet from debris
- After the first tremor, be prepared for aftershocks. Though less intense, aftershocks cause additional damages and may bring down weakened structures. Aftershocks can occur in the first hours, days, weeks, or even months after the quake.
- Check for fire hazards and use torchlights instead of candles or lanterns.
- If the building you live in is in a good shape after the earthquake, stay inside and listen for radio advises. If you are not certain about the damage to your building, evacuate carefully. Do not touch downed power line.
- Help injured or trapped persons. Give first aid where appropriate. Do not move seriously injured persons unless they are in immediate danger of further injury. In such cases, call for help.
- Remember to help your neighbours who may require special assistance-infants, the elderly, and people with disabilities.

- Listen to a battery-operated radio for the latest emergency information.
- Stay out of damaged buildings.
- Return home only when authorities say it is safe. Clean up spilled medicines, bleaches or gasoline or other flammable liquids immediately. Leave the area if you smell gas or fumes from other chemicals. Open closet and cupboard doors cautiously.
- If you smell gas or hear hissing noise, open windows and quickly leave the building. Turn off the switch on the top of the gas cylinder.
- Look for electrical system damages - if you see sparks, broken wires, or if you smell burning of amber, turn off electricity at the main fuse box. If you have to step in water to get to the fuse box, call an electrician first for advice.
- Check for sewage and water lines damage. If you suspect sewage lines are damaged, avoid using the toilets. If water pipes are damaged, avoid using water from the tap.
- Use the telephone only for emergency calls.
- In case family members are separated from one another during an earthquake (a real possibility during the day when adults are at work and children are at school), develop a plan for reuniting after the disaster. Ask an out of state / district relative or friend to serve as the "family contact". Make sure everyone in the family knows the name, address, and phone number(s) of the contact person (s).

SAFETY TIPS FOR CYCLONE

Before the Cyclone Season

Keep watch on weather and listen to radio or TV. Keep alert about the community warning systems – loudspeakers, bells, conches, drums or any traditional warning system.

- Get to know the nearest cyclone shelter / safe houses and the safest route to reach these shelters.
- Do not listen to rumours.
- Prepare an emergency kit containing:
    - A portable radio, torch and spare batteries;
    - Stocks dry food – Chura, Chhatua, Mudhi, gur, etc.
    - Matches, fuel lamp, portable stove, cooking utensils, waterproof bags
    - A first aid kit, manual, etc.
    - Katuri, pliers, small saw, axe and plastic rope
- Check the roof and cover it with net or bamboo. Check the walls, pillars, doors and windows to see if they are secure. If not, repair those at the earliest. In case of tin roofs, check the condition of the tin and repair the loose points. Cover the mud walls with polythene or coconut leaves mats or straw mats on a bamboo frame. Bind each corner of the roof with a plastic rope in case of thatched roof.
- Trim dry tree branches, cut off the dead trees and clear the place/courtyard of all debris, including coconuts and tree branches.
- Clear your property of loose materials that could blow about and cause injury or damage during extreme winds.
- If your area is prone to storm surge, locate safe high ground or shelter.
- Keep important documents, passbook, etc. in a tight plastic bag and take it along with your emergency kits if you are evacuating.
- Identify the spot where you can dig holes to store food grains, seeds, etc. in polythene bags.
- Keep a list of emergency addresses and phone numbers on display. Know the contact telephone number of the

government offices /agencies, which are responsible for search, rescue and relief operations in your area.

If you are living in an area where CBDP exercises have taken place, ensure:

- Vulnerability list and maps have been updated
- Cyclone drill including search & rescue, first aid training have taken place
- Stock of dry food, essential medicines and proper shelter materials maintained

Upon a cyclone warning

- Store loose items inside. Put extra agricultural products/ stock like paddy in plastic bags and store it by digging up a hole in the ground, preferably at a higher elevation and then cover it properly. Fill bins and plastic jars with drinking water.
- Keep clothing for protection, handy
- Prepare a list of assets and belongings of your house and give information to volunteers and other authorities about your near and dear ones.
- Fill fuel in your car/motorcycle and park it under a solid cover. Tie bullock carts, boats securely to strong posts in an area, which has a strong cover and away from trees. Fallen trees can smash boats and other assets.
- Close shutters or nail all windows. Secure doors. Stay indoors, with pets.
- Pack warm clothing, essential medications, valuables, papers, water, dry food and other valuables in waterproof bags, to be taken along with your emergency kit.
- Listen to your local radio / TV, local community warning system for further information.
- In case of warning of serious storm, move with your family to a strong pucca building. In case of warning of cyclones

of severe intensity, evacuate the area with your family, precious items and documents and emergency kit. Take special care for children, elders, sick, pregnant women and lactating mothers in your family. Do not forget your emergency food stock, water and other emergency items. **GO TO THE NEAREST CYCLONE SHELTER.**

- Do not venture into the sea for fishing.

On Warning of Local Evacuation

Based on predicted wind speeds and storm surge heights, evacuation may be necessary. Official advice may be given on local radio / TV or other means of communication regarding safe routes and when to move.

- Wear strong shoes or chappals and clothing for protection.
- Lock your home, switch off power, gas, water, and take your emergency kit.
- If evacuating to a distant place take valuable belonging, domestic animals, and leave early to avoid heavy traffic, flooding and wind hazards.
- If evacuating to a local shelter or higher grounds carry the emergency kit and minimum essential materials.

When the Cyclone Strikes

- Disconnect all electrical appliances and turn off gas.
- If the building starts crumbling, protect yourself with mattresses, rugs or blankets under a strong table or bench or hold on to a solid fixture (e.g. a water pipe)
- Listen to your transistor radio for updates and advice.
- Beware of the calm 'eye'. If the wind suddenly drops, don't assume the cyclone is over; violent winds will soon resume from the opposite direction. Wait for the official **"all clear"**.
- If driving, stop – but well away from the sea and clear of trees, power lines and watercourses. Stay in the vehicle.

After the Cyclone

- Do not go outside until officially advised it is safe.
- Check for gas leaks. Do not use electric appliances, if wet.
- Listen to local radio for official warnings and advice.
- If you have to evacuate, or did so earlier, do not return until advised. Use a recommended route for returning and do not rush.
- Be careful of snake bites and carry a stick or bamboo
- Beware of fallen power lines, damaged bridges, buildings and trees, and do not enter the floodwaters.
- Heed all warnings and do not go sightseeing.

SAFETY TIPS FOR FLOODS

This guide lists simple things you and your family can do to stay safe and protect your property from floods.

Before flooding occurs

- All your family members should know the safe route to nearest shelter/ raised pucca house.
- If your area is flood-prone, consider alternative building materials. Mud walls are more likely to be damaged during floods. You may consider making houses where the walls are made of local bricks up to the highest known flood level with cement pointing.
- Have an emergency kit on hand which includes a:
    - A portable radio, torch and spare batteries;
    - Stocks of fresh water, dry food (chura, mudi, gur, biscuits), kerosene, candle and matchboxes;
    - Waterproof or polythene bags for clothing and valuables, an umbrella and bamboo stick (to protect from snake), salt and sugar.
    - A first aid kit, manual and strong ropes for tying things

When you Hear a Flood Warning or if Flooding Appears Likely

- Tune to your local radio/TV for warnings and advice.
  - Keep vigil on flood warning given by local authorities
  - Don't give any importance to rumours and don't panic
  - Keep dry food, drinking water and clothes ready
- Prepare to take bullock carts, other agricultural equipments, and domestic animals to safer places or to higher locations.
- Plan which indoor items you will raise or empty if water threatens to enter your house
- Check your emergency kit

During Floods

- Drink boiled water.
- Keep your food covered, don't take heavy meals.
- Use raw tea, rice-water, tender coconut-water, etc. during diarrhoea; contact your ANM/AWW for ORS and treatment.
- Do not let children remain on empty stomach.
- Use bleaching powder and lime to disinfect the surrounding.
- Help the officials/volunteers distributing relief materials.

If You Need to Evacuate

- Firstly pack warm clothing, essential medication, valuables, personal papers, etc. in waterproof bags, to be taken with your emergency kit.
- Take the emergency kit
- Inform the local volunteers (if available), the address of the place you are evacuating to.
- Raise furniture, clothing and valuables onto beds, tables and to the top of the roof (electrical items highest).

- Turn off power.
- Whether you leave or stay, put sandbags in the toilet bowl and over all laundry / bathroom drain-holes to prevent sewage back-flow.
- Lock your home and take recommended/known evacuation routes for your area.
- Do not get into water of unknown depth and current.

If you stay or on your return

- Stay tuned to local radio for updated advice.
- Do not allow children to play in, or near, flood waters.
- Avoid entering floodwaters. If you must, wear proper protection for your feet and check depth and current with a stick. Stay away from drains, culverts and water over knee-deep.
- Do not use electrical appliances, which have been in floodwater until checked for safety.
- Do not eat food, which has been in floodwaters.
- Boil tap water (in cities) until supplies have been declared safe. In case of rural areas, store tube well water in plastic jars or use halogen tablets before drinking.
- Be careful of snakes, snakebites are common during floods.

TIPS ON FIRE ACCIDENTS

(a) High-Rise Fires

- Calmly leave the apartment, closing the door behind you. Remember the keys!
- Pull the fire alarm near the closest exit, if available, or raise an alarm by warning others.
- Leave the building by the stairs.
- Never take the elevator during fire!

If the Exit is Blocked by Smoke or Fire

- Leave the door closed but do not lock it.

- To keep the smoke out, put a wet towel in the space at the bottom of the door.
- Call the emergency fire service number and tell them your apartment number and let them know you are trapped by smoke and fire. It is important that you listen and do what they tell you.
- Stay calm and wait for someone to rescue you.

If There is a Fire Alarm in Your Building which Goes Off

- Before you open the door, feel the door by using the back of our hand. If the door is hot or warm, do not open the door.
- If the door is cool, open it just a little to check the hallway. If you see smoke in the hallway, do not leave.
- If there is no smoke in the hallway, leave and close the door. Go directly to the stairs to leave. Never use the elevator.

If Smoke is in Your Apartment

- Stay low to the floor under the smoke.
- Call the Fire Emergency Number which should be pasted near your telephone along with police and other emergency services and let them know that you are trapped by smoke.
- If you have a balcony and there is no fire below it, go out.
- If there is fire below, go out to the window. **DO NOT OPEN THE WINDOW** but stay near the window.
- If there is no fire below, go to the window and open it. Stay near the open window.
- Hang a bed sheet, towel or blanket out of the window to let people know that you are there and need help.
- Be calm and wait for someone to rescue you.

(A) Kitchen Fires:

It is important to know what kind of stove or cooking oven

you have in your home – gas, electric, kerosene or where firewood is used. The stove is the No. 1 cause of fire hazards in your kitchen and can cause fires, which may destroy the entire house, especially in rural areas where there are thatched roof or other inflammable materials like straw kept near the kitchen. For electric and gas stoves ensure that the switch or the gas valve is switched off/turned off immediately after the cooking is over. An electric burner remains hot and until it cools off, it can be very dangerous. The oven using wood can be dangerous because burning embers remain. When lighting the fire on a wooden fuel oven, keep a cover on the top while lighting the oven so that sparks do not fly to the thatched roof. After the cooking is over, ensure that the remaining fire is extinguished off by sprinkling water if no adult remains in the kitchen after the cooking. Do not keep any inflammable article like kerosene near the kitchen fire.

Important Do's in the Kitchen

- Do have an adult always present when cooking is going on the kitchen. Children should not be allowed alone.
- Do keep hair tied back and do not wear synthetic clothes when you are cooking.
- Do make sure that the curtains on the window near the stove are tied back and will not blow on to the flame or burner.
- Do check to make sure that the gas burner is turned off immediately if the fire is not ignited and also switched off immediately after cooking.
- Do turn panhandles to the centre of the stove and put them out of touch of the children in the house.
- Do ensure that the floor is always dry so that you do not slip and fall on the fire.
- Do keep matches out of the reach of children.

Important Don'ts

- Don't put towels, or dishrags near a stove burner.

- Don't wear loose fitting clothes when you cook, and don't reach across the top of the stove when you are cooking.
- Don't put things in the cabinets or shelves above the stove. Young children may try to reach them and accidentally start the burners, start a fire, catch on fire.
- Don't store spray cans or cans carrying inflammable items near the stove.
- Don't let small children near an open oven door. They can be burnt by the heat or by falling onto the door or into the oven.
- Don't lean against the stove to keep warm.
- Don't use towels as potholders. They may catch on fire.
- Don't overload an electrical outlet with several appliances or extension cords. The cords or plugs may overheat and cause a fire.
- Don't use water to put out a grease fire. ONLY use baking soda, salt, or a tight lid. Always keep a box of baking soda near the stove.
- Don't use radios or other small appliances (mixers, blenders) near the sink.

COMMON TIPS

- Do keep the phone number of the Fire Service near the telephone and ensure that everyone in the family knows the number.
- Do keep matches and lighters away from children.
- Do sleep with your bedroom closed to prevent the spread of fire.
- Do you know that you should never run if your clothes are on fire and that you should - "STOP – DROP-ROLL."

LANDSLIDE

During a Landslide

- Stay alert and awake. Many debris-flow fatalities occur

when people are sleeping. Listen to a Weather Radio or portable, battery-powered radio or television for warnings of intense rainfall. Be aware that intense, short bursts of rain may be particularly dangerous, especially after longer periods of heavy rainfall and damp weather.

- If you are in areas susceptible to landslides and debris flows, consider leaving if it is safe to do so. Remember that driving during an intense storm can be hazardous. If you remain at home, move to a second story if possible. Staying out of the path of a landslide or debris flow saves lives.
- Listen for any unusual sounds that might indicate moving debris, such as trees cracking or boulders knocking together. A trickle of flowing or falling mud or debris may precede larger landslides. Moving debris can flow quickly and sometimes without warning.
- If you are near a stream or channel, be alert for any sudden increase or decrease in water flow and for a change from clear to muddy water. Such changes may indicate landslide activity upstream, so be prepared to move quickly. Don't delay! Save yourself, not your belongings.
- Be especially alert when driving. Embankments along roadsides are particularly susceptible to landslides. Watch the road for collapsed pavement, mud, fallen rocks, and other indications of possible debris flows.

What to Do if You Suspect Imminent Landslide Danger:

- Contact your local fire, police, or public works department. Local officials are the best persons able to assess potential danger.
- Inform affected neighbors. Your neighbors may not be aware of potential hazards. Advising them of a potential threat may help save lives. Help neighbors who may need assistance to evacuate.
- Evacuate. Getting out of the path of a landslide or debris flow is your best protection.

Media and Community Education Ideas

- In an area prone to landslides, publish a special newspaper section with emergency information on landslides and debris flows. Localize the information by including the phone numbers of local emergency services offices, the Red Cross, and hospitals.
- Report on what city and county governments are doing to reduce the possibility of landslides. Interview local officials about local land- use zoning regulations.
- Interview local officials and major insurers. Find out if debris flow is covered by flood insurance policies and contact your local emergency management office to learn more about the program.
- Work with local emergency services to prepare special reports for people with mobility impairments on what to do if evacuation is ordered.
- Support your local government in efforts to develop and enforce land-use and building ordinances that regulate construction in areas susceptible to landslides and debris flows. Buildings should be located away from steep slopes, streams and rivers, intermittent-stream channels, and the mouths of mountain channels.

After the Landslide

- Stay away from the slide area. There may be danger of additional slides.
- Check for injured and trapped persons near the slide, without entering the direct slide area. Direct rescuers to their locations.
- Help a neighbour who may require special assistance - infants, elderly people, and people with disabilities. Elderly people and people with disabilities may require additional assistance. People who care for them or who have large families may need additional assistance in emergency situations.

- Listen to local radio or television stations for the latest emergency information.
- Watch for flooding, which may occur after a landslide or debris flow. Floods sometimes follow landslides and debris flows because they may both be started by the same event.
- Look for and report broken utility lines to appropriate authorities. Reporting potential hazards will get the utilities turned off as quickly as possible, preventing further hazard and injury.
- Check the building foundation, chimney, and surrounding land for damage. Damage to foundations, chimneys, or surrounding land may help you assess the safety of the area.
- Replant damaged ground as soon as possible since erosion caused by loss of ground cover can lead to flash flooding.
- Seek the advice of a geotechnical expert for evaluating landslide hazards or designing corrective techniques to reduce landslide risk. A professional will be able to advise you of the best ways to prevent or reduce landslide risk, without creating further hazard.

Media and Community Education Ideas

- In an area prone to landslides, publish a special newspaper section with emergency information on landslides and debris flows. Localize the information by including the phone numbers of local emergency services offices, the American Red Cross chapter, and hospitals.
- Report on what city and county governments are doing to reduce the possibility of landslides. Interview local officials about local land- use zoning regulations.
- Interview local officials and major insurers regarding the National Flood Insurance Program. Find out if debris flow is covered by flood insurance policies from the National Flood Insurance Program and contact your local emergency management office to learn more about the program.

- Work with local emergency to prepare special reports for people with mobility impairments on what to do if evacuation is ordered.
- Support your local government in efforts to develop and enforce land-use and building ordinances that regulate construction in areas susceptible to landslides and debris flows. Buildings should be located away from steep slopes, streams and rivers, intermittent-stream channels, and the mouths of mountain channels.

Before a Landslide: How to Plan

Develop a Family Disaster Plan. Please see the "Family Disaster Plan" section for general family planning information. Develop landslide-specific planning.

Learn about landslide risk in your area. Contact local officials, state geological surveys or departments of natural resources, and university departments of geology. Landslides occur where they have before, and in identifiable hazard locations. Ask for information on landslides in your area, specific information on areas vulnerable to landslides, and request a professional referral for a very detailed site analysis of your property, and corrective measures you can take, if necessary.

If You are at Risk from Landslides

- Talk to your insurance agent.
- Develop an evacuation plan.
- Discuss landslides and debris flow with your family. Everyone should know what to do in case all family members are not together. Discussing disaster ahead of time helps reduce fear and lets everyone know how to respond during a landslide or debris flow.

INFORMATION TECHNOLOGY AND NATURAL DISASTER MANAGEMENT IN INDIA

Introduction

It is a well known fact that natural disasters strikes countries, both developed and developing, causing enormous destruction and creating human sufferings and producing negative impacts on national economies. Due to diverse geo-climatic conditions prevalent in different parts of the globe, different types of natural disasters like floods, droughts, earthquakes, cyclones, landslides, volcanoes, etc. strikes according to the vulnerability of the area. India is considered as the world's most disaster prone country. It has witnessed devastating natural disasters in recent past like droughts, floods, cyclones, earthquakes, landslides, etc.

Natural Disasters in India:-

India is a large country and prone to a number of natural hazards. Among all the natural disasters that country faces, river floods are the most frequent and often devastating. The shortfall in the rainfall cause droughts or drought like situation in various parts of the country. The country has faced some severe earthquakes causing widespread damage to the life and property. India has a coastline of about 8000 km which is prone to very severe cyclonic formations in the Arabian Sea and Bay of Bengal. Another major problem faced by the country is in the form of landslides and avalanches.

With an increase in the perception towards spreading a culture of prevention in the disaster management scenario, considerable emphasis is now being placed on research and development activities in the area of information technology for disaster preparedness and prevention. This has brought in a significant positive change even though the multitude and frequency of disasters in the country has increased.

Application of Information Technology in Disaster Management

Though it is not possible to completely avoid the natural disasters, but the sufferings can be minimised by creating proper awareness of the likely disasters and its impact by developing a suitable warning system, disaster preparedness and management of disasters through application of information technology tools. The changing trends have opened up a large number of scientific and technological resources and skills to reduce disaster risk. The IT tools are discussed below:-

(A) GIS and Remote Sensing

GIS provides a tool for effective and efficient storage and manipulation of remotely sensed data and other spatial and non-spatial data types for both scientific management and policy oriented information. This can be used to facilitate measurement, mapping, monitoring and modelling of variety of data types related to natural phenomenon. The specific GIS application in the field of Risk Assessment are:- Hazard Mapping to show earthquake, landslides, floods or fire hazards. Thses map could be created for cities, districts or even for the entire country and tropical cyclone Threat Maps are used by meteorological departments to improve the quality of the tropical storm warning services and quickly communicate the risk to the people likely to get affected by the cyclone.

Remote sensing makes observation of any object from a distance and without coming into actual contact. Remote sensing can gather data much faster than ground based observation, can cover large area at one time to give a synoptic view. Remote sensing comprises Aerial Remote Sensing which is the process of recording information, such as photographs and images from sensor on aircrafts and Satellite Remote Sensing which consists of several satellite remote sensing system which can be used to integrate natural hazard assessments into development planning studies.These are: Landsat, SPOT Satellite, Satellite Radar System, Advanced Very High Resolution Radio. Some application of GIS and Remote Sensing in various disasters are as follows:-

(i) Drought

GIS and Remote Sensing can be used in drought relief management such as early warnings of drought conditions will help to plan out the strategies to organise relief work. Satellite data may be used to target potential ground water sites for taking up well-digging programmes. Satellite data provides valuable tools for evaluating areas subject to desertification. Film transparencies, photographs and digital data can be used for the purpose of locating, assessing and monitoring deterioration of natural conditions in a given area.

(ii) Earthquake

GIS and Remote Sensing can be used for preparing seismic hazards maps in order to assess the exact nature of risks.

(iii) Floods

Satellite data can be effectively used for mapping and monitoring the flood inundated areas, flood damage assessment, flood hazard zoning and post-flood survey of rivers configuration and protection works.

(iv) Landslides

Landslide zonation map comprise a map demarcating the stretches or area of varying degree of anticipated slope stability or instability. The map has an inbuilt element of forecasting and is hence of probabilistic nature. Depending upon the methodology adopted and the comprehensiveness of the input data used, a landslide hazard zonation map able to provide help concerning location,-extent of the slop area likely to be affected, and rate of mass movement of the slope mass.

(v) Search and Rescue

GIS can be used in carrying out search and rescue operations in a more effective manner by identifying areas that are disasters prone and zoning them accordingly to risk magnitudes.

(B) Internet

In the present era of electronic communication, the internet provides a useful platform for disaster mitigation communications. Launching of a well defined web site is a very cost-effective means of making an intra-national and international presence felt. It provides a new and potentially revolutionary option for the rapid, automatic, and global dissemination of disaster information. A number of individuals and groups, including several national meteorological services, are experimenting with the Internet for real-time dissemination of weather observation, forecasts, satellite and other data. In the most critical phase of natural disasters electronic communication have provided the most effective and in some instances perhaps the only means of communication with the outside world.

(C) Warning and Forecasting System

An advance system of forecasting, monitoring and issuing early warnings plays the most significant role in determining whether a natural hazard will assume disastrous proportions or not. The country have the following forecasting systems:

(*) Indian Meteorological Department (IMD)

IMD provides cyclone warnings from the Area Cyclone Warning Centres (ACWCs) It has developed the necessary infrastructure to originate and disseminate the cyclone warnings at appropriate levels. It has made operational a satellite based communication system called Cyclone Warning Dissemination System for direct dissemination of cyclone warnings to the cyclone prone coastal areas. IMD runs operationally a Limited-area Analysis and Forecast System (LAFS), based on an Optimal Interpretation (OI) analysis and a limited area Primitive Equation (PE) model, to provide numerical guidance.

(D) Role of Space Technology

Space systems from their vantage position have unambiguously demonstrated their capability in providing vital information and services for disaster management The Earth Observation satellites provide comprehensive, synoptic and multi temporal coverage of large areas in real time and at frequent intervals and 'thus' - have become valuable for continuous monitoring of atmospheric as well as surface parameters related to natural disasters. Geo-stationary satellites provide continuous and synoptic observations over large areas on weather including cyclone-monitoring. Polar orbiting satellites have the advantage of providing much higher resolution imageries, even though at low temporal frequency, which could be used for detailed monitoring, damage assessment and long-term relief management. The vast capabilities of communication satellites are available for timely dissemination of early warning and real-time coordination of relief operations. The advent of Very Small Aperture Terminals (VSAT) and Ultra Small Aperture Terminals (USAT) and phased - array antennae have enhanced the capability further by offering low cost, viable technological solutions towards management and mitigation of disasters. Satellite communication capabilities-fixed and mobile are vital for effective communication, especially in data collection, distress alerting, position location and co-ordinating relief operations in the field. In addition, Search and Rescue satellites provide capabilities such as position determination facilities onboard which could be useful in a variety of land, sea and air distress situations.

11

Role Of Community And Students In Disaster Management

Dr. Anita Nigam
Lecturer, Deptt. Of Geography,
D.B.S College, Kanpur

Since the time of Earth summit at Rio de Janeiro held in June 1992, the disaster management experts have focused on capacity building to mitigate the sufferings of most environment connected disasters. It was through only as a strategy to enhance domestic know-how essential to identify individuals and associations as well as resources in the underdeveloped world. It has since then been used as a basic component of Disaster Management. It has also been used as a tool to minimise risk. Risk is considered as an exposure to hazard. Negligence or ignorance may entail loss or injury. Disaster risk is considered as a product of hazard and vulnerability and can be minimised with capacity building.

ELEMENTS OF DISASTER MANAGEMENT

Disaster management is the group of many works in which many methods related to management comes. They are following:

(1) Relief and Response: Relief and response plays a crucial and important role in community based initiatives. Earlier the Government distributed relief and aid often with the help of outside volunteers. But the community help emphasise involvement of local community leaders and volunteers and equipping them with essential skills in providing relief to affected persons.

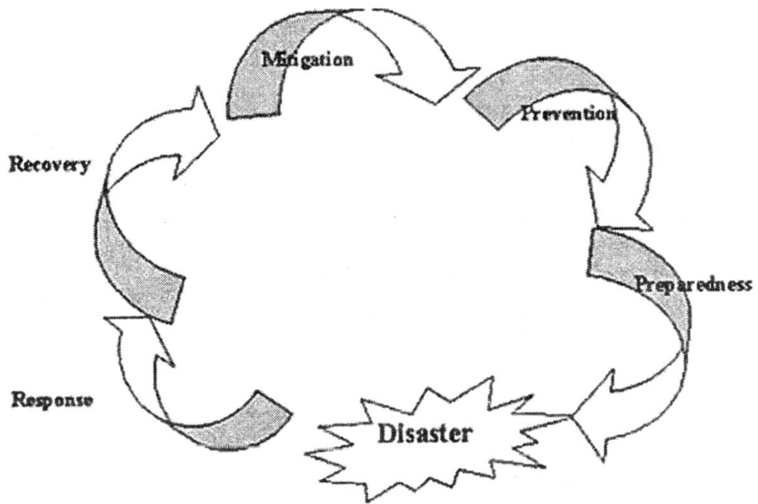

Fig : Elements of Disaster Management

(2) Recovery, Rehabilitation and Reconstruction: This phase involves giving touches to beginning the life again. Additional funds are provided to rebuild the houses often resistant to particular disasters in the disaster prone area. Essential services are restored and people are encouraged to restart their business or take up new employment.

(3) Prevention and Mitigation: This phase seeks environmental sound techniques to reduce the risk of potential disasters.

(4) Preparedness: It simply means being prepared to solve or face a hazard and initiative members are made capable (through capacity building) to manage with the disaster. Special measures are taken before a disaster strikes.

FORM OF DISASTER MANAGEMENT

Our country is a federal state where there is an organized arrangements for disaster management from national level to state, district and village level.

Following chart can be proved helpful in understanding this:

National Level

Home Department

(Central Relief Commissioner)

↓

State Level

Disaster Management Department

(State Relief Commissioner)

↓

District Level

Office of District Magistrate

(District Magistrate)

Block Level

Office of Panchayat Samiti

(Block Development Officer)

Village Level

Rural Disaster Management Committee

(Sarpanch/Head of the Village)

At National Level: The disaster management work at national level is assigned to home ministry. The Central Relief Commissioner, who is the officer of joint secretary level, looks after this complete relief works in centre and co-ordinates between the system and the various disaster management related officers. The following institutions giving decision and direction at the centre are responsible for disaster management work:

(1) Central cabinet which is presided by the Prime Minister.

(2) Group of specific ministers under the leadership of Prime Minister.

(3) Officers related to various ministers and officers invited from various departments. Other than home ministry, agriculture, railways, health and civil aviation ministries are given preference in it.

Other than these ministries, Meteorological Department, Central Water Commission, Public Works Department and Defence Ministry related officers fully help in various activities of disaster management.

The Central Disaster Management Committee thus made is responsible for the following important works:

(1) Co-ordination is to be made in all the necessary means and they are to be used for removing the effects of disaster.

(2) Central disaster project is to be established and state, district, blocks and small units are to be directed for making their disaster projects.

(3) Co-ordination is to be made in the works of disaster management. The workers are to be given proper training and all possible measures are to be made to prevent the disaster and weakening its effects.

(4) Valuation is to be done on national level and international help and assistance is to be controlled in proper manner.

At the State Level: The actual responsibility of disaster management in India is of the states where disaster has taken place; the Centre only helps in the efforts of the state. The Chief Secretary is to be the President of disaster management committee at the state level who is also called the Relief Commissioner. He works on the consultation with the Chief Minister. The state disaster management committee consists the secretaries of the various departments of the state, chief police officials, head of the fire department and the members of Civil Society Organizations.

Following are the main functions of state disaster management committee:

(1) Development of state disaster management projects.

(2) Contribution in the development of disaster management and responsible projects at district, block and ward level.

(3) Establishing disaster management committees at all the levels.

(4) Training is to be given in various disasters such as earthquake, cyclone, landslide, flood, fire accidents, industrial accidents, and terrorist attacks.

(5) Strengthening the disaster management parties established at all the levels.

(6) Doing co-ordination in the works of various local organizations.

At District Level: The disaster management committee established at district level consists district magistrate, head of the district police, chief fire officer and high officials of irrigation and health department. The representatives of some voluntary organizations are also the members of this committee who also give their required assistance. All these parties work under the direction of District Magistrate.

Following are the main functions of district disaster management committee:

(1) Assisting in the preparation of district disaster management by the administration.

(2) Providing proper training to the various disaster management parties of the district.

(3) Assisting the works of disaster management by the state and central governments and providing required information.

(4) Doing mock drills of disaster so that people get the training to face the disaster in advance.

Disaster Management Committee at the Block Level: Block Development Officer use to be the president of block disaster management committee. The other members of this committee are social welfare department, health department, rural water supply and sanitation department, fire department, senior citizens and the representatives of social service organizations.

Following are the main functions of the block disaster management committee:

(1) Assisting in preparing the disaster management project of block administration.

(2) Giving suggestions to prevent disaster.

(3) Training the various block disaster management parties and doing co-ordination in them.

(4) Doing mock drills to prevent the disaster.

Disaster Management Committee at the Village level: The Sarpanch or Pradhan use to be the chairman of village disaster management committee. There are 10 to 12 members of this committee. Representatives from all the classes are included in it. The engineers, doctors, teachers, senior citizens and young men living in the village are given representation in this committee.

The main function of this committee is to prepare disaster management projects for the village. Dividing people in various disaster management parties and giving training to them and making them to do mock drills.

ROLE OF THE COMMUNITY IN DISASTER MANAGEMENT

During and after Tsunami tragedy in December 2004, newspapers and electronic media screamed in bold letters "Disaster- the great leveler of rich and poor and of religions." These were not innovations in thought but happenings in practice to bind the people of the world together. Perhaps Karl Marx would have also called it the international brotherhood. It however, differed from Marx's thoughts. It was rightly globalization in practice and the world a global village in reality. Within this concept of globalization, there is great force on strengthening the role of base level element which are called communities. In matters of disaster mitigations the communities have also to play a role in reduction of effects.

Importance of Community Resources in India

Traditionally, Indian society in the starting of Aryan Civilization was ruled by community leaders. They also solved the social problems. In all matters including education of the children the members of the community worked together. The community system of education was known as gurukuls. As the villages grew in size two village institutions known as Sabha and Samiti helped the leaders indecision making. There are many episodes in the history of India when the members of the community under their leaders faced natural disasters together. The protection of the environment had become a cause for concern. It provided the communities a rationale for protection of their respective territories. These very territories later became political boundaries of kingdoms. Most of the cases of misuse of environment arose on account of conquests and annexations of small communities by the bigger ones. Political they came to be known Janapadas and Mahajanapadas which in later periods gave rise to empires. In the medieval period, foreign aggressions and conquests followed. It was only after 1947 when India got independence that this traditional wisdom was revived. Among these initiatives included involvement of community in decision making, revival of Panchayats and community based hazards mitigation plans. Study and importance of community resources has also been included in the school curriculae. This intimate relationship is visible in the slogan "Let us study the community, use the community resources, serve the community and involve the community in all decision processes."

Disaster Mitigation, Environment Protection and Community Resources:

(1) **Geographic Resources:** Protection of forests, hill landscapes, waterfall, lakes rivers, springs, meadows, sea ports, dams and river valleys. All these resources concern environment and the communities concerned. Saving these resources would mean saving the community from ecological disaster.

(2) **Historical Resources:** Historical monuments, sites, religious shrines relics, inscriptions, mines, rocks and gardens are our common heritage. It enjoins on the community to make a firm commitment to prevent or minimize any danger or damage of these structures.

(3) **Cultural Resources:** These include educational institutions, universities, theatres, emporia, newspapers, transport, television, telephone services and offices. All of them have been made with community resources and are associated with the intellectual and properly rights and areas pre-requisite for socio-economic development. Their protection should predominate all other issues.

ROLE OF SCHOOLS AND STUDENTS IN DISASTER MANAGEMENT

Disaster management is essentially an environment protection programme. Like in all such programmes, students have an important role to play in disaster management. First of all they cannot be separated from the community. Clearly the involvement of students is of paramount importance but precautions must be taken to stop unnecessary burden. No efforts should be made towards risk transfer or diffusion of risk. In disaster management, there is a certain requirement for efficiency. These standards must be related to valuation before applying to students.

School Planning

Students should not be involved in disaster management individually but through the institution of the school itself. It is of course true that there are much bravery on their own. Some of them also get national awards on 26th January the Republic day every year. These are real life stories, most daring and worth emulating but not all children can be expected to show their punch in the same manner. So it is necessary that involvement of students in disaster management must be done through careful planning at the school level. Some of the main elements of school planning disaster management are the following:

1. Integrate into the study of social sciences, information about vulnerability, risk reduction and management techniques.
2. Events selected should be suitable to particular age groups and categories of children like boys, girls, mentally and physically handicapped students.
3. Teachers selected to accompany students in the field must have the necessary motivation.
4. There should be no distortion of facts while dealing with young minds.
5. Suitability, efficiency and physical fitness must be strongly pressed and applied at every stage. There are many hazards like hitch-hiking, rock climbing, mountaineering, etc., which need complete physical fitness. Some criteria are also applied like suitability, efficiency and physical fitness as standards of sections.

Disaster Management Committee

Involving school students in disaster management clearly calls for certain preventions, standards and rules for selecting a team. The parents should know what is going on and their consent is needed. This cannot be left to the dictates or choice of any one teacher or the principal. It calls for collective action and combined decision. It goes by a saying care when they share. In other words, a committee is needed to share the responsibilities that can then care for the innocent minds. Often parents too need to be represented on the committee. Their construction involvement will be appreciated by all members of the community.

Organize task forces on each of the following objects:

1. Task Force on Disaster Warning.
2. Task Force on External Device
   (i) Evolve methods of using community resources.
   (ii) Selection of resource persons.

3. **Task Force on Field Service:** Evacuation and search as well as rescue
4. Task Force on Emergency and First Aid.
5. Task Force on Public Services and Awareness Generation.
6. Task Force on Mitigation Strategies.

Resource Personnel

Resource persons are those who have special skills, in the present case, in the field of disaster management. Since Disaster Management Committee will also have some specialists as its members they are better equipped with the knowledge of what they can expect from resource persons. They will obviously influence the work of DMC. They will also provide learning opportunities to students in many real life situations. The resource persons can also directly impress the decision of students to chose any specific work area like, for example, rescue and evacuation, distribution of relief, medical and hospital services and other such fields as mentioned in the box.

Advantages of Involving Students

Bellwether, meaning an indicator of future trends, is also how students react to today's challenges. The environment is getting nitty-gritty. The students are getting exposed to all sorts of hazards. Therefore Bellwether approach is described as the need of the hour. Other advantages are the following:

1. **Disaster Readiness:** Involving students through their respective schools is an important step in disaster preparedness. Through this preparedness, students will also learn how to care for their school property. For example, they can check seepage, leakage, unsafe electric connections, etc. Secondly, with the involvement of school, the school building can also play as a temporary disaster relief centre. Students who become familiar with disaster management technique will themselves ensure sufficient facilities and space. Thirdly, once it is known that the school is the centre of activity its capacity building will extend to

its own environment. For example, students will plant trees and create shelter-belts for the school which in turn is also an environment improvement measure. They will keep in touch with fire brigade and other emergency services and in the process improve the school's own safety standards.

2. **Extra Curricular Activities:** By involving students in disaster management the students will also come to know the importance of curricular activities like, for example, morning PT, games and sports activities, rock climbing, swimming which will come handy during disaster mitigation in the field. In addition, students will also learn skills like earthquake and fire drills, sounding alert, helping keep cool in the face of disaster and control panic and other rescue and evacuation skills especially during fire and floods.

CONCLUSION

The goal of any disaster management initiative is to build a disaster resistant/resilient community equipped with safer living and sustainable livelihoods to serve its own development purposes. The community is also the first responder in any disaster situation, thereby emphasizing the need for community level initiatives in managing disasters. To encourage such initiatives, the following are required:

(a) Creating awareness through disaster education and training and information dissemination are necessary steps for empowering the community to cope with disasters.

(b) Community based approach followed by most NGOs and Community Based Organizations (CBOs) should be incorporated in the disaster management system as an effective vehicle of community participation.

(c) Within a vulnerable community, there exist groups that are more vulnerable like women and children, aged and infirm and physically challenged people who need special care and attention especially during disaster situations. Efforts are required for identifying such vulnerable groups and providing special assistance in terms of evacuation, relief, aid and medical attention to them in disaster situations.

REFERENCES

UNCRD Disaster Management planning Hyogo office; people, communities and Disasters, proceedings on international workshop on earthquake safer world in the 21st century, Kobe, Japan, February 2003.

Drabek, T.E., Human System Responses to Disaster: An Inventory of Sociological Findings, Springer-Velar, New York, 1986.

Dynes, R.R. et. al., Organized Behavior in Disaster, Disaster Research Centre, University of Delaware New York, 1974.

12

The Role of Communication During Natural And Manmade Disaster

Dr. Chandra Prakash Singh
Department of English
D.B.S. (P.G.) College
Kanpur

Dr. Shankar Singh Solanki
Department of English
D.A-V. (PG) College
Kanpur

The word communication originates from communis a Greek word, meaning to 'make common'. Communication is the method by which people share their ideas, informations, opinions and feelings in natural and manmade disaster. Communication is a two way process, when you communicate' you perceive the other persons responses and react with your own thoghts and feelings. It is only by paying attention to the other person that you have any idea about what to say or do next. Right direction communication may be very useful but wrong communication is very harmful in disaster.

Chemical Smog (London Smog) : This type of smog is thought to be caused by sulphur dioxide. It is formed by combination of smoke, dust, fog and SO_2. Chemical smog is usually formed around some industrial and power plants. It is generally bad in early morning hours and become worse after sunrise, due to sunlight induced oxidation of SO_2 to SO_3 followed by reaction with humidity. Sulphuric acid is formed in this type of smog, which is very harmful to people suffering from bronchial diseases such as asthma or emphysema.

On Thursday, December 4, 1952, a high temperature air mass moved over Southern England and thus creates a temperature inversion and casued white fog to settle over London. As the particulate and sulphur dioxide levels rose,due to the extensive use of coal-fired heating and power production system, the fog began to blacken. The high pressure area stalled and the pollutant build-up worsened further, since there were no air currents to disperse the smog. By-Friday morning, visibility was zero. According to an eye-witness such was the state that white collar became almost black within 20-minutes.

The smog, so formed was intensely irritating to the human respiratory system. As a result, most of the people soon developed red eyes, hurning throats and nagging coughs. Soon reports of smog-related deaths began to come in the elderly and the people with chronic respiratory problems became the first casualty; followed by young and otherwise healthy persons. More than 4,0000 people died before the fog disappeared/lifted on December 9, 1952.

Los Angeles Smog (photochemical smog) - Photochemical smog is associated with adverse meteorological conditions (inversion conditions) when air movement is restricted in summers in highly motorized areas. The first noticed incidence of photochemical smog was is Log Angeles, USA, in the mid 1940's and thus, it is sometimes referred as Los Angeles smog.

Photo-chemical smog is oxidizing smog having a high concentration of oxidants. Photochemical smog is a mixture of reactants and products that result from the interaction betwen volatile organic compound (VOCs) and oxidant (such as NO_2, O_3-, CO etc.) the primary pollutants in photochemical smog are nitric oxide and hydrocarbons. These primary pollutants convert rapidly to the secondary pollutants like ozone, organic nitrtes (peroxyacetyl nitrate), oxidized hydrocarbons and photochemical aerosols int the presence of sunlight. It is characterized by brown and hazy fumes which reduce visibility, cuase-eye and lung irritation, damage crops, leads to the cracking of rubber, damage of plants, etc.

In India, Bombay and Calcutta are ideal conditions for the formation of photochemical smog, but it may be masked by smoke and SO_2.

Mine-Mata Diseases - In the early 1950s, people of Minamata (a small coastal town in Japan) noticed a strange behaviour of their cats. Their cats were twitching, stumbling and jerking that they called dancing cats but the fact was the cat were suffering from brain damage known as 'methyl mercury poisoning'.

The Chisso chemical plant used to release the residues containing mercury into Mina-maa bay. It was assumed that elemental mercury, which is insoluble in water, would sink into the bottom sediments converts the elemental mercury into soluble methyl mercury. This soluble methyl mercury was finally absorbed by the tissues of aquatic organisms, particularly fishes. These fishes, containing about 50 ppm of mercury, when consumed by people lead to an epidemic of nervous problem including numbness, tingling sensation, headaches, blurred vision, loss of muscle control and slurred speech. About 50 people died and more than 3500 were affected. Mina-mata tragedy was probably the first water pollution episode of modern times.

Japan, Sweden and Canada are still suffering from 'Mina-mata Diseases' due to widespread use of mercury compounds as algicdes and fungicides in agriculture, pulp and paper industries and chloro-alkali plants.

Solid Waste Management - All solid and semi-solid waste arising from human and animal activities, except-human excrete and sullage (liquid wastes from bathroom and kitchen) etc.) are discorded as useless or unwanted are included in the term solid wastes. The term solid wastes encompasses the highly heterogeneous mass of discarded materials or throwaway from urban community as well as the more homogeneous accumulation of waste generated by agricultural, industrial and mining activities. Solid waste (waste other than liquid or gaseous) can be classified as municipal, industrial, agricultural, medical, mining waste and sewage sludge.

The greenhouse effect is a warming of the Earth's surface and lower atmosphere that tends to intensify with an increase in atmosphere carbon dioxide. The atmosphere allows a large percentage of the rays of visible light from the Sun to reach the Earth's surface and heat it. A part of this energy is reradiated by the Earth's surface in the form of long-wave infrared 9TR) radiation, much of which is absorbed by molecules of carbon dioxide and wate vapour in the atmosphere and which is reflected back to the surface as heat. This is roughly analogous to the effect produced by the glass panes of a greenhouse, which transmit sunlight in the visible range but hold in heat. The trapping of this infrared radiation causes the Earth's surface and lower atmospheric layers to warm to a higher temperture than would otherwise be the case. An increase in atmospheric concentrations of other trace gases such as chlorofluorocarbons (Freons), nitrous oxide, and methane, due again largely to human activity, may also aggravate greenhouse conditions and the IR active gases responsible for the effect are likewise referred to as **greenhouse gases**. They are mainly

CO_2 – 52%, CH_4 – 24%, N2O – 18%, CFC'S – 6%

Acid Rain - Acid rain is one of the most dangerous and widespread forms of pollution. Sometimes called "the nseen plague", acid rain can go undetected in an area for years. Technically, acid rain is rain that has a larger amount of acid in it than what is normal. The acidity of rain in parts of Europe and North America has dramatically increased over the past few decades. It is now common in many places for rain and non-living systems become harmed and damaged as a result of acid rain.

Effect on Human - Humans can become seriously ill, and can even die from the effects of acid rain. One of the major problems that acid rain can cause in a human being is respiratory problems. Many can find it difficult to breathe, especially people who have asthma. Asthma, along with dry cough, headaches and throat irritations can be caused by the sulfur dioxides and nitrogen oxides from acid rain. Acid rain can be absorted by both plants (through soil and/or direct contact) and animals (from thins they eat and/or direct contact). When humans eat these plants or animals, the toxiny inside of their meals can affect them. Brain damage, kidney problems, and "alzheimer's disease has been linked to people eating "toxic" anumals/plants.

Ozone Layer Depletion - The term Ozone depletion is used to describe two distinct, but related observations, a slow, steady decline of about 3% per decade, in the total amount of ozone in the earth's stratosphere during the past twenty years, and a much larger, but seasonal, decrease in stratospheric ozone over the earth's polar regions during the same period. (The latter phenomenon is commonly rerred to as the "ozone tide"). The detailed mechanism by which the plar ozone holes form is different from that for he mid-latitude thinning, but the proximate cause of both trends is believed to be catalytic destruction of ozone by atomic chlorine and bromine. The primary source of these haologen atoms in the stratopshere is photodissociation of chloroflurocarbon (CFC) compounds, commonly called Freons, and bromofluorocarbon compounds known as Halons, which are transported into the stratosphere after being emitted at the surface. Both ozone depletion mechanisms strengthened as emissions of CFCs and Halons increased.

Since the ozone layer prevents most harmful UVB wavelengths (270-315 nm) of ultra-violet light from passing through the Earth's atmosphere, observed and projected decreases in ozone have generated worldwide concern, leading to adoption of the Montreal Protocol banning the production of CFCs and halons as well as related ozone depleting chemicals such as carbon tetrachloride and trichloroethane (also known as methyl chloroform). It is suspected that a variety of biological consequences, including, for example, increases in skin cancer, damage to plants, and reduction of plankton populations in the ocean's photic zone, may result from the increased UV exposure due to ozone depletion.

Ozone Creation - Three form (or allotropes) of oxygen are involved in the ozone-oxygen cycle Oxygen atoms. O, or atomic oxygen, oxygen molecules, O_2, and ozone, O_3, Ozone is formed in the stratosphere when oxygen molecules photodissociate after absorbing an ultraviolet photon whose wavelength is sharter than 240 nm. This produces two oxygen atoms. The atomic oxygen then combines with O_2 to create O_3. Ozone molecules strongly absorb UV light between 310 and 200 nm, following which ozone splits into a molecule of O_2 and an oxygen atom. The oxygen atom then joins up with an oxygen molecule to regenerate ozone. This is a continuing process which terminates when an oxygen atom "recombines" with an ozone molecule to make $2O_2$ molecules. Prior to the begnning of the depletion trend, the amount of ozone in the stratosphere was kept roughly constant by a balance between the rates of creation and destruction of ozone molecules by UV light.

$$O_2 + hv \rightarrow O + O$$
$$O_2 + O + M \rightarrow O_3 + M$$
$$O_3 + hv \rightarrow O_2 + O$$

Ozone Destruction - Ozone can be destroyed by a number of free radical catalysts, the most important of whicha re hydroxyl (OH) , nitric oxide (NO) and atomic chlorine (Cl) and bromine (Br). All of these radicals have both natural and anthropogenic (manmade) sources. At the present time, most of the OH and NO in the stratosphere is of natural origin, but human activity has dramatically increased the chlorine and bromine. These elements are found in certain stable organic compounds, especially chlorofluorocarbons (CFCs), which may find their way to the stratosphere without being destroyed in the troposphers. Once in the stratosphere, the Cl and Br atoms are liberated from the parent compounds by the action of ultraviolet light, and can destroy ozone molecules in a catalytic cycle. In this cycle, a chlorine atom reacts with an ozone molecule, taking an oxygen atom with it (forming CIO) and leaving a normal oxygen molecule. A free oxygen atom than takes away the oxygen from the CIO, and the final result is an oxygn molecule and a chlorine atom, which then reinitiates the cycle.

Antarctica Ozone Hole - In the area over Antarctica, there are stratospheric cloud ice particles that are not present at warmer latitudes. Reactions occur on the surface of the ice particles that accelerate the ozone destruction caused by stratospheric chlorine. Polar Regions get a much larger variation in sunlight than anywhere else, and during the 3 months of winter spend most of time in the dark without solar radiation. Temperatures stay close around or below – 80°C for much of the winter and the extremely low antarctic temperatures cause cause cloud formation in the relatively ":dry" stratosphere. These Polar Stratospheric Clouds (PSC's) are composed of ice crystals that provide the surface for a multitude of reactions, many of which speed the degradation of ozone molecules. This phenomenon has caused documented decreases in ozone concentrations over Antarctica.

In fact, ozone levels drop so low in spring in the Southern Hemisphere that scientists have observed what they call a "hole" in the ozone layer. The ozone destruction process requires conditions cold enough for stratospheric clouds to form. Once these stratospheric clouds from the process can take place, even in warmer conditions.

It was first notices by a research group from The British Antarctic Survey in the 1970's. Joseph, Farman, Brian Gardiner and Jonathan Shanklin, are the BAS scientists who discovered the Antarctic ozone hole. In the 1980s the first measurements of this loss were actually documented. In October 1984, when the British first reported their findings, ozone levels were about 35 percent lower than the average for the 1960s.

The United Nations has described the humanitarian disaster that followed the 12 Janaury 2010 earth-quake that struck Haiti as the worst since the founding of the organisation. The Haitian government has said that it fears more than 200,000 people have already perished More than 300,000 people have been rendered homeless. Health Minister "Alex Larsen said that the death toll from the earthquake could eventually reach half a million, with another 250,000 injured. The quake measured 7.0 on the Richter scale and had the force of 500,000 tonnes of TNT (trinitrotaluene).

Even as aid efforts were continuing. Haiti was hit by a stron aftershock measuring 6.1 on the Richter scale on the morning of 20 January 2010.

The U.N. itself was badly hit. Five hundred of its peacekeepers were missing a week after the quake. Forty-six personnel, including Hedi Annabi the Head of the U.N. mission in the capital Port-au-Prince, were confirmed dead by the third week fo January.

Haiti has been under virtual U.N. guardianship since 2004 after governance in the Caribbean country collapsed. The U.N. mission comprised 9,000 peacekeepers and 2,000 civilian administrators. The tremor completely or partially destroyed most of the government offices, the presidential palace and the U.N. premises. The houses of the comparatively well-off Haitians, located on the hills surrounding the capital, were mostly unscathed. It was the poor who bore the brunt of the quake.

Both the U.N. and the government of President Rene Preval have been rendered even more powerless by the force of the quake. Even at relatively normal times, the U.N. peacekeepers were finding it difficult to maintain law and order.

There is no Haitian army to lend a helping hand in the rescue and relief operations. The army was disbanded in 1994 by President Jean-Bertrand Aristide because of its undisciplined ways and its penchant for staging coups and backing right-wing figures. The local police force, underpaid and numbering a few hundred, is in no position to cope with the magnitude of the disaster.

Natural disaster - In Chili, due to Earthquake 122 people killed on 28 Feb. 2010. Vehicles are seen overturned along a highway that collapsed during the earthquake near Santiago on Saturday (27 Feb. 2010). The trenor measured 8.8 on the Richter Scale. Officials warned of possible widespread damage from walls of water that way reach as high as three metres (nine feet).

Bhopal gas tragedy : Many years have gone by since the Bhopal gas tragedy. The victims of the biggest industrial accident are yet to receive succour. In the early morning of December 3, 1984 a Union Carbide pesticide producing plant leaked a highly toxic cloud of methyl isocyanate onto the densely populated region of Bhopal. Nobody knew exactly what had happened except that some gas had engulfed Bhopal and as the sun rose the gas diffused and finally dispersed leaving in its wake thousads of humans choking, coughing and blinded.

The Bhopal Gas Tragedy is a catastrophe that has no parallel in industrial history. In the early morning hours of December 3, 1984 a rolling wind carried a poisonous grey cloud past the walk of the Union Carbide C plant in Bhopal, Madhya Pradesh, India. Forty tons of toxic gases were released from Carbide's Bhopal plant and spread throughout the city. The cause was the contamination of Methyl Isocyanate (mic) storage tank no. 610 with water carrying catalytic material. Residents awoke to clouds of suffocating gas and began a desperate flight through the dark streets. The leak was caused by a series of mechanical and human errors. A portion of the safety equipment at the plant had been non-operational for four months and the rest failed. The city health officials had not been informed of the toxicity of the chemicals used at the Union Carbide factory. There were no emergency plans or procedures in place and no knowledge of how to deal with the poisonous cloud.

No alarm ever sounded a warning and no evacuation plan was prepared. Dead bodies of humans and animals blocked the streets, leaves turned black, and the smell of burning Chili peppers lingered in the air. Between one-half and two-thirds of the skilled engineers who were fully familiar with the plant right from the project stage and certainly since the the commissioning, had left the Union Carbide Bhopal establishment before the accident.

Of the 800,000 people living in Bhopal at the time, 2000 died immediately, 30,000 were injured and as many as 8,000 have died since. Many of the survivors were still suffering from one or several of the several of the following ailments partial or complete blindness, gastrointestinal disorders, impaired immune systems, post traumatic stress disorders, and menstrual problems in women. A rise in spontaneous abortions, still births, and offsprings with genetic defects was also noted.

Production - Methyl isocynate is the starting material for the production of carbaryl. Methulamine and phosgene on heating yield MIC and HCI. The products are chilled, the gaseous HCI is separated in an absorber and the liquid MIC is transferred to carbamate production unit or strorage tank.IMIC is associated with about 2% unreacted $COCl_2$. The latter checks the reaction between MIC and water and also inhibits polymerization. Phosgene also provide a source of CO_2- which can act on container walls (of stainless steel alloy) to form substances that can serve as catalysts for reaction of MIC.

$$CH_3NH_2 + COCl_2 \rightarrow CH_3-N=C=O+HCl$$

Methyl amine Hydrocloric acid

REFERENCES

1. Hindustan times 28 Feb. 2010.
2. Front Line 12 Feb. 2010, p. 33.
3. Smirit Srivastava, Environment and Ecology, Publishes S.K. Kataria & Sons, New Delhi
4. Civil Services Times, October 2009, p. 49.

13

How does Disaster Management Work and its Effectiveness

Deepti gupta
Lecturer-Socialogy
Brahmavart College Mandhan, Kanpur

India has been traditionally vulnerable to natural disasters on account of its unique geo-climatic conditions. Floods, droughts, cyclones, earthquakes and landslides have been a recurrent phenomena. About 60% of the landmass is prone to earthquakes of various intensities; over 40 million hectares is prone to floods; about 8% of the total area is prone to cyclones and 68% of the area is susceptible to drought. In the decade 1990-2000, an average of about 4344 people lost their lives and about 30 million people were affected by disasters every year. The loss in terms of private, community and public assets has been astronomical.

At the global level, there has been considerable concern over natural disasters. Even as substantial scientific and material progress is made, the loss of lives and property due to disasters has not decreased. In fact, the human toll and economic losses have mounted. It was in this background that the United Nations General Assembly, in 1989, declared the decade 1990-2000 as the International Decade for Natural Disaster Reduction with the objective to reduce loss of lives and property and restrict socio-economic damage through concerted international action, specially in developing countries.

The super cyclone in Orissa in October, 1999 and the Bhuj earthquake in Gujarat in january, 2001 underscored the need to adopt a multi dimensional endeavour involving diverse scientific, engineering, financial and social processes; the need to adopt multi disciplinary and multi sectoral approach and incorporation of risk reduction in the developmental plans and strategies.

Over the past couple of years, the Government of India have brought about a paradigm shift in the approach to disaster management. The new approach proceeds from the conviction that development cannot be sustainable unless disaster mitigation is built into the development process. Another corner stone of the approach is that mitigation has to be multi-disciplinary spanning across all sectors of development. The new policy also emanates from the belief that investments in mitigation are much more cost effective than expenditure on relief and rehabilitation.

Disaster management occupies an important place in this country's policy framework as it is the poor and the under-privileged who are worst affected on account of calamities/ disasters. Disasters retard socio-economic development, further impoverish the impoverished and lead to diversion of scarce resources from development to rehabilitation and reconstruction.

The steps being taken by the Government emanate from the approach outlined above. The approach has been translated into a National Disaster Framework [a roadmap] covering institutional mechanisms, disaster prevention strategy, early warning system, disaster mitigation, preparedness and response and human resource development. The expected inputs, areas of intervention and agencies to be involved at the National, State and district levels have been identified and listed in the roadmap. This roadmap has been shared with all the State Governments and Union Territory Administrations. Ministries and Departments of Government of India, and the State Governments/UT Administrations have been advised to develop their respective roadmaps taking the national roadmap as a broad guideline. There is, therefore, now a common strategy underpinning the action being taken by all the participating organisations/stakeholders. The changed approach is being put into effect through:

(a) Institutional changes

(b) Enunciation of policy

(c) Legal and techno-legal framework

(d) Mainstreamin; Mitigation into Development process

(e) Funding mechanism

(f) Specific schemes addressing mitigation

(g) Preparedness measures

(h) Capacity building

(i) Human Resource Development and, above all, community participation.

Institutional and Policy Framework

The institutional and policy mechanisms for carrying out response, relief and rehabilitation have been well-established since Independence. These mechanisms have proved to be robust and effective insofar as response, relief and rehabilitation are concerned. However, the increasing frequency and ferocity, the rising extent and sweep as well as the mounting human and economic toll has necessitated a reappraisal and re-orientation of existing institutional and policy frameworks along with creation of newer frameworks for holistic disaster management. The changed policy/approach mandates a priority to pre-disaster aspects of mitigation, prevention and preparedness and new institutional mechanisms are being put in place to address the policy change.

Although, the primary responsibility for disaster management is of the concerned State Governments, the Central Government plays a key role by providing financial and logistic support in case of major disasters and co-ordinate the effort of all Central Ministries/Departments/Organizations. At the apex level, the Cabinet Committee on Drought Management has been re-constituted and converted into a Cabinet Committee on Natural Calamities. The scope of the Committee has been enlarged so as to address itigation and preparedness measures also. A High Level Committee of Ministers under the Chairmanship of Minister of

Agriculture deals with financial support required to be provided to the State Governments from the National Calamity Contingency Fund, if the funds available with the State Governments under Central Relief Fund are not adequate. The matters relating to nuclear, biological and chemical emergencies are looked after by the Cabinet Committee on Security.

Cabinet Secretary, who is the highest executive officer, heads the National Crisis Management Committee (NCMC). Secretaries of all the concerned Ministries/ Departments as well as organizations are the members of the Committee. The NCMC gives direction to the Crisis Management Group as deemed necessary. The Secretary, Ministry of Home Affairs is responsible for ensuring that all developments are brought to the notice of the NCMC promptly. The NCMC can give directions to any Ministry/ Department/Organization for specific action needed for meeting the crisis situation.

The Central Relief Commissioner in the Ministry of Home Affairs is the Chairman of the Crisis Management Group (CMG) consisting of senior officers (called nodal officers) from various concerned Ministries. The CMG's functions are to review every year contingency plans formulated by various Ministries/ Departments/Organizations in their respective sectors, measures required for dealing with a natural disaster, coordinate the activities of the Central Ministries and the State Governments in relation to disaster preparedness and relief and to obtain information from the nodal officers on measures relating to above. The CMG, in the event of a disaster, meets frequently to review the relief operations and extend all possible assistance required by the affected States to overcome the situation effectively. The Resident Commissioner of the affected State is also associated with such meetings.

Mitigation, preparedness and response are multi-disciplinary functions, involving a number of Ministries/Departments. Institutional mechanisms which would facilitate this inter-disciplinary approach are being put in place. It is proposed to create Disaster/ Emergency Management Authorities, both at the National and State levels, with representatives from the relevant Ministries/ Departments to bring about this coordinated and multi-disciplinary approach with experts covering a large number of branches.

The National Emergency Management Authority is proposed to be constituted. The organization will be multi-disciplinary with experts covering a large number of branches. The National Emergency Management Authority is proposed as a combined Secretariat/Directorate structure – a structure which will be an integral part of the Government while, at the same time, retaining the flexibility of a field organization. The Authority will be headed by an officer of the rank of Secretary/ Special Secretary to the Government in the Ministry of Home Affairs with representatives from the Ministries/Departments of Health, Water Resources, Environment & Forest, Agriculture, Railways, Atomic Energy, Defense, DRDO, External Affairs, Space, Information and Broadcasting, Chemicals, Science Technology, Telecommunication, Urban Employment and Poverty alleviation, Rural Development and Indian Meteorological Department as Members. The authority would meet as often as required and review the Status of warning systems, mitigation measures and disaster preparedness. When a disaster strikes, the Authority will coordinate disaster management activities. The Authority will be responsible for:-

- Providing necessary support and assistance to State Governments by way of resource data, macro-management of emergency response, specialized emergency response teams, sharing of disaster related data base etc.
- Coordinating/mandating Government's policies for disaster reduction/mitigation
- Ensuring adequate preparedness at all levels in order to meet disasters
- Coordinating response to a disaster when it strikes
- Assisting the State Governments in coordination post disaster relief

- Coordinating resources of all Central Government Departments/agencies involved.
- Monitor and introduce a culture of building requisite features of disaster mitigation in all development plans and programmes.
- Any other items of work which may be entrusted to it by the Government.

The States have also been asked to set up Disaster Management Authorities under the Chief Minister with Ministers of relevant Departments [Water Resources, Agriculture, Drinking Water Supply, Environment & Forests, Urban Development, Home, Rural Development etc.] as members. 11 States and UTs – Tamil Nadu, Arunachal Pradesh, Uttaranchal, Orissa, Gujarat, Kerala, Nagaland, Rajasthan, Delhi, A&N administration and Chandigarh Administration have notified the authority. The other States are in the process of setting up similar authorities.

Re-structuring of the Relief Department in the States: At the State level, the work of post calamity relief was being handled by the Departments of Relief & Rehabilitation. The Government of India is working with the State Governments to restructure the Departments of Relief & Rehabilitation into Departments of Disaster Management with an enhanced area of responsibility to include mitigation and preparedness apart from their present responsibilities of relief and rehabilitation. The changeover has already happened in 11 States/UTs – Andhra Pradesh, Arunachal Pradesh, Bihar, Himachal Pradesh, Rajasthan, Tamil Nadu, Uttaranchal, Nagaland, Andaman & Nicobar Administration, Sikkim and Lakshadweep. The change is under process in other States.

The States have been advised to restructure/re-group the officers/staff within the Department of Disaster Management with definite functions to pursue the holistic approach to disaster management. The four functional groups to be assigned with specific tasks within the departments are as indicted below:-

- Functional Group 1: Hazard Mitigation
- Functional Group 2: Preparedness and Capacity Building
- Functional Group 3: Relief and Response
- Functional Group 4: Administration and Finance

At the district level, the District Magistrate who is the chief coordinator will be the focal point for coordinating all activities relating to prevention, mitigation and preparedness apart from his existing responsibilities pertaining to response and relief. The District Coordination and Relief Committee is being reconstituted/ re-designated into Disaster Management Committees with officers from relevant departments being added as members. In view of its enhanced mandate of mitigation and prevention, the district heads of the departments engaged in development are now being included in the Committee so that mitigation and prevention is mainstreamed into the district plan. The existing system of drawing up preparedness and response plans will continue. There will, however, also be a long term mitigation plan. District Disaster Management Committees have already been constituted in 256 districts and are in the process of being constituted in the remaining districts.

Similarly, sub-divisional and Block/Taluka level Disaster Management Committees are also being constituted. At the village level Disaster Management Committees and Disaster Management Teams are being constituted. Each village in a multi-hazard prone district will have a Disaster Management Plan. The process of drafting the plans at all levels has already begun. The Disaster Management Committee which draws up the plans consists of elected representatives at the village level, local authorities; Government functionaries including doctors/paramedics of primary health centres located in the village, primary school teachers etc. The plan encompasses prevention, mitigation and preparedness measures. The Disaster Management Teams at the village level will consist of members of youth organisations like Nehru Yuvak Kendra Sangathan (NYKS) and National Service Scheme (NSS) and other non-governmental organisations as well as able bodied volunteers from the village. The teams are provided basic training in evacuation, search and rescue, first aid trauma counseling etc. The Disaster Management Committee will review the disaster management plan at least once in a year. It would also generate awareness among the people in the village about dos' and don'ts for specific hazards depending on the vulnerability of the village. A large number of village level Disaster Management Committees and Disaster Management Teams have already been constituted.

Disaster Management Policy: Disaster management is a multidisciplinary activity involving a number of Departments/ agencies spanning across all sectors of development. Where a number of Departments/agencies are involved, it is essential to have a policy in place, as it serves as a framework for action by all the relevant departments/agencies. A National Policy on Disaster Management has been drafted, and is in the process of being finalized. After interministerial consultations, it will be submitted to the Cabinet for approval. In the line with the changed focus, the policy proposes to integrate disaster mitigation into development planning. The policy shall inform all spheres of Central Government activity and shall enjoin upon all existing sectoral policies. The broad objectives of the policy are to minimize the loss of lives and social, private and community assets because of natural or man-made disasters and contribute to sustainable development and better standards of living for all, more specifically for the poor and vulnerable section by ensuring that the development gains are not lost through natural calamities/ disaster.

The policy notes that State Governments are primarily responsible for disaster management including prevention and mitigation, while the Government of India provides assistance where necessary as per the norms laid down from time to time and proposes that this overall framework may continue. However, since response to a disaster requires coordination of resources available across all the Departments of the Government, the policy mandates that the Central Government will, in conjunction with the State Governments, seek to ensure that such a coordination mechanism is laid down through an appropriate chain of command so that mobilization of resources is facilitated.

The broad features of the draft National Policy on Disaster Management are enunciated below:-

(i) Adoption of a holistic and pro-active approach towards prevention, mitigation and preparedness.

(ii) Incorporation of mitigation measures in the on-going schemes/programmes.

(iii) Each Ministry/Department of the Central/State Government will set apart an appropriate quantum of funds under the Plan for specific schemes/projects addressing vulnerability reduction and preparedness.

(iv) Where there is a shelf of projects, projects addressing mitigation will be given priority.

(v) Each project in a hazard prone area to have mitigation as an essential term of reference and to include a statement indicating as to how the project addresses vulnerability reduction.

(vi) Community involvement and awareness generation, particularly that of the vulnerable segments of population and women has been emphasized as necessary for sustainable disaster risk reduction. This is a critical component of the policy since communities are the first responders to disasters and, therefore, unless they are empowered and made capable of managing disasters, any amount of external support cannot lead to optimal results.

(vii) Interaction with the corporate sector, non-governmental organizations and the media in the national efforts for disaster prevention/vulnerability reduction.

(viii) Building up institutional structures/appropriate chain of command and imparting appropriate training to disaster managers at various levels to ensure coordinated and quick response and development of inter-State arrangements for sharing of resources during emergencies.

(ix) Inculcating a culture of planning and preparedness at all levels for capacity building measures.

(x) Formulation of Standard Operating Procedures (SOPs) and disaster management plans at state and district levels as well as by relevant central government departments.

(xi) Compliance with construction designs laid down in relevant Indian Standards.

(xii) Evaluation and, where necessary, retrofitting of lifeline buildings in seismic zones III, IV & V – hospitals, railway stations, airports/airport control towers, fire station buildings, communication network, major administrative buildings.

(xiii) Conversion of relief codes into disaster management codes for institutionalizing the planning process.

(xiv) Promotion of international cooperation in the area of disaster response, preparedness and mitigation in tune with national strategic goals and objectives.

The States have also been advised to formulate State DM Policies with the broad objective to minimize the loss of lives and social, private and community assets and contribute to sustainable development. The States of Gujarat and Madhya Pradesh have State Policies for Disaster Management in place while other States are in process.

The policy and the funding mechanism for provision of relief assistance to those affected by natural calamities are clearly laid down. These are reviewed by the Finance Commission appointed by the Government of India every five years.

The Finance Commission makes recommendation regarding the division of tax and non-tax revenues between the Central and the State Governments and also regarding policy for provision of relief assistance and their share of expenditure thereon. A Calamity Relief Fund (CRF) has been set up in each State as per the recommendations of the Eleventh Finance Commission. The size of the Calamity Relief Fund has been fixed by the Finance

Commission after taking into account the expenditure on relief and rehabilitation over the past 10 years. The Government of India contributes 75% of the corpus of the Calamity Relief Fund in each State. 25% is contributed by the State. Relief assistance to those affected by natural calamities is granted from the CRF. Overall norms for relief assistance are laid down by a national committee with representatives of States as members.

Different States can have State-specific norms to be recommended by State level committee under the Chief Secretary. Where the calamity is of such proportion that the funds available in the CRF will not be sufficient for provision of relief, the State seeks assistance from the National Calamity Contingency Fund (NCCF) – a fund created at the Central Government level. When such requests are received, the requirements are assessed by a team from the Central Government and thereafter the assessed requirements are cleared by a High Level Committee chaired by Minister of Agriculture. In brief, the institutional arrangements for response and relief are well-established and have proved to be robust and effective.

Legal and Techno-legal Framework

Disaster Management Act: The States have been advised to enact Disaster Management Acts to provide for authorities coordinating mitigation, preparedness and response as well as for various mitigation/preparedness measures required to be undertaken. Two States, Gujarat & Bihar, have already enacted such a law.

Other States are in the process. A proposal for enacting a National Disaster Management Act is under examination.

Disaster Management Code: In line with the changed approach, the State Governments have also been advised to convert their Relief Codes into Disaster Management Codes by building into it the process necessary for drawing up disaster management and mitigation plans as well as elements of preparedness apart from response and relief. A Committee constituted under the Executive Director, National institute of Disaster Management has drafted a Model Disaster Management Code which is being circulated to the States so as to assist them in this process. Some States have constituted committees to revise the codes as per GOI guidelines. The revised codes will ensure that the process of drawing up disaster management plans and mitigation and preparedness measures gets institutionalized.

With the above-mentioned institutional mechanisms and policy frameworks in position and the actions taken to implement the policy guidelines, it is expected that the task of moving towards vulnerability reduction will be greatly facilitated.

Disaster Prevention and Mitigation

The Yokohama message emanating from the International Decade for Natural Disaster Reduction in May, 1994 underlined the need for an emphatic shift in the strategy for disaster mitigation. It was inter-alia stressed that disaster prevention, mitigation, preparedness and relief are four elements which contribute to and gain from the implementation of the sustainable development policies.

These elements along with environmental protection and sustainable development, are closely inter related, and it was therefore, recommended that Nations should incorporate them in their development plans and ensure efficient follow up measures at the community, sub-regional, regional, national and international levels. The Yokohama strategy also emphasized that disaster prevention, mitigation and preparedness are better than disaster response in achieving the goals and objectives of vulnerability reduction. Disaster response alone is not sufficient as it yields only temporary results at a very high cost. Prevention and mitigation contribute to lasting improvement in safety and are essential to integrated disaster management.

Mainstreaming Disaster Management into Development: The Government of India have adopted mitigation and prevention as essential components of their development strategy. The Tenth Five Year Plan document has a detailed chapter on Disaster Management.

The plan emphasizes the fact that development cannot be sustainable without mitigation being built into developmental process. Each State is supposed to prepare a plan scheme for disaster mitigation in accordance with the approach outlined in the plan. In brief, mitigation is being mainstreamed into developmental planning.

Flood Preparedness and response: Measures for flood mitigation were taken from 1950 onwards. As against the total of 40 million hectares prone to floods, area of about 15 million hectares have been protected by construction of embankments. A number of dams and barrages have been constructed. The State Governments have been assisted to take up mitigation programmes like construction of raised platforms etc. Floods continue to be a menace however mainly because of the huge quantum of silt being carried by the rivers emanating from the Himalayas. This silt has raised the bed level in many rivers to above the level of the countryside. Embankments have also given rise to problems of drainage with heavy rainfall leading to water logging in areas outside the embankment. In order to respond effectively to floods, Ministry of Home Affairs have initiated National Disaster Risk Management Programme in all the floodprone States. Assistance is being provided to the States to draw up disaster management plans at the State, District, Block/Taluka and Village levels.

Awareness generation campaigns to sensitize all stakeholders on the need for flood preparedness and mitigation measures are being undertaken. Elected representatives and officials are being trained in flood disaster management under the programme. Bihar, Orissa, West Bengal, Assam and Uttar Pradesh are among the multi-hazard prone States where this programme is being implemented with assistance from UNDP, USAID and European Commission.

Earthquake Risk Mitigation: A comprehensive programme has been taken up for earthquake risk mitigation. Although the BIS has laid down the standards for construction in the seismic zones, these were not being followed.

The building construction in urban and suburban areas is regulated by the Town and Country Planning Acts and Building Regulations. In many cases, the Building regulations do not incorporate the BIS codes. Even where they do, the lack of knowledge regarding seismically safe construction among the architects and engineers as well as lack of awareness regarding their vulnerability among the population led to most of the construction in the urban/sub-urban areas being without reference to BIS standards. In the rural areas, the bulk of the housing is non-engineered construction. The mode of construction in the rural areas has also changed from mud and thatch to brick and concrete construction thereby increasing the vulnerability. The increasing population has led to settlements in vulnerable areas close to the river bed areas which are prone to liquefaction. The Government have moved to address these issues.

National Core Group for Earthquake Risk Mitigation: A National Core Group for Earthquake Risk Mitigation has been constituted consisting of experts in earthquake engineering and administrators. The Core Group has been assigned the responsibility of drawing up a strategy and plan of action for mitigating the impact of earthquakes; providing advice and guidance to the States on various aspects of earthquake mitigation; developing/organizing the preparation of handbooks/pamphlets/ type designs for earthquake-resistant construction; working out systems for assisting the States in the seismically vulnerable zones to adopt/integrate appropriate Bureau of Indian Standards codes in their building byelaws; evolving systems for training of municipal engineers as also practicing architects and engineers in the private sector in the salient features of Bureau of Indian Standards codes and the amended byelaws; evolving a system of certification of architects/engineers for testing their knowledge of earthquakeresistant construction; evolving systems for training of masons and carrying out intensive awareness generation campaigns.

Review of building bye-laws and their adoption: Most casualties during earthquakes are caused by the collapse of structures. Therefore structural mitigation measures are the key to make a significant impact towards earthquake safety in our country. In view of this the States in earthquake prone zones have been requested to review, and if necessary, amend their building bye-laws to incorporate the BIS seismic codes for construction in the concerned zones. Many States have initiated necessary action in this regard. An Expert Committee appointed by the Core Group on Earthquake Risk Mitigation has already submitted its report covering appropriate amendments to the existing Town & Country Planning Acts, Land Use Zoning Regulation, Development Control Regulations & Building Bylaws, which could be used by the State Governments & the local bodies there-under to upgrade the existing legal instruments. The Model Building Bylaws also cover the aspect of ensuring technical implementation of the safety aspects in all new constructions & upgrading the strength of existing structurally vulnerable constructions. To facilitate the review of existing building byelaws and adoption of the proposed amendments by the State Governments & UT administrations, discussion workshops at regional level in the country are being organized. It is expected that all planning authorities and local bodies will soon have development control regulations and building byelaws which would include multi-hazard safety provisions.

Development and Revision of Codes: The Bureau of Indian Standard (BIS) codes are relevant for multi-hazard resistant design and construction. Some of the codes need to be updated. There are some areas for which codes do not exist. An action plan has been drawn up for revision of existing codes, development of new codes and documents/commentaries and making these codes and documents available all over the country including on-line access to these codes. An Apex committee consisting of representatives of Ministry of Consumer Affairs, BIS and MHA has been constituted to review the mechanism and process of development of codes relevant to earthquake risk mitigation and establish a protocol for revision by BIS.

Hazard Safety Cells in States: The States have been advised to constitute Hazard Safety Cells (HSC) headed by the Chief

Engineer, State PWD with necessary engineering staff so as to establish mechanism for proper implementation of the building codes in all future Govt. constructions, and to ensure the safety of buildings and structures from various hazards. The HSCs will also be responsible for carrying out appropriate design review of all Government buildings to be constructed in the State, act as an advisory cell to the State Government on the different aspects of building safety against hazards and act as a consultant to the State Government for retrofitting of the lifeline buildings. Rajasthan, West Bengal, Delhi and Chhatisgarh have already constituted these cells and other States are in the process.

National Programme for Capacity Building of Engineers and Architects in Earthquake Risk Mitigation: Two National Programmes for Capacity Building in Earthquake Risk Mitigation for Engineers and Architects respectively, have been approved to assist the State Governments in building up capacities for earthquake mitigation. Under these two programmes 10,000 engineers and 10,000 architects in the States will be given training in seismically safe building designs and related techno-legal requirements. Assistance is being provided to the State/UTs to build the capacities of more than 125 State Engineering Colleges and 110 Architecture Colleges to be able to provide advisory services to the State Governments to put in place appropriate technolegal regime, assessment of buildings and infrastructures and their retrofitting. These institutions will function as State Resource Institutions. Twenty-one Engineering and Architecture Institutions have been designated as National Resource Institutes to train the faculty members of selected State Engineering and Architecture colleges. 450 engineering faculty members and 250 architecture faculty members of these State Resource Institutions will be trained during the current year.

Training of rural masons: A programme to assist the States/ UTs in training and certification of 50000 masons has been formulated in consultation with Housing and Urban Development Corporation (HUDCO) and the Ministry of Rural Development. The training module for masons to include multi-hazard resistant construction has also been prepared by an expert committee and revised curriculum will be introduced in the vocational training programme of Ministry of Human Resource Development.

Earthquake Engineering in Undergraduate Engineering/ Architecture Curricula: The role of engineers and architects is crucial in reducing earthquakerisks by ensuring that the construction adheres to the norms of seismic safety. In view of this, the elements of earthquake engineering are being integrated into the undergraduate engineering and architecture courses. Model course curricula have been developed for adoption by various technical institutions and universities and circulated to the Universities and Technical Institutions for integration into the undergraduate curriculum. Ministry of Home Affairs is working with All India Council of Technical Education (AICTE) and Council of Architecture (COA) for introduction of revised curricula for engineering and architecture course from 2005-2006.

Retrofitting of Lifeline buildings: While these mitigation measures will take care of the new constructions, the problem of unsafe existing building stock would still remain. It will not be possible to address the entire existing building stock, therefore the life line buildings like hospitals, schools or buildings where people congregate like cinema halls, multi-storied apartments are being focused on. The States have been advised to have these buildings assessed and where necessary retrofitted. The Ministries of Civil Aviation, Railways, Telecommunication, Power and Health and Family Welfare have been advised to take necessary action for detailed evaluation and retrofitting of lifeline buildings located in seismically vulnerable zones so as to ensure that they comply with BIS norms. Action plans have been drawn up by these Ministries for detailed vulnerability analysis and retrofitting/ strengthening of buildings and structures.

The Ministry of Finance has been requested to advise the financial institutions to give loans for retrofitting on easy terms. Accordingly the Ministry of Finance had advised Reserve Bank of India to issue suitable instructions to all the Banks and Financial Institutions to see that BIS codes/bye laws are scrupulously followed while financing/refinancing construction activities in seismically vulnerable zones.

Accelerated Urban Earthquake Vulnerability Reduction Programme: An accelerated Urban Earthquake Vulnerability Reduction Programme has been taken up in 38 cities in seismic zones III, IV & V with a population of half a million and above. These cities are Dehradun, Delhi, Jamnagar, Rajkot, Bhavnagar, Surat, Greater Mumbai, Bhiwandi, Nasik, Pune, Bhubaneswar, Cuttack, Chennai, Patna, Asansol, Guwahati, Vadodara, Coimbatore, Ahmedabad, Agra, Varanasi, Bareily, Meerut, Lucknow, Kanpur, Kolkatta, Srinagar, Jammu, Indore, Jabalpur, Amritsar, Jalandhar, Vijayawada, Dhanbad, Mangalore, Kochi, Kozhikod and Trivandrum. 474 Orientation programmes have been organized for senior officers and representatives of the local planning and development bodies to sensitize them on earthquake preparedness and mitigation measures. Training programmes have been organized for engineers and architects to impart knowledge about seismically safe construction and implementation of BIS norms.

Awareness generation programmes, community and neighbourhood organizations have been started in these cities. These cities are also being assisted to review and amend their building bye-laws to incorporate multi hazard safety provisions. City Disaster Management Plans are being developed under the project. Nine Cities have prepared city Disaster Management Plans so far.

Mainstreaming Mitigation in Rural Development Schemes: Rural housing and community assets for vulnerable sections of the population are created on a fairly large scale by the Ministry of Rural Development under the Indira Awas Yojna(IAY) and Sampooran Grameen Rojgar Yojna(SGRY). About 250 thousand small but compact housing units are constructed every year, besides community assets such as community centres, recreation centres, anganwadi centres etc. Technology support is provided by about two hundred rural housing centers spread over the entire country. The Ministry of Home Affairs is working with the Ministry of

Rural Development for changing the guidelines so that the houses constructed under IAY or school buildings/community buildings constructed under SGRY are earthquake/cyclone/flood resistant; as also that the schemes addressing mitigation are given priority under SGRY. Ministry of Rural Development is carrying out an exercise for this purpose. This initiative is expected to go a long way in popularization of seismically safe construction at village/ block level.

Core Group on Cyclone Mitigation: A National Core Group on Cyclone Monitoring & Mitigation has been constituted. Experts from Indian Meteorological Department, National Centre for Medium Range Weather Forecasting, Central Water Commission, National Remote Sensing Agency and Indian Space Research Organisation have been made the Members of the Core Group, besides administrators from the relevant Ministries/Departments and State Governments vulnerable to cyclones. The Group has been assigned the responsibility of looking at warning protocols for cyclones; coordination mechanism between different Central and State Ministries/ Departments/ Organisations; mechanism for dissemination of warning to the local people and; cyclone mitigation measures required to be taken for the coastal States. The Group will also suggest short-term and long-term measures on technology up-gradation. The cyclone warning formats have been revised to ensure that the warning is more meaningful to the community at risk. A project has been taken up with the United States for upgradation of models for cyclone track prediction.

Landslide Hazard Mitigation: A National Core Group has been constituted under the Chairmanship of Secretary, Border Management and comprising of Secretary, Department of Science and Technology, Secretary, Road Transport & Highways, and the Heads of Geological Survey of India and National Remote Sensing Agency for drawing up a strategy and plan of action for mitigating the impact of landslides, provide advise and guidance to State Governments on various aspects of landslide mitigation, monitor the activities relating to landslide mitigation including landslide hazard zonation and to evolve early warning systems and protocols for landslides/landslide risk reduction. The Government have designated Geological Survey of India (GSI) as the nodal agency responsible for coordinating/undertaking geological studies, landslides hazard zonation, monitoring landslides/avalanches, studying the factors responsible and suggesting precautionary and preventing measures. The States/Union Territories have been requested to share the list of habitations close to landslide prone areas in order to supplement Geological Survey of India's ongoing assessment of such areas based on the Survey of India's Toposheet and their existing data base on landslides for the purpose of landslide hazard zonation being carried out by them. A national strategy for mitigating landslide hazard in the country is being drawn up in consultation with all the agencies concerned.

Awareness generation: Recognizing that awareness about vulnerabilities is a sine qua non for inducing a mindset of disaster prevention, mitigation and preparedness, the Government has initiated a nation-wide awareness generation campaign as part of its overall disaster risk management strategy. In order to devise an effective and holistic campaign, a steering committee for mass media campaign has been constituted at the national level with due representation of experts from diverse streams of communication. The Committee has formulated a campaign strategy aimed at changing peoples' perception of natural hazards and has consulted the agencies and experts associated with advertising and media to instill a culture of safety against natural hazards.

Apart from the use of print and electronic media, it is proposed to utilize places with high public visibility viz. hospitals, schools, railway stations and bus terminals, airports and post offices, commercial complexes and municipality offices etc. to make people aware of their vulnerabilities and promote creation of a safe living environment.

3.25 A novel method being tried is the use of government stationery viz. postal letters, bank stationery, railway tickets, airline boarding cards and tickets etc. for disseminating the message of disaster risk reduction. Slogans and messages for this purpose have already been developed and have been communicated to concerned Ministries/agencies for printing and dissemination. The mass media campaign will help build the knowledge, attitude and skills of the people in vulnerability reduction and sustainable disaster risk management measures.

Preparedness

Mitigation and preparedness measures go hand in hand for vulnerability reduction and rapid professional response to disasters. The Bhuj earthquake in January, 2001 brought out several inadequacies in the system. Professionally trained search and rescue teams were not available; specialized dog squads to look for live bodies under the debris were not available and there was no centralized resource inventory for emergency response. Although army played a pivotal role in search and rescue and also set up their hospital after the collapse of Government hospital at Bhuj, the need for fully equipped mobile hospitals with trained personnel was felt acutely. Despite these constraints, the response was fairly well organized. However, had these constraints been taken care of beforehand, the response would have been even more professional and rapid which may have reduced the loss of lives. Specialist search and rescue teams from other countries did reach Bhuj. However, precious time was lost and even with these specialist teams it was not possible to cover all severely affected areas as quickly as the Government would have desired. It was, therefore, decided that we should remove these inadequacies and be in a state of preparedness at all times.

Setting up of Search and Rescue Teams in States: The States have been advised to set up their own Specialist Teams for responding to disasters. Ministry of Home Affairs will provide assistance for the training of the State trainers. Many States/Union Territories have initiated action for setting up of specialized SAR units. Ten States have identified the Training Centers for training in Search and Rescue in the States. They have also identified trainers who will be imparted training at CPMF training institutions. Some states e.g. Maharashtra, Orissa, Gujarat and Delhi have trained search and rescue teams. It has been provided that 10% of the annual inflows into the CRF can be used for procurement of search and rescue equipment and communication equipment. States have been advised to include training in search and rescue in the training of State Armed Police.

Emergency Operation Centres: The States are being assisted to set up control rooms/emergency operations centres at the State and district level. Assistance for this is being given under the GOI – UNDP project in the States covered by the project. Assistance under the Modernization of Police Scheme is also available for setting up EOCs. The control rooms, which will function round the clock, will be composite control rooms to look after law and order issues as well as disaster management. Equipments are also being provided for these control rooms under the disaster risk management programme. Hazard zone-wise standard layout, structural design and construction drawings have been developed for State and District EOCs and shared with all the States. Construction work has started for multi-hazard resistant EOCs in six States and 64 districts.

National Emergency Operation Centre: To coordinate the entire disaster/emergency operations effectively, the existing Control Room at the national level has been upgraded as National Emergency Operations Center (NEOC). The National EOC is equipped with satellite phones, GPS, computers, emergency lights, GIS information system etc in five on-site emergency coordination kits in ready-to-use mode. Staffs in the NEOC have been trained. A State of the art underground and all-hazard resistant, National EOC with superior structural features and communication facilities is being set up. A Committee of CPWD/BARC/DRDO has been constituted to finalize the design parameters.

National Emergency Communication Network: The communication network between the national and the state EOCs and the site of the emergency/crises are currently based on the DOT network. It has been observed that in a calamity/hazard, communication is the first casualty. It has therefore been decided to put in place multi-mode and multi-channel communication system so that enough redundancy is available. It has been decided that the POLNET will also be used for disaster management; and for this the POLNET communication facility will be extended to SDMs and Collectors as well as the Emergency Operation Centers. For emergency communications, discussions have also been held with the Department of Space (ISRO). They will be making available alternate satellite communication units to connect with State EOCs and mobile units which can be transported to the site of a disaster. A Group had been set up for drawing up a communication plan for disaster management and the said Group has submitted its report. This provides for a dedicated communication system for disaster management with built in redundancies. Phase I of the National Disaster Management Communication Plan to provide satellite based mobile voice/data/ video communication between National EOC/State EOCs/ mobile EOCs and remote disaster/emergency sites is under implementation. Phase II of the communication plan to connect National/State/District EOCs with disaster/emergency sites is proposed to be completed. The communication backbone to be used will include terrestrial link (DOT), POLNET, NICNET, ISDN and SPACENET

CONCLUSION

Disaster Management requires multi-disciplinary and pro-active approach. Besides various measures for putting in place institutional and policy framework, disaster prevention, mitigation and preparedness measures enunciated in this paper and initiatives being taken by the Central and State Governments, the community, civil society organizations and media also have a key role to play in achieving our goal of moving together, towards a safer India. The message being put across is that in order to move towards safer and sustainable national development, development projects should be sensitive towards disaster mitigation.

This mission is vulnerability reduction to all types of hazards, be it natural or manmade. This is not an easy task to achieve, keeping in view the vast population, and the multiple natural hazards to which this country is exposed. However, if we are firm in our conviction and resolve that the Government and the people of this country are not prepared to pay the price in terms of massive casualties and economic losses, the task, though difficult, is achievable and we shall achieve it.

We have taken the first few but significant steps towards vulnerability reduction, putting in place prevention and mitigation measures and preparedness for a rapid and professional response. With a massive awareness generation campaign and building up of capabilities as well as institutionalization of the entire mechanism through a techno-legal and techno-financial framework, we are gradually moving in the direction of sustainable development.

The various prevention and mitigation measures outlined above are aimed at building up the capabilities of the communities, voluntary organizations and Government functionaries at all levels. Particular stress is being laid on ensuring that these measures are institutionalized considering the vast population and the geographical area of the country. This is a major task being undertaken by the Government to put in place mitigation measures for vulnerability reduction. This is just a beginning. The ultimate goal is to make prevention and mitigation a part of normal day-to-day life.. We have a firm conviction that with these measures in place, we could say with confidence that disasters like Orissa cyclone and Bhuj earthquake will not be allowed to recur in this country; at least not at the cost, which the country has paid in these two disasters in terms of human lives, livestock, loss of property and means of livelihood.

India and Disaster Management

14

Natural Disasters in India

Vineeta Singh
Head of the Department Geography, JDVM PG College, Kanpur, UP

Hema Kashyap
Lecturer, Geography All Saints Convent School New Tehri Uttarakhand

P. S. Kashyap
Asstt. Prof., Agril. Engg., GBPUA&T, Hill Campus Pantnagar, Uttarakhand

Natural disasters in India, many of them related to the climate of India, cause massive losses of Indian life and property. Droughts, flash floods, cyclones, avalanches, landslides brought on by torrential rains, and snowstorms pose the greatest threats. Other dangers include frequent summer dust storms, which usually track from north to south; they cause extensive property damage in North India (Balfour, 1976) and deposit large amounts of dust from arid regions. Hail is also common in parts of India, causing severe damage to standing crops such as rice and wheat.

Landslides are common in the Lower Himalayas. The young age of the region's hills result in labile rock formations, which are susceptible to slippages. Rising population and development pressures, particularly from logging and tourism, cause deforestation. The result is denuded hillsides which exacerbate the severity of landslides, since tree cover impedes the downhill flow of water (Allaby, 1998). Parts of the Western Ghats also suffer from low-intensity landslides. Avalanches occurrences are common in Kashmir, Himachal Pradesh, and Sikkim.

Floods are the most common natural disaster in India. The heavy southwest monsoon rains cause the Brahmaputra and other rivers to distend their banks, often flooding surrounding areas. Though they provide rice paddy farmers with a largely dependable source of natural irrigation and fertilisation, the floods can kill thousands and displace millions. Excess, erratic, or untimely monsoon rainfall may also wash away or otherwise ruin crops (Allaby, 1998). Almost all of India is flood-prone, and extreme precipitation events, such as flash floods and torrential rains, have become increasingly common in central India over the past several decades, coinciding with rising temperatures. Mean annual precipitation totals have remained steady due to the declining frequency of weather systems that generate moderate amounts of rain. Keeping in view some of the important natural disasters are discussed here.

1. Cyclones

Tropical cyclones, which are severe storms spun off from the Intertropical Convergence Zone, affect thousands of Indians living in the coastal regions. Tropical cyclogenesis is particularly common in the northern reaches of the Indian Ocean in and around the Bay of Bengal. Cyclones bring with them heavy rains, storm surges, and winds that often cut affected areas off from relief and supplies. In the North Indian Ocean Basin, the cyclone season runs from April to December, with peak activity between May and November (Atlantic Oceanographic and Meteorological Laboratory, Hurricane Research Division). Each year, an average of eight storms with sustained wind speeds greater than 63 kilometres per hour (39 mph) form; of these, two strengthen into true tropical cyclones, which have sustained gusts greater than 117 kilometres per hour (73 mph). On an average, a major (Category 3 or higher) cyclone develops every other year.

During summer, the Bay of Bengal is subject to intense heating, giving rise to humid and unstable air masses that produce cyclones. Many powerful cyclones, including the 1737 Calcutta cyclone, the 1970 Bhola cyclone, and the 1991 Bangladesh cyclone, have led to widespread devastation along parts of the eastern coast of India and neighboring Bangladesh. Widespread death and property destruction are reported every year in exposed coastal states such as Andhra Pradesh, Orissa, Tamil Nadu, and West Bengal. India's western coast, bordering the more placid Arabian Sea, experiences cyclones only rarely; these mainly strike Gujarat and, less frequently, Kerala.

In terms of damage and loss of life, Cyclone 05B, a super cyclone that struck Orissa on 29 October 1999, was the worst in more than a quarter-century. With peak winds of 160 miles per hour (257 km/h), it was the equivalent of a Category 5 hurricane. Almost two million people were left homeless, another 20 million people lives were disrupted by the cyclone. Officially, 9,803 people died from the storm, unofficial estimates place the death toll at over 10,100 (Naval Maritime Forecast Center).

Table 1
Some Severe Cyclones in India

S. No.	*Location*	*Occurrence*	*Damages*
1.	Bengal	Oct, 1847	75,000 people and 6000 cattle killed, Damage to property
2.	Bengal	October, 1874	80,000 people killed heavy loss to property and communication disrupted
3.	Andhra Pradesh	November, 1946	750 people and 30,000 cattle lost life, Damage to property and roads also reported
4.	Tamil Nadu	December, 1972	80 people and 150 cattle killed and communication disrupted
5.	Bengal	September, 1976	10 people and 40,000 cattle lost life, Damage to property including communication
6.	Andhra Pradesh	November, 1977	8547 people and 40,000 cattle lost life, Communication disrupted heavy loss to property
7.	Tamil Nadu	May, 1979	700 people and 300,000 cattle lost life, Communication disrupted

8.	Orissa	September, 1985	84 people and 2600 cattle lost life, Land of 4.0 has damaged
9.	Andhra Coast	November, 1987	50 people and 25,800 cattle lost life, 84,00 houses, roads, and other communication disrupted
10.	Orissa	June, 1989	61 people and 27,000 cattle lost life, 145,000 houses, communication disrupted
11.	Andhra Pradesh	May, 1990	928 human lives lost, 14,000 houses damaged
12.	Tamil Nadu	November, 1991	185 people and 540 cattle dead. Property including roads worth 300 crores damaged
13.	Bengal	April, 1993	Over 100 causalities, communication system including road disrupted and damaged
14.	Bengal	November, 1994	More than a thousand houses damaged in 26 villages, damage to lake and fisheries, disrupted all communication
15.	Andhra Coast	October, 1996	1057 causalities, 647,000 houses damaged road network completely damaged
16.	Gujarat	June, 1998	1261 casualties, 2.57 lakh houses damaged
17.	Orissa	October, 1999	10,086 Casualties, 21.6 Lakh houses damaged

2. Floods

Floods are any high stream flow which overlap natural or artificial banks of a river or a stream and are markedly higher than the usual as well as inundation of low land. Sometimes copious monsoon rains combine with massive flows from the rivers, then the floods indeed become calamitous. Through geophysical studies, it has been found that more than one half billion people on our planet reside on river side and coastal flood plains where they produce 1/3 of world's food production and on any day at least-some fraction of these plains go under flood water and hence causing widespread losses to human lives and heads of cattle dead, devastated homes, destroyed the agricultural crops and disrupted the communication links such as railways, roads as well as damage to health hazards. Even after the receding of floods it takes several months or even years before the community comes to the pre-flood level. So floods are a natural and inevitable phenomenon of life in almost all the states of India.

Floods depend on many things such as climate, nature of the collecting basin, nature of the streams, soil, vegetative cover, amount of snow melt and over all rainfall. Annually, the Indian land mass receives on precipitation of 88-89 cm with very high variation from region to region. In the state of Rajasthan, the rainfall is almost nil where as in the state of Meghalaya, an average rainfall of 1000 cm occurred every year. So this variation in the occurrence of rainfall makes the country prone towards the situations like floods and droughts.

India is the most flood affected nation in the world after Bangladesh. It accounts for one fifth (1/5) of global deaths due to floods and on an average thirty million people are evacuated every year. So floods, in India are not a new phenomenon. "Unprecedented floods" take place every year in one state or other state of the country. The vulnerability of states or union territories of India due to floods was not observed severely in the past due to low developmental activities and population pressure. However, in the present time, unabated population and high rate of developmental activities forced on the occupation of flood plains and making the society highly vulnerable for flood losses.

Other factors like lack of adequate refugee sites above flood levels, accessible routes for reaching at sites, lack of public Information about escape routes and other appropriate response activities renders communities more vulnerable. The protected area (32 m.ha.) is also vulnerable to floods as the flood control structures mainly embankments may breach during a severe flood and the protected areas may be inundated. In India, 22 states and one Union territory (Andaman & Nicobar) are vulnerable to Floods. However, the most vulnerable state of India are Uttar Pradesh, Bihar, Assam, West Bengal, Gujarat, Orissa, Andhra Pradesh, Madhya Pradesh, Maharashtra, Punjab and Jammu & Kashmir. At district wise (as on 1991), there are 137 districts are vulnerable to floods.

Table 2
Some Severe Floods in India

S. No.	*Date*	*Area affected*	*Synoptic System*
1.	17-23 July 1980	East Uttar Pradesh	Low Pressure area
2.	17-23 July 1980	Central & Southwest Uttar Pradesh	Land depression
3.	4-10 September 1980	Southeast Uttar Pradesh	Land depression
4.	18-24 September 1980	South Orissa	Deep Depression
5.	18-24 September 1980	Andhra Pradehs	Deep Depression
6.	18-24 September 1980	Central Uttar Pradesh	Deep Depression
7.	9-15 July 1981	Gujarat	Low pressure are
8.	16-22 July 1981	Rajasthan	Low pressure area
9.	9-29 July 1981	Uttar Pradesh	Low pressure area
10.	6-12 August 1981	East Uttar Pradesh	Cyclonic Strom
11.	3-9 September 1981	East Uttar Pradesh	Land depression
12.	19-25 August 1982	East Madhya Pradesh	Well marked low pressure area
13.	28-31 August 1982	North Orissa	Depression
14.	30 Aug-3 Sept 1982	Uttar Pradesh	Land Depression
15.	20-23 June 1983	Gujarat	Land Depression
16.	11-17 August 1983	West Maharashtra	Trough off Maharashtra Coast
17.	18-31 August 1983	Northeast Uttar Pradesh	Low pressure area
18.	15-19 September 1983	Marathwada and West Maharashtra	Low pressure area

19.	8-14 September 1983	Southeast Uttar Pradesh	Land depression
20.	21-27 June 1984	West Bengal pressure area	Well marked low
21.	28 June – 11 July 1984	Uttar Pradesh	Low pressure area
22.	23 August- 5 Sept 1985	Bihar	Low pressure area
23.	12-25 September 1985	East Uttar Pradesh	Land Depression
24.	11-18 September 1985	Bihar	Well marked low pressure are
25.	17-23 July 1986	Bihar	Land Depression
26.	7-20 August 1986	North Andhra Pradesh	Deep Depression
27.	23-29 July 1987	Bihar	Low Pressure area
28.	30 July-20 Aug 1987	North Bengal	Cyclonic circulation
29.	3-16 September 1987	Bihar Plateau	Well marked low pressure are
30.	15-19 July 1988	North Gujarat	Cyclonic Storm
31.	25 Aug – 7 September	1988	Nrth Gujarat Cyclonic Storm
32.	21-28 September, 1988	Punjab	Low pressure area
33.	19-26 July, 1989	Coastal Andhra Pradesh	Depression
34.	13-26 July 1989	Western Maharashtra	Depression
35.	1-6 July, 1990	North West Rajasthan	Low pressure Area
36.	16-29 August 1990	Vidarbha	Depression
37.	23-29 August 1990	Gujarat	Depression
38.	25-31 July 1991	Vidarbha	Deep depression
39.	5-13 September 1991	North Bengal	Cyclonic Circulation
40.	16-22 July 1992	Gujarat	Cyclonic Circulation
41.	10-16 September 1992	Jammu & Kashmir	Cyclonic Circulation
42.	10-16 September 1992	East Uttar Pradesh	Well marked low pressure area

43.	1-14 July 1993	Gujarat	Cyclonic Circulation
44.	8-14 July 1993	Punjab	Cyclonic circulation
45.	15-20 July 1993	Bihar Plateau	Well marked low pressure area
46.	15-21 July 1993	North Bengal	Well marked low pressure area
47.	9-15 September, 1993	Uttar Pradesh	Well marked low pressure area
48.	14-27 July 1994	Gujarat	Low pressure area
49.	1-7 September 1994	Orissa	Low pressure area
50.	1-7 September 1994	Vidarbha	Well marked low pressure area
51.	17-23 August 1995	Bihar	Low pressure area
52.	5-15 September, 1995	Haryana	Low pressure area
53.	20-26 June 1996	Rajathan	Low Pressure area
54.	25 July – 7 August 1996	Bihar	Low Pressure area

3. Droughts

Indian agriculture is heavily dependent on the monsoon as a source of water. In some parts of India, the failure of the monsoons result in water shortages, resulting in below-average crop yields. This is particularly true of major drought-prone regions such as southern and eastern Maharashtra, northern Karnataka, Andhra Pradesh, Orissa, Gujarat, and Rajasthan. In the past, droughts have periodically led to major Indian famines, including the Bengal famine of 1770, in which up to one third of the population in affected areas died; the 1876–1877 famine, in which over five million people died; the 1899 famine, in which over 4.5 million died; and the Bengal famine of 1943, in which over five million died from starvation and famine-related illnesses.

All such episodes of severe drought correlate with El Niño-Southern Oscillation (ENSO) events. El Niño-related droughts have also been implicated in periodic declines in Indian agricultural output. Nevertheless, ENSO events that have coincided with abnormally high sea surfaces temperatures in the Indian Ocean—in one instance during 1997 and 1998 by up to 3 °C (5 °F)—have resulted in increased oceanic evaporation, resulting in unusually wet weather across India. Such anomalies have occurred during a sustained warm spell that began in the 1990s. A contrasting phenomenon is that, instead of the usual high pressure air mass over the southern Indian Ocean, an ENSO-related oceanic low pressure convergence center forms; it then continually pulls dry air from Central Asia, desiccating India during what should have been the humid summer monsoon season. This reversed air flow causes India's droughts. The extent that an ENSO event raises sea surface temperatures in the central Pacfic Ocean influences the degree of drought.

4. Earthquakes

The Indian subcontinent has a history of devastating earthquakes. The major reason for the high frequency and intensity of the earthquakes is that India is driving into Asia at a rate of appromately 47 mm/year. Geographical statistics of India show that almost 54% of the land is vulnerable to earthquakes. The latest version of seismic zoning map of India given in the earthquake resistant design code of India [IS 1893 (Part 1) 2002] assigns four levels of seismicity for India in terms of zone factors. In other words, the earthquake zoning map of India divides India into 4 seismic zones (Zone 2, 3, 4 and 5) unlike its previous version which consisted of five or six zones for the country. According to the present zoning map, Zone 5 expects the highest level of seismicity whereas Zone 2 is associated with the lowest level of seismicity. The latest seismic zoning map can be accessed from The India Meteorological Department website.

The MSK (Medvedev-Sponheuer-Karnik) intensity broadly associated with the various seismic zones is VI (or less), VII, VIII and IX (and above) for Zones 2, 3, 4 and 5, respectively, corresponding to Maximum Considered Earthquake (MCE). The

IS code follows a dual design philosophy: (a) under low probability or extreme earthquake events (MCE) the structure damage should not result in total collapse, and (b) under more frequently occurring earthquake events, the structure should suffer only minor or moderate structural damage. The specifications given in the design code (IS 1893: 2002) are not based on detailed assessment of maximum ground acceleration in each zone using a deterministic or probabilistic approach. Instead, each zone factor represents the effective period peak ground accelerations that may be generated during the maximum considered earthquake ground motion in that zone. Each zone indicates the effects of an earthquake at a particular place based on the observations of the affected areas and can also be described using a descriptive scale like Modified Mercalli intensity scale or the Medvedev-Sponheuer-Karnik scale. The areas prone to earthquake have been divided into 5 zones numbered from 1 to 5.

Zone 5: Zone 5 covers the areas with the highest risk zone that suffers earthquakes of intensity MSK IX or greater. The IS code assigns zone factor of 0.36 for Zone 5. Structural designers use this factor for earthquake resistant design of structures in Zone 5. The zone factor of 0.36 is indicative of effective (zero period) peak horizontal ground accelerations of 0.36 g (36 % of gravity) that may be generated during MCE level earthquake in this zone. It is referred to as the Very High Damage Risk Zone. The state of Kashmir, Punjab,the western and central Himalayas, the North-East Indian region and the Rann of Kutch fall in this zone. Generally, the areas having trap or basaltic rock are prone to earthquakes.

Zone 4: This zone is called the High Damage Risk Zone and covers areas liable to MSK VIII. The IS code assigns zone factor of 0.24 for Zone 4. The Indo-Gangetic basin and the capital of the country(Delhi, Jammu) fall in Zone 4.

Zone 3: The Andaman and Nicobar Islands, parts of Kashmir, Western Himalayas fall under this zone. This zone is classified as Moderate Damage Risk Zone which is liable to MSK VII. The IS code assigns zone factor of 0.16 for Zone 3.

Zone 2: This region is liable to MSK VI or less and is classified as the Low Damage Risk Zone. The IS code assigns zone factor of 0.10 (maximum horizontal acceleration that can be experienced by a structure in this zone is 10 % of gravitational acceleration) for Zone 2.

Zone 1: The regions in zone 1 are least prone to the affect of earthquake. Buildings in Seismic Zone 1 fall into a code exception to the moment-resisting frame requirement and the system could be used intact to any height, limited only by the available shear walls' capacity to withstand local wind pressures.

Table3.
Some Major Earthquake Events in India

S. No.	*Year*	*Place*	*Intensity*	*Damage*
1.	1618	Bombay	-	2000 lives lost
2.	1720	Delhi	6.5	some lives lost
3.	1737	Bengal	-	300,000 lives lost
4.	1803	Mathura	6.5	The shock felt up to Calcutta
5.	1803	Kumaon	6.5	Killed 200-300 people
6.	1819	Kutchch	8.0	Chief towns of Tera, Kathara and Mothala razed to the ground
7.	1828	Srinagar	6.0	1000 people killed
8.	1833	Bihar	7.7	Hundreds of people killed
9.	1848	Mt.Abu	6.0	Few people killed
10.	1869	Assam	7.5	Affected an area of 2,50,000 Sq. miles
11.	1885	Srinagar	7.0	Kamiarary area destroyed
12.	1897	Shillong	8.7	Wide spread destruction in Shillong
13.	1905	Himachal Pradesh	8.0	Thousands of people killed
14.	1906	Himachal Pradesh	7.0	Heavy damage
15.	1916	Nepal	7.5	All houses collapsed at Dharchulla

16.	1918	Assam	7.6	Heavy damage
17.	1930	Dhubri, Meghalaya	7.1	Heavy damage in Dhubri
18	1934	Bihar, Nepal	8.3	Large number of border area people killed
19	1935	Quetta (in Pakistan)	7.5	25,000 people killed
20	1941	Andaman	8.1	Very heavy damage
21	1947	Dibrugarh	7.8	Heavy damage
22	1950	Assam	8.6	Heavy damage to life and property .
23	1952	NE India	7.5	Heavy damage
24	1956	Bulandshahar, U.P.	6.7	Many people killed
25	1956	Anjar, Gujarat	7.0	Hundreds of people killed
26	1958	Kapkote, U.P.	6.3	Many people killed
27	1967	Koyna,	6.1	Koyna Nagar razed
28	1969	Bhadrachalam	6.5	Heavy damage
29	1986	Dharamshala (H.P)	5.7	Koyna Nagar razed, lots of damage
30	1988	Assam	7.2	Few people killed
31	1988	Bihar- Nepal	6.5	Large number of people killed
32	1991	Uttarkashi	6.6	Lots of damage to life and property
33	1993	Latur	6.4	Heavy damage to life and property about ,000 people killed
34	1997	Jabalpur	6.0	Lots of damage to property, about 39 lives lost
35	1999	Chamoli	6.8	Lots of damage to property about 100 people lost lives
36	2001	Bhuj	6.9	Huge devastation , about 14000 people lost lives

Summary & Conclusions

It is a well known fact that natural disasters are inevitable. Natural disasters strikes countries, both developed and developing, causing enormous destruction and creating human sufferings and producing negative impacts on national economies. Different types of natural disasters like floods, droughts, earthquakes, cyclones, landslides, and volcanoes, etc. strikes according to the vulnerability of the area. India is considered as one of the the world's most disaster prone country. It has witnessed devastating natural disasters in recent past like droughts, floods, cyclones, earthquakes, landslides, etc.

Among all the natural disasters that country faces, river floods are the most frequent and often devastating. The shortfall in the rainfall causes droughts or drought like situation in various parts of the country. The country has faced some severe earthquakes causing widespread damage to the life and property. India has a coastline of about 8000 km, which is prone to very severe cyclonic formations in the Arabian Sea and Bay of Bengal. Though it is not possible to completely avoid the natural disasters, but the sufferings can be minimized by creating proper awareness of the likely disasters and its impact by developing a suitable warning system, disaster preparedness and management of disasters through application of information technology tools.

CITATIONS

Allaby, M. (1998). Flood, facts on file, Cosmo Publications, New Delhi, India, ISBN 0-8160-3520-2. p15-42.

Atlantic Oceanographic and Meteorological Laboratory (2010), Hurricane Research Division. (http://www.aoml.noaa.gov/hrd/tcfaq/G1.html).

Balfour, E (1976), Encyclopaedia Asiatica: Comprising Indian Subcontinent, Eastern and Southern Asia, Cosmo Publications, ISBN 8170203252, p995.

Goswami BN, Venugopal V, Sengupta D, Madhusoodanan MS, Xavier PK (2006). "Increasing trend of extreme rain events over India in a warming environment". Science 314 (5804): 1442–1445.

Kumar KK, Rajagopatan B, Hoerling M, Bates G, Cane M (2006). "Unraveling the Mystery of Indian Monsoon Failure During El Niño". Science 314 (5796): 115–119.

Natural disasters in India. (2010). http://www.wikipedia.org.

Naval Maritime Forecast Center (2010). "Tropical Cyclone 05B". (Joint Typhoon Warning Center).(http://www.usno.navy.mil.pdf).

15

Natural Disaster Management India : A Review

Dr. Dipti Shukla
Assistent Professor
Dept. of English
DBS(PG) College, Kanpur

Everything appears to be all right when you go back home from your work place in the evening and relax over a cup of tea. But the moment TV is switched on, we often see a nightmare. The pictures of crumbling houses, collapsing bridges, inundated villages/cities, heart-breaking scenes of relatives crying over dead/ charred bodies, mass cremation etc. etc. instantly puts you down. A disaster strikes, mostly it is natural and sometimes it is man-made. Not only India, but also the entire world suffers from disasters arising from the interplay of human activities and natural hazards. In this article we are focussing on Natural Disasters and their management. For the sake of clarity let us have a look at the definition of natural disaster:

A natural disaster is any natural phenomenon which causes such widespread human material or environmental losses that the stricken community cannot recover without external assistance Examples include earthquakes, cyclones, storms, floods, drought, bush/ forest fire, avalanches etc.

At regular but unpredictable intervals, people around the world are affected by natural hazards. These may be caused by climate (e.g. drought, flood, cyclone) geology (eg earthquake, volcano, tidal wave, landslide) the environment (e.g. pollution, deforestation, desertification, pest infestation) or combinations of these. Hazards become disasters when people's homes and livelihoods are destroyed. Poverty, population pressures and environmental degradation mean that increasing numbers of people are vulnerable to natural hazards. Increasing population and urbanisation is increasing the world's exposure to natural hazards, especially in coastal areas (with greater exposure to floods, cyclones and tidal waves). Although worldwide disaster occurrence seems to follow an upward trend, some of their impacts on societies (victims and economic damages) have not increased as preparedness has improved.

A natural disaster is the effect of a natural hazard (e.g. flood, tornado, volcano eruption, earthquake, or landslide) that affects the environment, and leads to financial, environmental and/or human losses. The resulting loss depends on the capacity of the population to support or resist the disaster, and their resilience. This understanding is concentrated in the formulation: "disasters occur when hazards meet vulnerability." A natural hazard will hence never result in a natural disaster in areas without vulnerability, e.g. strong earthquakes in uninhabited areas. The term natural has consequently been disputed because the events simply are not hazards or disasters without human involvement.

With the tropical climate and unstable landforms, coupled with high population density, poverty, illiteracy and lack of adequate infrastructure, India is one of the most vulnerable developing countries to suffer very often from various natural disasters, namely drought, flood, cyclone, earth quake, landslide, forest fire, hail storm, locust, volcanic eruption, etc. Which strike causing a devastating impact on human life, economy and environment? Though it is almost impossible to fully recoup the damage caused by the disasters, it is possible to

- Minimize the potential risks by developing early warning strategies

- Prepare and implement developmental plans to provide resilience to such disasters
- Mobilize resources including communication and telemedicine services, and
- To help in rehabilitation and post-disaster reconstruction.

Space technology plays a crucial role in efficient mitigation of disasters. While communication satellites help in disaster warning, relief mobilization and tele-medicinal support, earth observation satellites provide required database for pre-disaster preparedness programmes, disaster response, monitoring activities and post-disaster damage assessment, and reconstruction, and rehabilitation. The article describes the role of space technology in evolving a suitable strategy for disaster preparedness and operational framework for their monitoring, assessment and mitigation identifies gap areas and recommends appropriate strategies for disaster mitigation vis-à-vis likely developments in space and ground segments.

Various disasters like earthquake, landslides, volcanic eruptions, fires, flood and cyclones are natural hazards that kill thousands of people and destroy billions of dollars of habitat and property each year. The rapid growth of the world's population and its increased concentration often in hazardous environment has escalated both the frequency and severity of natural disasters. With the tropical climate and unstable land forms, coupled with deforestation, unplanned growth proliferation non-engineered constructions which make the disaster-prone areas mere vulnerable, tardy communication, poor or no budgetary allocation for disaster prevention, developing countries suffer more or less chronically by natural disasters. Asia tops the list of casualties due to natural disaster. Among various natural hazards, earthquakes, landslides, floods and cyclones are the major disasters adversely affecting very large areas and population in the Indian sub-continent.

These natural disasters are of:

- Geophysical origin such as earthquakes, volcanic eruptions, landslides and

- Climatic origin such as drought, flood, cyclone, locust, forest fire.

Though it may not be feasible to control nature and to stop the development of natural phenomena but the efforts could be made to avoid disasters and alleviate their effects on human lives, infrastructure and property. Rising frequency, amplitude and number of natural disasters and attendant problem coupled with loss of human lives prompted the "General Assembly of the United Nations to proclaim 1990s as the International Decade for Natural Disaster Reduction (IDNDR) through a resolution 44/236 of December 22, 1989"[1] to focus on all issues related to natural disaster reduction. In spite of IDNDR, there had been a string of major disaster throughout the decade. Nevertheless, by establishing the rich disaster management related traditions and by spreading public awareness the IDNDR provided required stimulus for disaster reduction. It is almost impossible to prevent the occurrence of natural disasters and their damages. However it is possible to reduce the impact of disasters by adopting suitable disaster mitigation strategies.

The disaster mitigation works mainly address the following:

- Minimise the potential risks by developing disaster early warning strategies,
- Prepare and implement developmental plans to provide resilience to such disasters,
- Mobilise resources including communication and tele-medicinal services and
- To help in rehabilitation and post-disaster reduction.

Disaster management on the other hand involves:

- Pre-disaster planning, preparedness, monitoring including relief management capability.
- Prediction and early warning.
- Damage assessment and relief management.

Disaster reduction is a systematic work which involves with

different regions, different professions and different scientific fields, and has become an important measure for human, society and nature sustainable development.

India has been traditionally vulnerable to natural disasters on account of its unique geo-climatic conditions. Floods, droughts, cyclones, earthquakes and Landslides have been recurrent phenomena. "About 60% of the landmass is prone to floods; about 8% of the total area is prone to cyclones and 68% of the area is susceptible to drought. In the decade 1990-2000, an average of about 4344 earthquakes of various intensities; over 40 million hectares is prone to people lost their lives and about 30 million people were affected by disasters every year. The loss in terms of private, community and public assets has been astronomical."[2]

1.2At the global level, there has been considerable concern over natural disasters. Even as substantial scientific and material progress is made, the loss of lives and property due to disasters has not decreased. In fact, the human toll and economic losses have mounted.

It was in this background that the United Nations General Assembly, in 1989, declared the decade 1990-2000 as the International Decade for Natural Disaster Reduction with the objective to reduce loss of lives and property and restrict socio-economic damage through concerted international action, especially in developing countries.

Disaster management

Disaster management is a complex series of activities that include risk assessment, prevention measures, and preparedness to cope with future disasters, emergency response to a disaster, recovery and reconstruction.

Good development and community preparedness can reduce the impact of a disaster especially for the most vulnerable people, such as those living in hazard-prone areas with few financial resources to help them recover if they lose their means of livelihood.

Emergency Response

When disaster strikes the first response is to save lives (humanitarian action). While each disaster creates unique circumstances and the response needs to be tailored to meet the specifics of the situation the following general areas will usually form part of the response:

- Search and rescue - finding those who may be trapped under debris;
- Assessment of needs - working out what is required, in what quantities, and for whom;
- Health – providing medical care and preventing the spread of disease through immunisation, the provision of safe water and food, waste disposal and burial of the dead;
- Basic needs - procuring and distributing food, shelter and clothing;
- Gender - understanding the roles of men and women in families and communities to identify needs and ensure the fair distribution of resources;
- Livelihood and economy - assisting people earn a living to speed their recovery;
- Emotional support - counselling and reuniting separated families;
- Logistics - transporting people and equipment;
- Finance - obtaining, allocating and accounting for money;
- Communication - providing affected people with information, informing the, fundraising;
- Infrastructure - rebuilding roads, electricity and telephone networks, water pipelines, and waste disposal systems.

Few countries have all the resources necessary to meet the demands of a large-scale disaster. International assistance can provide expert knowledge and resources, but survivors and people living in the area can also do much to help if they are prepared. .

Any emergency response needs to be coordinated to ensure the survival of the maximum possible number of victims.Some of the issues to be considered in the disaster response include:

- respecting local knowledge while using international best practice;
- meeting survival needs in a culturally appropriate manner (e.g. types of food, clothing, shelter);
- limiting the effects of aid on the local economy;
- training people, organisations and communities to manage development fairly;
- prioritising the distribution of limited supplies;
- Gaining funding for long-term redevelopment and disaster preparedness, rather than simply responding to the current emergency situation.

In the chaos of a disaster, the pressure to make quick decisions and balance the specific interests of victims, governments, Non Government Organisations (NGOs) and donors may mean that best practice standards are not always achieved.

Disaster Recovery

Once the immediate danger is over, people may need assistance to rebuild their lives and their livelihoods. Communities may need to rebuild their social and physical infrastructure and revitalise the economy. It takes time and money to plan and ensure that long-term redevelopment and future disaster preparedness are appropriate for everyone. Damaged structures and services may not necessarily be restored in their previous locations or forms as the disruptions can be an opportunity to make improvements. Seasonal factors must be considered; for example, seeds need to be distributed during the planting season and the type of temporary shelter used will depend on the climate and season.

Disaster Preparedness

Much can be done to prepare for future disasters by:

- modifying or removing the causes of any likely hazard - for example by building houses away from hazard prone areas, building leavy banks in flood prone areas and upgrading stoves to reduce the risk of fire;
- taking measures to reduce the effects of a hazard - for example by building houses to standards that will protect people during a hazard, developing early warning systems that can function without power systems, developing response plans, defining the roles and training of emergency services personnel, collecting and storing resources and equipment to ensure a quick response, educating the public and rehearsing for a hazard (eg evacuation drill).

Development

Reconstruction after a disaster provides significant opportunities for improved development including:

- planning the response and recovery to prepare for future hazards;
- upgrading infrastructure, including roads, communication networks and water and sanitation systems to withstand disasters and assist in emergency response;
- building hazard resistant public buildings and housing to reduce the impact of hazards;
- developing the skills of local personnel to increase their capacity to respond to an emergency;
- poverty alleviation to reduce the vulnerability of those with limited resources;
- Expansion and modernisation of the economic base.

Care must be taken to ensure that changes do not increase an area's susceptibility to disasters. For example environmental factors need to be considered when creating job opportunities so that the people do not move to hazard-prone areas such as floodplains or unstable hillsides; introduction of new agricultural practices needs to avoid leading to land degradation.

Institutional and Policy Framework

The institutional and policy mechanisms for carrying out response, relief and rehabilitation have been well-established since Independence.These mechanisms have proved to be robust and effective insofar as response, relief and rehabilitation are concerned. However, the increasing frequency and ferocity, the rising extent and sweep as well as the mounting human and economic toll has necessitated a reappraisal and re-orientation of existing institutional and policy frameworks along with creation of newer frameworks for holistic disaster management. The changed policy/approach mandates a priority to pre-disaster aspects of mitigation, prevention and preparedness and new institutional mechanisms are being put in place to address the policy change. Although, the primary responsibility for disaster management is of the

Concerned State Governments, the Central Government plays a key role by Providing financial and logistic support in case of major disasters and co-ordinate the effort of all Central Ministries/ Departments/Organizations. At the apex level, the Cabinet Committee on Drought Management has been re-constituted and converted into a Cabinet Committee on Natural Calamities. The scope of the Committee has been enlarged so as to address mitigation and preparedness measures also. A High Level Committee of Ministers under the Chairmanship of Minister of Agriculture deals with financial support required to be provided to the State Governments from the National Calamity Contingency Fund, if the funds available with the State Governments under Central Relief Fund are not adequate.

The matters relating to nuclear, biological and chemical emergencies are looked after by the Cabinet Committee on Security. Cabinet Secretary, who is the highest executive officer, heads the National Crisis Management Committee (NCMC). Secretaries of all the concerned Ministries/Departments as well as organizations are the members of the Committee. The NCMC gives direction to the Crisis Management Group as deemed necessary. The Secretary,

Ministry of Home Affairs is responsible for ensuring that all developments are brought to the notice of the NCMC promptly. The NCMC can give directions to any Ministry/Department/ Organization for specific action needed for meeting the crisis situation.

Disaster Management Policy

Disaster management is a multidisciplinary activity involving a number of Departments/agencies spanning across all sectors of development. Where a number of Departments/agencies are involved, it is essential to have a policy in place, as it serves as a framework for action by all the relevant departments/agencies. A National Policy on Disaster Management has been drafted, and is in the process of being finalized. After interministerial consultations, it will be submitted to the Cabinet for approval. In the Line with the changed focus, the policy proposes to integrate disaster mitigation into development planning. The policy shall inform all spheres of Central

Government activity and shall enjoin upon all existing sectoral policies. The broad objectives of the policy are to minimize the loss of lives and social, private and community assets because of natural or man-made disasters and contribute to sustainable development and better standards of living for all, more specifically for the poor and vulnerable section by ensuring that the development gains are not lost through natural calamities/ disaster.

Our individual responses

Money is the best way to help.

The most useful form of assistance during a humanitarian crisis is the donation of money to non-government overseas aid organisations. This is because such organisations:

- May have qualified people already working in the affected country who understand what is needed in the emergency situation, understand the peoples' cultures, and know the local languages.

- have strong local networks so they know where to buy emergency relief goods at the best prices with the least long-term negative impact on the affected country and can manage timely and cost-effective transportation have controls in place to check that as much money as possible is spent on goods or services for the people in need.

What not to give:

Items such as food, clothing, blankets, medicines and toys can cause problems for relief authorities. The costs of sorting, storing, and packing, labelling (in English and in the recipient country's language) and then transporting these items may be higher than the cost of buying them in the country of need or from a country nearby. Sometimes such donations may also be culturally inappropriate.

Natural disasters are not bound by political boundaries and have no social or economic considerations. They are borderless as they affect both developing and developed countries. They are also merciless, and as such the vulnerable tend to suffer more at the impact of natural disasters. For example, the developing countries are much more seriously affected in terms of the loss of lives, hardship borne by population and the percentage of their GNP lost. Since 1991, two-third of the victims of natural disasters was from developing countries, while just 2 percent were from highly developed nations. Those living in developing countries and especially those with limited resources tend to be more adversely affected. With the alarming rise in the natural disasters and vulnerability per se, the world community is strengthening its efforts to cope with it.

REFERENCES

1. Annual Reports, Natural Disaster Management Division, Ministry of Agriculture
2. Ibid.

16

Natural Disasters in India and Vulnerable Group: Role Of NGOs

Dr. Ranjana Srivastava
Asst. Professor
Dept. of English
D.B.S.(P.G.) College
Kanpur

Dr. Seema Nigam
Lecturer
Dept. of English
D.B.S. (P.G.) College
Kanpur

The earth has been an unstable proposition throughout its existence. Man who entered the seen has been exploring during his short existence to unravel the various mysteries which are mysteries till date. These mysteries have been understood to some extent, by and confined to, the intellectual community but when the victims of these unexplored mysteries are the people then they need to know what the mysteries are and the impact that the mysteries can have on them.

India is one of the countries most prone to natural calamities. Geographical and natural position of India has made it one of the most hazard-prone lands in the world. It is particularly highly vulnerable to storms, landslides, droughts, floods and cyclones. Every year, number of lives and good chunk of property worth several million rupees are lost because of these calamities. Generally most of the regions of the country are disaster-prone of either type. Such disasters result into various social, economic and health problems causing affliction and isolation to all age group in general but elderly people in particular. During last two decades

India suffered some major natural disasters, including the earthquake at Gujarat. Drought in Rajasthan and Orissa and floods in Bihar, heavy rainfall in Maharashtra and man made disasters such as ethnic and civil conflicts in Assam and war conflict in Kargil, Bhopal Gas tragedy, Casualty at Hotel Taj and Petroleum fire tragedy at Jaipur.

India is the second most populous country in the world. Improved life expectancy has given rise to an increase in the number of persons above 60 years. During the next 25 years, the number of people over the age of 60 in India is estimated to reach 178 million. Over 75 per cent of the elderly live in the rural areas.

Older poor people are at high levels of risk in the world's increasing number of conflicts and natural disasters, but are not as yet systematically identified and catered for as a vulnerable group. In recent years, there has been an explosion of different natural disasters apart from a few other man-made disasters. In all emergencies, a psychological study shows, older people identify the social and psychological traumas that afflict them. Separation from, or loss of, family members leads them to isolation bereavement and loss of support. "Older people try to hide their sorrows and bad experiences, they are patient, they gather together in groups to support each other and try to cope. Older people want to built not to destroy"(Community leader, Rwanda).The elderly population may experience a number of common ailments which may become worse in disaster situation, including heart disease, strokes, cancer, arthritis, poor vision and hearing, depression and dementia. Understanding the high risk the elderly population is paramount. Particular attention should be paid to the possible vision deficit, hearing loss, cognitive changes and acute illness. Precaution should be taken to prevent new or further injuries from falling during relocation. Older people are often left to care for younger children or other dependents in the obscene of middle generation adults. The destruction of social structure because of disasters may cause,loss of family and community support as well as loss of self respect for older people, as cultural and social value break down .Therefore, they need strong pole of sympathy to prop up.

The Administration of Aging (AoA) responds to the special need of older disaster victims. Older people often have difficulty in obtaining necessary assistance because of progressive physical and mental impairments and other frailties that often accompany aging.

Thus the need of hour to be aware of the disasters has been recognized prima-facie which resulted into non government organizations. In India there are several types of NGOs performing a particular job or jobs. The sectors have been wide spread across the country especially in rural and remote areas. The types of NGOs in India include volunteer sector, civic society, grassroots organizations, transnational social movement organizations, private voluntary organizations, self-help groups (SSG) and many other related organizations. NGOs cover areas that include welfare of street children, women and old people, youth, slum dwellers, child laborers, sex workers, and landless workers. India is estimated to have more than 2 million NGOs at present. NGOs play significant role in emergencies.

In the past years approach of government had been only to provide immediate help for basic needs. Emergency relief was seen as a separate intervention, unrelated to development activities. Aid agencies and Governments often focused on rapid and efficient distribution of medical and material aid and paid little attention to longer-term issues, such as dislocation and loss of employment which are aftermath of natural catastrophe which in rural areas can include a complete loss of livelihoods.

The super cyclone that lashed the coast of Orissa at a speed of 350 kilometres an hour on 29 October 1999 left thousands of people and livestock dead, hundreds of thousands of human beings and cattle wounded, collapsed houses, and millions of hectares of croplands destroyed in no time. About 19 million people of 126 blocks and 44 urban local bodies in 14 districts were severely affected by the super cyclone, which was accompanied by heavy rain and floods.

About 100,000 water purification tablets were distributed in the worst affected Erasama Block of the Jagatsinghpur district through the Mobile Medicare Unit .A total of 187.6 metric tons of rice, 22.48 metric tons of dhal, 5 metric tons of edible oil and 5 metric tons of iodized salt was distributed to 5,000 families of older persons in six districts as emergency dry rations for 15 days. There was no reported loss of commodities, either owing to mishandling, improper storage, packaging loss or pilferage. Realizing the need for food supplementation for needy older people, another 130 day supply of food, along with essential household items, were provided to 4,100 elderly families. Food for 60 days was also distributed to another 5,500 elderly families with the financial support of the European Community Humanitarian Organization in the cyclone affected areas.

On reassessing the provision of shelter materials, NGOs decided that the most viable and immediate shelter material available to provide cover to houses of the affected families whose roof had been blown away, would be plastic sheets, 15 foot by 12 foot. About 10,200 plastic sheets were distributed among the targeted population. Five thousand good quality blankets were also provided to the targeted population.

Older persons, were given emergency medical treatment and preventive health care. The concerned district medical officer was told in advance of the operational sites to be covered by the medical team to ensure better coordination.

Before the actual relief distribution, the volunteers of the partner agencies had undertaken a thorough household rapid assessment and selected 5,000 older persons based on the following criteria. Preference was given to those who were in the age above 60 selection was on the basis of loss of extended and earning family members The relief programme was intended to reach the unreached and thus more preference was given to those areas inaccessible to relief services provided by the Government and other agencies

The programme also identified the most vulnerable caste groups, such as the scheduled caste and scheduled tribes, and more weightage was given to them for relief distribution All the older persons who were categorized as below the poverty line were given more preference than those who were not. "In times of such intense stress and uncertainty older adults have historically being considered on at risk group." Physically weak, disabled, and frail older persons were selected so as to enhance their dignity in the family.

In a disaster situation, when communities recover, older people typically face difficulties in accessing land and other scarce resources. Exclusion from credit, income generation and food-for-work programme is common and this exacerbates their loss of independence, status and dignity. The income-generation programme was undertaken to ensure that older people could have full and equal support in rebuilding their livelihoods.

Help Age India undertook a massive income-generation programme for 1,400 elderly families. Seven agencies partnered this programme. Different income-generating trades were identified after physical verification of feasibility and viability. The agencies carefully selected the beneficiaries of the income-generation programme, seeing to it that the beneficiaries met all the set criteria, Groups were formed by taking the beneficiaries of similar income-generating activities. The groups were limited to 15 to 20 members each to ensure proper coordination among members. In villages there were few beneficiaries, with different trade options, the agencies clubbed them to other groups carrying related income-generating activities. The agencies formed the groups using the Self-Help Groups scheme so that they could saves something out of the profit earned to create a village fund.Some contributions from the beneficiaries were sought by each agency to ensure participation. The beneficiaries contributed to cattle feed, medicines and other costs involved in constructing sheds for goats, sheep and cows. To start a grocery shop or other petty businesses, the beneficiaries had to bear the cost of the building. In some cases, they were also provided bicycles, containers etc. to do petty trading. The income-generating programme initiated by Help Age India had a long-term impact on the lives of the older persons. A total of 120 older people joined the Self-help Groups Scheme. These groups also served as a forum to look after the future disaster preparedness of their respective communities. In addition, these small groups of older persons served as a common platform to share their problems and become united in advocating their cause at the local level. This could be considered as a revival of the traditional village governance system.

The aftermath of the super cyclone resulted in a huge loss of human life as well as loss of houses and property. With the onset of the winter and rainy season, older persons become more vulnerable. Help Age India thought of constructing one core room for each of the older persons selected. With the aim to restore their dignity by providing a safe shelter Help Age undertook the construction of 395 houses in cyclone-affected areas. The single and disabled older persons were given priority. The beneficiaries formed groups so that they could mutually share their labour in construction activities. The formation of groups helped the older persons who did not have family support, or who were too frail to construct houses. In addition, the agencies provided mason and carpenter support for construction activities. The beneficiaries, on the other hand, contributed the labour components to rebuild the houses .The agency's material support, however, varied from case to case. The housing programme had positive and negative impacts. As all the programme supports were channeled through the older persons, their dignity in the family as well as in the community was enhanced. The once isolated older persons were seen happily staying near or with their dear ones. The programme was implemented in a community-based approach, which had a positive impact – all the older persons of the village became united and contributed their labour for each other. In a few instances, they were seen putting in some extra labour to construct a bigger house than was originally planned. Another positive impact of the programme was the timely support that the distressed people received. As far as the negative impact of the programme is concerned, the small support of Help Age India restricted a few villages from receiving more support from other agencies. The Indira Awas Yojana Programme also restricted older persons from obtaining more benefits as they were supported by Help Age. Though support was only given to some selected beneficiaries in the village, the whole village had to suffer because of the reluctance of the government to enter into such villages where there was already some kind of support provided by other agencies.

A major earthquake struck the State of Gujarat in western India on 26 January 2001, the tremors of which were felt throughout India. The quake, which was perhaps the strongest in 50 years, led to widespread devastation on a scale never seen before. The epicentre was 20 kilometres north-east of Bhuj district and measured from 6.9 to 7.9 on the Richter scale. Several regions of the State and neighboring areas were badly affected. This led to widespread devastation in Gujarat and 7,904 villages. According to the United Nations Office for the Coordination of Humanitarian Affairs, it is estimated that up to 30,000 deaths may have occurred and that more than 146,000 people were reported injured. Most of the people who were affected lived in the rural areas. They were the people who live below the poverty line and many of whom depend upon their daily wages for their livelihood. They are the same people who were very recently affected by drought in the area.. Infrastructure and public facilities suffered significant damage.

One of the most active groups assisting the earthquake victims was the Rashtriya Swayamsevak Sangh (RSS), which set up coordination points and directed the flow of aid very effectively. RSS has hugely increased its reputation for being organized when all others fail – a role which puts it in a position to challenge the Government itself, if the occasion arose.

Without doubt, the international response to the earthquake was rapid and massive .According to the United Nations Disaster Assessment and Coordination, by 10 February 2001, relief had arrived from 38 countries and the presence of 245 agencies had been registered, including at least 99 international NGOs, 55 national NGOs, 20 donor government teams, 10 United Nations and intergovernmental organizations and Red Cross representatives from 10 countries.

The medical items provided through the mobile medicare units were orthopedic treatments and other related medicines: antibiotics, saline drips, medical dressings, bleaching powder, water purification tablets, anti-diarrhoea, anti-asthmatic, anti-histamine tablets, etc. They also provided immediate medical assistance for injuries resulting from the earthquake .Medical support included check-ups, preventive health care and counseling, and the administration of medication for common problems such as viral diseases, diabetes, blood pressure and arthritis. One outreach worker from the mobile medicare unit visited the camps once a week to provide psychosocial support and referred serious cases to partners or families that could look after them. Most of the worst affected areas were in the western desert that experiences extreme weather conditions during winters. Following an initial assessment, it was clear that the provision of blankets to older persons was immediately needed. A total of 7,500 blankets were purchased and distributed by the partner organizations and other voluntary groups.

Older persons were provided with temporary shelters through the distribution of 7,500 plastic sheets (size: 15 feet by 12 feet), and 1,000 tents among the elderly and other people, and their families, who had been left homeless by the earthquake. NGOs distributed 4,500 lamps to provide lighting for the beneficiaries and their families. Kerosene for the lamps was provided by the Government. A total of 3,000 stoves were also distributed.

Most people lost everything and there was an urgent need for basic household items such as a cooking pot, bucket, cooking utensils and steel water carriers. About 7,500 sets of these items were distributed. One of the critical factors faced by older persons during the aftermath of the earthquake was how to rebuild their houses within the communities. The dilemma they faced was whether they should build their houses in the same location or shift to another area that had more potential for development.

NGOs assisted 1,575 families of older persons who needed to rebuild their houses and supported them with 17,000 rupees per house, as a partial support to the overall rebuilding process. The process of implementation had primary importance, as it was aimed at galvanizing local resources and enhancing the participation of older persons and the community in the reconstruction of their houses. Community support was ensured with support for the removal of rubble and the salvaging of materials, which could be recycled as wooden doors, beams, bricks, etc. Wherever possible, women and others were motivated to participate in a community type of intervention where the sharing of responsibilities was encouraged at all levels. Most of all, the perceptions of older persons were paramount in any kind of rebuilding process.

The needs assessment clearly highlighted that rebuilding of livelihoods through traditional handicrafts, particularly encouraging handicrafts such as embroidery, handloom and leather craft, would be an important part of rebuilding lives. As a result of the earthquake, a number of artisans died and lot of machines and tools were damaged or destroyed. Help Age India, through its partner NGOs, encouraged the revival of these activities in selected villages so as to preserve the traditional crafts of these communities.

The other income-generating activities were in the area of animal husbandry, for example, poultry, goat rearing, bee-keeping, piggeries, duck rearing and dairy. Older persons were formed into groups so that they could undertake combined activities, which were self-sustaining in nature, such as productions of pickle and *papad*. The group activity of income generation was encouraged so that the community could feel ownership of their project. The economic feasibility of each income-generating activity was worked out by the partner agency in consultation with the communities and the older persons. The partner NGO was responsible for coordination and for facilitating group formation and forging linkages with markets Help Age India and Help Age International worked closely with the other humanitarian agencies to ensure that they were aware of the needs of older people in their relief activities In the family, as well as in the community, as all the support was channeled through them, the older persons were again seen staying with their family and friends with their dignity retained. Most of the NGOs are to extend hand of help to all but especially to vulnerable groups and to ensure older persons' rights and their equitable access to all types of relief during emergencies in all type of disasters. Any emergency situation is considered as a platform and a catalyst for change, bringing to the forefront the hidden vulnerabilities of older people during emergencies and finding suitable options and choices within the community to mitigate such vulnerability .This will be the prime focus of our future endeavors. NGOs seek to advocate for older people's needs, contributions, bringing their plight to the attention of national- and state-level coordination committees and ensuring the inclusion of older people as a vulnerable group in emergencies. Although partnering with local and grass-roots NGOs is suggested for effective programme implementation, the process of selecting

Timely need assessment not only helps in reaching the most affected and needy population, it is also necessary to access funds for emergency operations. This is a critical lesson learned by Help Age India in both the responses. This was developed in Orissa and fine-tuned in Gujarat (i.e., rapid assessments, mobile medicare unit assessments for logistics, and initial programme design) As the disaster situation changes at a rapid rate, there is a need to update it regularly to have a thorough idea about future interventions Survey techniques for household assessment is important In the transitory phase of relief to rehabilitation, needs assessment becomes paramount in the selection of priority interventions. Commodity management is very essential in emergencies as food intervention is a common need in most emergencies.

REFERENCES

1. "Gujrat's unlearnt lessons" in ***Front Line*** at www.indiaserver.com
2. www.Gujrat- earthquake.gov.in
3. "Lifespan perspective on Natural Disasters", K.E.Cherry

17

Natural Disaster and National Management System

Alka Saxena
Deptt. of B.Ed.
D.B.S. College, Kapur

Loss of life and property due to natural disasters like tropical cyclones, floods, droughts, tornadoes, earthquakes, volcanic eruptions etc, is very large. Fortunately warning facilities are available today and by mitigation measures, loss of lives and properties can be minimised. National Meteorological Services of the world to provide warnings to the public for some of the weather related natural disasters. It is not possible to forecast a long period ahead precisely when and where a dangerous natural pphenomenon will take place. While natural disasters cannot be prevented, the loss of life and property can be minimized by taking proper long-term and short-term disaster mitigation measures.

Disaster management has been organized into four phases called disaster management cycle. Prevention, Preparedness, Response and Recovery. It seeks to motivate societies at risk to become engaged in conscious disaster management, beyond the traditional response to disasters. Disaster reduction is multi-sectoral and interdisciplinary in nature and involves a wise variety of interrelated activities at the local, national, regional and international level. Access to information is crucial for the effective management of disasters. All those who are concerned with managing disasters necessarily have the need to access timely and accurate information. Understanding the potential risks and impacts of natural disasters requires sound knowledge concerning the features of the landscape, the patterns of human development, and a scientific understanding of natural disasters.

Some common disasters known to occur in our country are as under:

A tsunami is wave-chain that is generated in a water body by an impulsive disturbance that displaces water column. Landslides, explosions, earthquakes and volcanic eruptions all can generate tsunami. Tsunamis can savagely attack coastlines, causing devastating property damage and loss of life. As recent as 26th December, 2004, the multiple tsunamis struck and ravaged coastal regions all over the Indian Ocean, devastating parts of Indonsia, Sri Lanka, India, Thailand and other countries causing immeasurable loss to life and property.

Important Features of Tsunami

- All low lying areas are prone to Tsunami strikes.
- A Tsunami is a series of sea-waves caused by an underwater earthquake, landslide or volcanic eruption. At times, the first wave may not be the largest. But danger from following Tsunami waves may last for several hours after the arrival of the first wave.
- Tsunami waves can be very long (as much as 60 miles or 100 km) and be as far as one hour.
- The tsunami wave force is enormous. It can carry large rocks weighing many tons along with other debris and can move them several metres inland. Homes and other structures that fall is its way are destroyed. The force of floating material and water can kill or injure people.
- Tsunamis have not fixed schedule. They can take place anytime of the day or night.
- Tsunami could travel up rivers and streams that lead to oceans.

- In some places a tsunami may cause the sea to rise vertically only a few inches or feet, but in other places tsunami have been known to scourge vertically as high as 100 feet. Most tsunamis cause the sea to rise no more than 10 feet.

The advent of satellite technology has made it feasible to provide advance knowledge about the arrival of a potentially tsunamigenic earthquakes. The warning time depends upon the distance between the epicentre and the coast time. It gives advance information about the predicted times at selected coastal communities where the tsunami is likely to travel in a few hours.

During a Tsunami

High multi-storey, reinforced concrete hotels are located in many low-lying coastal areas. The upper floors of such hotels can provide a safe place. Take refuge there is case of a tsunami warning and you cannot move quickly enough to reach higher ground.

Off shore reefs and shallow areas may help in breaking the force of tsunami waves, but coastal residents in these areas may still face the threat from large and dangerous tsunami waves. It is advisable to stay away from the coastal area, it there is a tsunami threat or warning.

Tsunamis in South Asia

Tsunamis in South Asia

Date	*Location*
1524	Near Dabhol, Maharashtra
02 April 1762	Arakan Coast, Myanmar
16 June 1819	Rann of Kachchh, Gujarat
31 October 1847	Great Nicobar Island
31 December 1881	Car Nicobar Island
26 August 1883	Krakatoa volcanic eruption
28 November 1945	Mekran coast, Balochistan

26 December 2004	Banda Aceh, Indonesia; Tamil Nadu, Kerala, Andhra Pradesh, Andaman and Nicobar Islands, India; Sri Lanka; Thailand; Malaysia; Somalia; Kenya; Tanzania

Floods

Flood are defined as a relatively high flow of water discharged from river and stream network, which sets the riverbank margins to overflow and lead to the inundation of low land areas surrounding the riverbed. It is essentially a physical phenomenon. Floods arise from abnormally heavy rains, dam failures, snow melts, river blockages. Flood disasters rank second only to droughts in the total number of people affected worldwide.

Types of Floods

Floods can be classified into three categories as under:-

(i) River floods – Rivers get charged due to heavy rains over large catchments areas or by melting of snow or sometimes both especially in the mountainous tracts. The floods take place in river systems with tributaries that may drain into large geographic areas and encompass many independent river basins. Amount of flooding depends on moisture in the soil, vegetation cover, and depth of snow and size of catchments basin.

(ii) Coastal flood- Coastal flooding is associated with tropical cyclones/ harsh winds arising at the ocean surface. Coastal floods are often aggravated by wind induced storm surges along the coastline. Sea and ocean water floods the inland coasts affecting kilometres of tracts. Ocean tides, storm surges or tsunamis play a definite role. Prolonged and indefinite rains in the rainy season marked from June-September results in extreme flood in coastal river basins.

(iii) Flash floods- These floods occur within six hours of the beginning of rainfall and are characterised with rising clouds, thunderstorms and tropical cyclones. These result from runoff from a torrential downpour, particularly if the catchments slope is unable to absorb and hold a significant part of water. Other causes of flash floods include dam failure, sudden break up of glaciers etc. These offer potential threats in the areas where the terrain is steep, surface runoff is high, water flows through canyons and where severe rainstorms are likely.

Flood Control

1. Depth and width of the riverbed could be increased as its capacity to carry larger loads increases manifold and thus reduce the area of the flood plain.
2. A network of canals can be established from the river systems, which generally leads to floods. This would also benefit the agricultural economy/section. Care must be taken in the design and construction because of the possible environmental impact and necessary safety features.
3. Reservoirs should be made for storing floodwater and releasing them at manageable rates. This would require careful engineering. Dams and reservoirs would further lead to generation or resources.
4. Newly constructed residential as well commercial buildings should have foundations, which are strong enough to respond to flood conditions.
5. Rivers and streambeds should be stabilized with stone, masonry or vegetation at the banks. This should strictly be followed where rivers pass through cities, specially near bridges.

Earthquakes and Seismology

An earthquake is a motion of the ground surface, ranging from a faint tremor to a wild motion capable of shaking buildings apart and causing gaping fissures to open in the ground. The magnitude or intensity of energy released by an earthquake is measured by the Richter Scale devised by Charles F. Richter in 1935. Good

Friday Earthquake of March 27, 1964 in Alaska (USA) measuring 8.4 to 8.6 on Richter scale is among the greatest earthquakes of the world ever recorded.

The science that studies the behaviour and patterns of seismic waves is called seismology. The place of origin of an earthquake is called focus, which is always hidden inside the earth, but its depth varies from place to place. The place of the origin of an earthquake is called 'focus' which is always hidden inside the earth. The deepest earthquake may have its focus at a depth of even 700 km below the ground surface. The waves generated by an earthquake are called 'seismic waves' which are recorded by an instrument called seismograph. The lines joining the places of equal intensity of seismic waves on the maps are called isoseismal lines.

Causes of Earthquakes

Earthquakes are caused mainly due to disequilibria in any part of the crust of the earth. A number of causes have been assigned to cause disequilibria in the earth's crust such as volcanic eruptions, faulting and folding, gaseous expansion and contraction inside the earth, hydrostatic pressure of man-made water bodies like reservoirs and lakes, and plate movements.

Effect of Earthquake Hazardous

Earthquakes and their hazards are determined on the basis of the magnitude of seismic intensity as determined by Richter scale but are decided in the basis of quantum of damages done by a specific earthquake to human lives and property.

(i) Landslides : Weaker landmasses and tectonically sensitive land margins cause landslides and debris falls, which damage settlements and transport systems on the lower slope segments.

(ii) Damage to Life and property: Structures such as buildings, roads, rails, factories, dams, bridges suffer a huge damage thus causing a heavy loss of human life and property both. Two major earthquakes of Bihar-Nepal border in 1934 and 1988 explain the impact of earthquake disasters on human structures and human lives. The damage caused by the Bihar earthquake of 15 January 1934, measuring 8.4 on Richter scale, include 10,700 human deaths, landslides and slumping in an area of 250 km length and 60 km width, ruptures and faults in the ground surface etc.

(iii) Damages to Government Infrastructure: Cities and towns are worst affected due to large concentration of human population, commercial complexes and residential areas. Due to collapse of buildings ground water pipes are bent and damaged thus water supply is disrupted, electric and telephone poles are uprooted and there is total disruption of power and communication. Other side effects are collapsed sewer system causing epidemics, road blocks etc.

(iv) Fire hazard : Earthquakes strongly shake the buildings and thus strong oscillations cause severe fires in houses, mines and factories because of overturning of cooking gas cylinders, contact of live electric wires, churning of blast furnaces, displacement of other electric and fire- related appliances.

(v) Landmass deformation: Severe earth tremors and resultant vibrations caused by severe earthquakes result in the deformation of ground surface because of crusts and troughs in the ground surface and faulting activity.

(vi) Flash floods : Strong seismic events result in the damages of dams and cause severe flash floods. Severe floods are also caused because of blocking of water flow of rivers due to rock blocks and debris produced by severe tremors on the hill slopes facing the river valleys.

Cyclones

Cyclones are the centres of low pressure surrounded by closed isobars having increasing pressure outward and closed air circulation from outside towards the central low pressure in such a way that air blows inward in anticlockwise on northern hemisphere and clockwise in southern hemisphere. They range in shape from circular, elliptical to V shape. From locational viewpoint cyclones are classified into two principal types e.g. (i) extra-tropical cyclones/temperate cyclones (ii) tropical cyclones.

Temperature cyclones are of different shapes e.g. circular, semi-circular, elliptical, elongated or V, but all of them are characterized by low pressure in their centres and closed isobars. The pressure difference between the centre and periphery is about 10-35 mb. It means that pressure increases from the centre towards outer margin. Average large diameter of an ideal cyclone is about 1900 km while short diameter measures 1000 km. The temperate cyclones move eastward under the influence of westerly winds with average velocity of 32 km per hour in summer and 48 km per hour in winters.

Tropical Cyclones developed in the regions lying between the tropics of Capricorn and Cancer are called tropical cyclones which are not regular and uniform like extra tropical cyclones which are not regular and uniform like extra tropical or temperate cyclones. There are numerous forms of these cyclones, which vary considerably in shape, size, velocity and weather conditions. The weather conditions of low latitudes mainly rainfall regimes are largely controlled by tropical cyclones.

Environmental Impact of Tropical Cyclones

Tropical cyclones are very severe disastrous natural hazards which inflict heavy loss to human lives and property in terms of destruction of buildings, transport systems, water and power supply systems, disruption of communication system, destruction of standing agricultural crops, domestic and wild animals, natural vegetation, private and public institutions etc.

Anticyclones

Surrounded by circular isobars anticyclone is such a wind system which has highest air pressure at the centre and lowest at the outer margin and winds blow from the centre outward in clockwise direction in the northern hemisphere and anticlockwise in the southern hemisphere. Thus, anticyclones are high-pressure systems and more common in the subtropical high pressure belts but are practically absent in the equatorial regions. Anticyclones were classified into (i) warm anticyclones, and (ii) cold anticyclones by Hanzilk in 1909.

Wind system is not fully developed in anticyclones because of weak pressure wherein winds spread in all directions from high pressure centre to low-pressure periphery. The winds are very much sluggish in the rear portion in comparison to the front portion. The centre is characterized by light breeze. Anticyclones are generally of circular shape but are very large in size. They become so large in size that their diameters become 9,000 km.

Landslides

Among physiographic units, the two northern units of the Greater Himalayas (7500-8500m), and the Inner Himalayas (Trans-Himalayan zone), an intervening system of high plateau and valleys lying between the two great mountain ranges, are considered along with middle mountains, the traditional centres of population. The upper northern section of these middle mountains remains largely under upper montane forest (2900-400 m), below which is the belt of intensive agriculture. Lithology is highly varied, including sedimentary, metamorphics, and granites. However, there are extensive areas of phyllites and schists; these are deeply weathered and the prevailing steep slopes render them highly susceptible to erosion and slope failure (mostly through landslides). Presently, according to gross yet reliable estimate, the landslides occupy about 1% of land surface in only five central districts of Himachal Pradesh. They have a total volume of more than $2.2 \times 10^6 m^3$ and a mean age of 6.5 years. This helps to evaluate the denudation rate, which is about 2.5-mm/year denudation rate. One of the main causes of landslides is road construction.

National Management System

Sharing happiness and sorrows develop oneness in people and infuse confidence in them to face any eventuality. Thus sharing responsibilities during national disasters and hazards reduce the intensity of sufferings. Disasters bring closer all bodies-Government and non-government to join hands to work cohesively at all levels from national, state, district, block, villages to individuals to fight and overcome the devastations created by disasters.

Managing Disasters

Collective and concerted efforts coupled with close coordination among various government and non-government agencies can efficiently mange disasters. Now what are these agencies that are working for our safety.

In the federal Setup of India, the basic responsibility for undertaking rescue, relief and rehabilitation measures in the event of natural disasters is that of the State Government concerned. The role of the Central Government is supportive, in terms of physical and financial resources and complementary measures in sectors such as transport, warning and inter-state movement of food grains. The dimensions of the response at the level of Central Government are determined in accordance with the existing policy of financing the relief expenditure, based on the recommendations of the Finance Commissions appointed after every five years. The country has an integrated administrative machinery for management of disasters at the National, State, District and Sub-District levels.

National Level

The gravity of the disaster, the scale of the relief operation required and the needs of the central assistance for augmenting financial resources and logistics support at the disposal of the State Government helps the Central Government to determine its response.

Based on the past experience, an integrated administrative response mechanism has been evolved. A broad view of the administrative response at national, state and district levels is given below:

National Level Organization

Control Room (Emergency Operation Room)- An Emergency Operations Center (Control Room) exists in the nodal Ministry of Home Affairs, which functions round the clock, to assist the Central

Relief Commissioner in the discharge of his duties. During crisis period, providing additional manpower and equipment, as per the need, strengthens it.

Other Line Ministries

India Meteorological Department, Central Water Commission, Ministry of Home Affairs, Ministry of Defense, Ministry of Finance, Ministry of Rural Development, Ministry of Urban Development, Department of Communications, Ministry of Health, Ministry of Water Resources, Ministry of Petroleum, Department of Agriculture & Cooperation. Ministry of Power, Department of Civil Supplies, Ministry of Railways, Ministry of Information and Broadcasting, Planning Commission, Cabinet Secretariat, Department of Surface Transport, Ministry of Social Justice, Department of Women and Child Development, Ministry of Environment and Forest, Department of Food. Each Ministry/ Department/Organization has their sectoral. Action Plan as Emergency Support System. The institutional mechanism at the National Level is as under.

Cabinet Committee/Task Force:

The Union Cabinet may set up a Cabinet Committee/Task Force/Group of Ministers for effective coordination and implementation or relief measures in the wake of a natural disasters. Such Committees/Task Force/ Group of Ministers had been set up in the wake of Super Cyclone of Orissa in 1999, Earthquake of Gujarat 2001, severe floods in 2000 and drought in 2002.

National Crises Management Committee (NCMC)

Cabinet Secretary, which is the highest executive officer, heads the NCMC. Secretaries of all the concerned Ministers/Departments as well as organizations are the members of the Committee. The NCMC gives direction to the Crisis Management Group as deemed necessary.

Crisis Management Group (CMG)

The Central Relief Commissioner in the Ministry of Home Affairs is the Chairman of the CMG, consisting of senior officers (called as nodal officers) from various concerned Ministries. The CMG's functions are to review.

Every year contingency plans formulated by various Ministries/ Departments/Organizations in their respective sectors, measures required for dealing with a natural disaster, coordinate the activities of the Central Ministries and the State Governments in relation to disaster preparedness and relief and to obtain information from the nodal officers on measures relating to above.

State Level Organization

At the State level, a State Crisis Management Committee has been set under the Chairmanship of the Chief Secretary, who is the highest executive functionary in the State. The Committee is required to take into consideration the instructions and guidance received, from time to time, from the Government of India and formulates action plans dealing with the different natural disasters.

An officer of the level of Secretary in the State Government is designated as Relief Commissioner, which is the nodal officer in the State is the coordinator of all activities/programs for disaster management.

District Level

District level is the key level for disaster management related activities. District Collector, the highest administrator in the district, is the focal point for preparation of the district level plans and for directing, supervising and monitoring relief measures for the natural disasters. A District Level Co-ordination and Relief Committee is constituted and is headed by the Collector as Chairman with participation of all other related government and non governmental agencies and departments in addition to the elected representative such as officials from the health department, Irrigation Department, Veterinary Department, Department of Water and Sanitation, Fire Services, representatives from Natioanl and International NGOs etc. The Disaster Management operation takes the help of Disaster Management Teams to help the administration for preparation of District Disaster Management Plan to coordinate in training the members of the Disaster Management Team at the district and to carry out mock drills.

Contingency Action Plan

A National Contingency Action Plan (CAP) for dealing with contingencies arising in the wake of natural disasters has been formulated by the Government of India and it had been periodically updated. It facilitates the launching of relief operations without delay. The CAP identifies the initiatives required to be taken by various Central Ministries/Departments in the wake of natural calamities, sets down the procedure and determines the focal points in the administrative machinery.

Village

The Disaster Management Plan at the village level is prepared by village Disaster Management Committee headed by the Sarpanch/village Headman who also coordinated with various agencies for providing training to the Disaster Management Teams. It is the duty of the members to ensure that mock drills are carried out at regular intervals by the villagers for various hazards.

It is not out of place to mention that the Government alone cannot take on the whole responsibility of Disaster Management. In addition to National, State District and Local levels, there are other institutions which are involved in the management of disasters at different levels in the country. Agencies like Civil Defence, Home Guards, Para-military Forces, Police, Fire-Services, National Cadet Corps (NCC), Youth Organization, UN Agencies, National and International groups, Private and Public Sector Enterprises, Media etc. play a major role in managing disasters. Some of the organizations functions are mentioned below.

Un Disaster Management Team (UNDMT) – INDIA

The UN General Assembly mandate has made UN office for Coordination of Humanitarian Affairs (UNOCHA) responsibly for all International disaster response. In view of the recurrent and widespread impact of national disasters in the country and the presence of 18 UN Organization with their related specialized

Agencies, India provide an important plateform for the UNDMT. This was done to implement disaster preparedness and mitigation effects and strength Government's disaster risk management capacities. Various UN Agencies such as FAO, ILO, UNFPA, UNICEF and WHO represent the UNDMT.

CONCLUSION

The mankind has been suffering the havocs and devastations created by natural disasters for many centuries and is still facing the fury of frequent floods, cyclones, earthquakes and landslides. Though it is beyond the capacity of the mankind to control the natural calamities, yet it is making all out efforts to minimize its vulnerability against them by planning ahead.

REFERENCE

1. Anonymous, 1990, Global Atmospheric Change and Public Health, Elsevier, New York.
2. Cunningham, W.P. and Saigo, B.W., 1055. Environmental Science. Wm. C. Brown Publishers, Dubuque.
3. Negi, B.S., 1991. Geography of Resources, Kedar Nath Ram Nath, Meerut.
4. Sharma, P.D., 1997. Ecology and Environment, Rastogi Publications, Meerut.
5. Trivedi, P.R., 1999. Encyclopaedia of Ecology and Environment, 1-10, Indian Institute of Ecology and Environment, New Delhi.
6. Jain Suman, 2005. Disaster Management, Prachi Publication, Delhi.

18

Disaster Management in India (A Case Study on Cyclone and Flood)

Ashutosh Agnihotri
Research Scholar
P.P.N. College
Kanpur

India has been traditionally vulnerable to natural disasters to account of its unique geo-climatic conditions Flood, droughts, cyclones earthquakes and landslides have been a recurrent phenomena. About 60% of the landmass is prone to earthquakes of various intensities; over 40 million hectares is prone to floods; about 8% of the total area is prone to cyclones and 68% of the area is susceptible to drought. In the decade 1990-2000, an average of about 4344 people lost their lives and about 30 million people were affected by disasters every year. The loss in terms of private, community and public assets has been astronomical.

At the global level, there has been considerable concern over natural disasters. Even as substantial scientific and material progress is made, the loss of lives and property due to disaster has not decreased. In fact, the human toll and economic losses have mounted. It was in this background that the United Nations General Assembly, in 1989. declared 1990-2000 as the international Decade for Natural Disaster Reduction with the objective to reduce loss of lives and property and restrict socio-economic damage thought concerted international action, specially in developing countries.

The super cyclone in Orissa in October, 1999 and the Bhuj earthquake in Gujrat in January, 2001 underscored the need to adopt a multi dimensional endeavor involving diverse scientific engineering, financial and social processes the need to adopt multi disciplinary and multi sectoral approach and incorporation of risk reduction in the developmental plans and strategies. Over the past couple of years, the Government of India have brought about a paradigm shift in the approach to disaster management. The new approach proceeds from the conviction that development cannot be sustainable unless disaster mitigation is built into the development process. Another corner stone of the approach is that mitigation has to be multi-disciplinary spanning across all sectors of development. the new policy also emanates from the belief that investments in mitigation are much more cost effective that expenditure on relief and rehabilitation.

Disaster management occupies an important place in this country's policy frameworks as it is the poor and the under privileged who are worst affected on account of calamities/ disasters. With the above mentioned institutional mechanism and policy framework. It is expected that the task of moving towards vulnerability reduction will be greatly facilitated.

In India cyclone, flood, earthquake drought are the major natural disaster.

Cyclone

Tropical Cyclones are intense low pressure systems which develop over sea. They are capable of causing immense damage due to strong winds heavy rains and storm surges. The frequency of the TC in the Bay of Bengal is 4 of 5 times more than in the Arabian Sea. About 35% of initial disturbances in the north Indian ocean reach TC strage of which 45% become severe.

Indian Meteorological Department (IMD) mandated to monitor and give warnings regarding Tropical Cyclone (TC). Monitoring process has been revolutionized by the advent of remote sensing techniques. A TC intensity analysis and forecast scheme has been worked our using satellite image interpretation techniques which facilitate forecasting of storm surges.

Dynamic forecasting of TCS requires knowledge of the vertical structure of both the Cyclone and the surrounding environment. The rawin sonde remains the principal equipment for sounding. The Doppler Radar wing profiler provides hourly soundings. A mesosphere, stratosphere (MST) radar has also been installed at Thirupati. Another profiler is being developed and will be deployed at IMD Pune. Another important source of upper level data is the aircraft reports. Increasing number of commercial jet aircraft are equipped with the Aircraft Meteorological Data Relay system. This data is being made available is also being used by the IMD for analysis and predictions.

Radars have been used to observe TCS since long. Surveillance of the spiral rain bands and the eye of the TC is important function of the coastal radars. 10 Cyclones Detection Radars have already been installed. These radars are providing useful estimates of centres upto to range 300-400 km. Doppler radar provide direct measurements of wind fields in TCS. INSAT data has also been used to study the structures of different TCS in the Bay of Bengal.

Flood

Flooding is caused by the inadequate capacity within the banks of the rivers to contain the high flow brought down from the upper catchments due to heavy rainfall. It is also caused by accumulation of water resulting from heavy spells of rainfall over areas, which have got poor drainage characteristic.

Flooding is accentuated by erosion and silting leading to meandering of the rivers in plains and reduction in carrying capacity of the river channel. It is also aggravated by earthquakes and land slides, leading to changes in river course and obstruction to flow. Synchronization of flood in the main rivers and tributaries and retardation of flow due to tidal effects lead to major floods. Cyclones bring in their wake considerable loss of life and property.

The flood forecasting and warning system is used for alerting the likely damage centres well in advance of the actual arrival of floods, to enable the people to move and also to remove the moveable property to safer places or to raised platforms specially

Constructed for the Purpose

A beginning in scientific flood forecasting was made in November, 1958 by Central Water Commission (them known as Central Water & Power Commission) when a Flood Forecasting Centre was set up at its Headquarters, at Delhi, for giving timely Forecasts and Warning of the incoming floods to the villages located in the river areas around the National Capital, Delhi. The network has been expanding and by now the Flood forecasting Network of the Central Water Commission (CWC) covers all the major flood prone inter-state river basins in the country.

Disaster Prevention and Mitigation

The Yokohama message emanating from the international decade for natural disaster reduction in May, 1994 underlined the need for an emphatic shift in the strategy for disaster mitigation. It was inter alia stressed that disaster prevention, mitigation, preparedness and relief are four elements which contribute to and gain, from the implementation of the sustainable development policies. These elements alongwith environment protection and sustainable development , are closely inter related. Therefore nations should incorporate them in their development plans and ensure efficient follow up measures at the community sub-regional, regional, national and international levels. The Yokhohama Strategy also emphasized that disaster prevention, mitigation and preparedness are better than disaster response in achieving. the goals and objectives of vulnerability reduction. Disaster response alone is not sufficient as it yields only temporary results at a very high cost. Prevention and mitigation contribute to lasting improvement is safety and are essential to integrated disaster management.

The Govenment of India have adopted mitigation and preventions essential components of their development strategy. The Tenth Five Year plan document has detailed chapter of Disaster Management. The plan emphasizes the fact that development process. Each State is supposed to prepare a plan scheme for disaster mitigation in accordance with the approach outlined in the plan. In brief mitigation is being institutionalized into developmental planning.

Finance Commission makes recommendations with regard to devolution of funds between the Central Government and State Government as also outlays for relief and rehabilitation. the earlier finance Commission were mandated to look at relief and rehabilitation. The Terms of Reference of the Twelfth Finance Commission have been changed and the Finance Commission has been mandated to look at the requirements for mitigation and prevention apart from its existing mandate of looking at relief and rehabilitation. A memorandum has been submitted to the Twelveth Finance Commission after Consultation with States. The Memorandum proposes a Mitigation Fund.

Measures for flood mitigation were taken from 1950 onwards. As against the Total of 40 million hectares prone to floods, area of about 15 million hectares have been protected by construction of embankments. A number of dams and barrages have been constructed. The State Governments have been assisted to take up mitigation programmes like construction of raised platforms etc. Floods continue to be menace however mainly because of the huge quantum of silt being carried by the rivers emanating from the

Himalayas. This silt has raised the bed level in many rivers to above the lever of the countryside. Embankments have also gives rise to problems of drainage with heavy rainfall leading to water logging in areas outside the embankment. Due to erratic behavior of monsoons, both low and medium rain fall regions, which constitute about 68% of the total area, are vulnerable to periodical flood.

Preparedness

Mitigation and preparedness measures go hand in hand for vulnerability reduction and rapid professional response to disasters. The Bhuj earthquake in January, 2001 brought out several inadequacies in the system. The search and rescue teams had not been trained professionally ; specialized dog squad to look for live bodies under the debris were not available and there was no centralized resource inventory for emergency response. Although army played a pivotal role in search and rescue and also set up their hospital after the collapse of Government hospital at Bhuj. the need for fully equipped mobile hospitals with trained personnel was felt acutely. Despite these constraints, the response was fairly well organized. However, had these constraints been taken care of before hand. the response would have been even more professional and rapid which may have reduced the loss of lives. Specialist search and rescue teams from other countries did reach Bhuj. However, precious time was lost and even with these specialist teams it was not possible to cover all severely affected areas as quickly as the Government would have desired. it was therefore, decided that we should removes these inadequacies and be in a stage of preparedness at all times.

The Central Government are now in the process of training and equipping 96 specialist search and rescue teams, with each team consisting of 45 personnel including doctors, paramedics, structural engineers etc, Ten teams have already been trained. These teams will be located at various centres around the country for specialised response. These teams will have the latest equipments as also dog squads for locating survirors in the debris.

Apart from specialist search & rescue units, it has been decided that personnel of Central Police organization should also be imparted training in searchm and rescue so that they can be requisitioned to the site of incident without loss of time. Pending arrival of the specialist teams, the battalions located near the site of incident would deployed immediately. For this purpose a curriculum has been drawn up and integrated into the training curriculum of CPMFs.

The states have also been advised to set up their own specialist teams for responding to disasters. Assistance will be provided to the State Government for training their trainers at the national institutes already designated for this purpose. The state Government search and rescue teams to be constituted from State Governments have been authorised to utilize 10% of the annual allocation made under the contingency Relief fund for purchase of equipments.

Fourteen Regional Response Centres are being set up in different parts of the country. these centres will have response teams and equipment and resources for being able to response to any hazard/calamity in the neighbouring States.

A Steering committee has been constituted in the Ministry to oversee the creation of capabilities for emergency response.

A 200 bedded mobile hospital, fully trained and equipped is being set up by the Ministry of Health and attached to a leading Government hospital in Delhi. Three additional mobile hospitals with all medical and emergency equipments are propsed to be located in different part of the country. These mobile hospitals will also be attached to the leading Government hospitals in the country. This will enable the mobile hospitals to extend assistance to the hospitals with which they are attached in normal time.

CONCLUSION

Disaster Management has to be a multi-disciplinary and pro-active approach. Besides various measures for putting in place institutional and policy framework, disaster prevention, mitigation and preparedness enunciated in this paper and initiatives being taken by the Central and State Government, the community, civil society organisations and media also have a key role to play in achieving our goal of moving together a safer India. The message being put across is that, in order to move towards safer and sustainable national development projects should be sensitive towards disaster mitigation.

Our mission should be vulnerability reduction to all types of hazards, be it natural or manmade. This is not an easy task to achieve, keeping in view the vast population and the multiple natural hazards to which this country is exposed However, if we are firm in our conviction and resolve that the Government and the people of this country are not prepared to pay the price in terms of massive casualties and economic losses, the task, though is achievable and we shall achieve it.

We should take the first but significant steps towards vulnerability reduction, putting in place prevention and mitigation measures and preparedness for a rapid and professional response. With a massive awareness generation campaign and building up of capabilities as well as institutionalization of the entire mechanism through a techno legal and techno financial framework, we are gradually moving in the direction of sustainable development.

REFERENCE

1. Disaster management by G.K. Ghosh, A.P.H. Publishing Corporation.
2. Disaster management by R.B. Singh, Rawat Pubications.
3. Disaster management Through the New Millennium by Ayaz Ahmad.

4. Emergency medical Services and Disaster Management: A Holistic Approach By P.K.Dave

5. Disaster management by B Narayan A.P.H. Publishing Corporation.

6. Modern Encyclopedia of Disaster and Hazard Management By B.C.Bose Rajat Publications.

7. Disaster management by Nikuj Kumar Alfa Publications.

8. Environmental Studies by Savindra Singh, Prayag Publications House Allahabad. P.P. 346-348.

9. Physical Geography by D.S. Lal Prayag Publications House Allahabad. P.P. 120-125.

Disasters Management and States

19

Orissa: The Disaster Capital Of India

Dr. Ranjana Bajpai,
Assistant Professor
Department of Geography
D.B.S. College, Kanpur.

Introduction

Located on the east coast of India, Orissa is blessed with a rich mineral wealth, forests, lakes and rivers, besides being home to a large number of indigenous people. But, with around 85 percent of Orissa's 37 million people living in the rural areas, the state is the second poorest in the country having one of the lowest levels of urbanization. Ever since independence, Orissa has been one of the most poor states and currently over 45% of the state's population lives below the poverty line, despite its rich natural and cultural heritage(India: Transition in Orissa, 2006). With an annual Per Capita Income of Rs. 13, 329 in 2004-2005, Orissa is ranked 17th among all states. Much has been said and written about Orissa's deplorable state of economy. Pradhan (1979) feels its poverty can be explained by the frequent incidences of natural disasters like floods, droughts and cyclones. Over the years these incidences have directly or indirectly affected the development efforts in the state.

Vulnerability to Natural Disasters

Orissa is quite often called as disaster capital of India. According to Orissa State Disaster Management Authority

(OSDMA), natural disasters kill about 1300 people every year in Orissa. The state has lost nearly 50,000 people in natural hazards like floods, cyclones, lightning and heat wave in 38 years between 1970 and 2007. Around 30 lakh people, about 10 per cent of the State's population are annually affected by natural disasters. About 51 per cent deaths have been caused by epidemics and 32 deaths by cyclones. Lightning and heat waves each account 6 per cent of total number of lives followed by flood (3 %) and fire (2 %)(Book on Super Cyclone released, 2009). According to Orissa State Disaster Management Authority (OSDMA), natural disasters kill about 1300 people every year in Orissa. On account of widespread exposure to natural hazards and disasters, on an average more than 36,000 houses are fully destroyed and more than 85,000 houses are partially destroyed per year. In Orissa, the loss of property during the period 1970-2007 on account of disasters has been estimated at Rs. 8,814 crore with an annual average of Rs. 232 crore. During this period 83 per cent of property loss has occurred due to floods, followed by 15 per cent due to cyclone and 2 per cent due to fire.

Orissa is vulnerable to multiple disasters. Its sub-tropical location makes it prone to sporadic natural disasters like tropical cyclones, storm surges, tsunamis, floods, droughts and even heat waves that damage the crops, cattle and human habitats alike. Floods, tropical cyclones, fires and health hazards are the worst disasters, claiming around 88% of the total lives lost to disasters. While floods and cyclones are common in the coastal districts of Orissa, Western Orissa is prone to acute droughts; a large part of the State is also prone to earthquakes. In addition, the State is also affected by disasters like heat waves, epidemics, forest fire, road accidents etc.

The history of disasters in Orissa substantiates the fact that about 80% of the State is prone to one or more forms of natural disasters. Over more than a century, the state has been declared disaster prone for not less than 95 years. Floods have occurred for 50 years, droughts for 32, and cyclones have stuck the state for 11years. Since 1965, these calamities have not only become more frequent, they are striking areas that have never experienced such conditions before. For instance, a heat wave in 1998 killed around 2,200 people: most of the casualties were from Coastal Orissa, a region known for its moderate climate. Since 1998, almost 3,000 people died due to heat stroke.

The 1999 super cyclone affected places like Bhubaneswar and Nayagarh, which were never traditionally cyclone-prone. While the 2001 drought parched fields in coastal districts, the unprecedented floods of 2001 submerged 25 of the 30 districts of the state. Many of these areas had never witnessed floods before. Between 1963 and 1999, Orissa experienced 13 major disasters, which killed 22,228 people and rendered 34, 21,000 people homeless. During 1997-2002, Orissa saw a series of disasters. Between 2003-2003, the entire state experienced a severe drought. The total loss of livelihood and damage to capital stock due to disasters from 1998 to 2003 was around Rs. 13, 230.47 crore, as the Tenth Plan document of the Government of Orissa reveals. Natural disasters have seriously affected livelihoods in the state and the income level of households (Mahapatra, 2006).

Common Natural Disasters

A close look into each of these disasters reveals how Orissa has become disaster capital of India with far reaching socio-economic implications.

Floods

Floods are the most recurrent disasters in the State. On an average, nearly 16 lakh people are exposed every year to flood risk and Kendrapara, Jajpur, Balasore, Bhadrak, Puri and Cuttack have relatively higher vulnerability. Before draining into the Bay of Bengal, all the major rivers of Orissa flow over long distances. The topography of the state, the drainage system with low channel capacity, low flood slope, sand bank mouths and high concentration of rainfall in a very short period in the catchment area are the prominent factors that determine the intensity of floods inundating the rivers. Heavy rainfall during monsoon causes floods in the rivers. Around 80% of its total annual rainfall is concentrated over a period of three months. Flow of water from neighbouring States of Jharkhand and Chattisgarh also contributes to flooding. The flat coastal belts with poor drainage, high degree of siltation of the rivers, soil erosion, breaching of the embankments and spilling of floodwaters over them, cause severe floods in the river basin and delta areas of the state. Rivers such as the Mahanadi, Subarnarekha, Brahmani, Baitarani, Rushikulya, Vansadhara and their many tributaries and branches flowing through the State expose vast areas to floods. Of these, damages are caused due to floods mainly in the Mahanadi, the Brahmani, and the Baitarani. These rivers have a common delta where flood waters mix together, and when flooded simultaneously, inflict extensive destruction. This problem becomes even more acute when floods coincide with high tide. The water level rises due to deposits of silt on the river-bed. Rivers often overflow their banks or water rushes through new channels causing heavy damages. Floods and drainage congestion also affect the lower reaches along the Subarnarekha.

A chronology of floods in Orissa clearly depicts the frequency of this natural disaster. During a hundred-year period from 1868-1967, there were 262 flood events in the state, of which 68 were high floods, 77 medium floods and 117 low floods(Sarangi and Penthoi, 2005). Mahanadi river has the distinction of having most floods, that is, 99 times, followed by Baitarani (86 times) and Brahmani (77 times) (Sarangi and Penthoi, 2005). Yearwise, 1881, 1894, 1896, 1907, 1920, 1926, 1927, 1934, 1940, 1941, 1943, 1955,

Table 1
Recent Floods in Orissa and the Damage Caused

	2006	*2007*	*2008*	*2009*
No. of Districts Affected	27	12(July) 15(Aug) 10(Sept)	21	15
Population Affected (in Lakh)	67.39	78.14	60.17	3.94
Human Lives Lost	105	91	110	56
Crop Area Affected(in Lakh Ha)	4.65	3.18	N.A.	1.29

Source: Compiled from OSDMA website www.osdma.org

1960, 1961 were the prominent as far as grimness of the situation is concerned. During the last 25 years, floods have occurred 12 times with varying intensity.

Table 1 presents recent incidences of floods in the state. Of late the floods have been more sporadic, even occurring in districts which had traditionally been drought prone. The floods of 2008, (especially in the month of September) were unprecedented, causing a significant loss of life and property. During September, 19 districts namely, Angul, Bargarh, Bhadrak, Bolangir, Boudh, Cuttack, Gajapati, Jagatsinghpur, Jajpur, Kalahandi, Kendrapara, Keonjhar, Khurda, Nayagarh, Puri, Rayagada, Sambalpur ,Nuapara and Subarnapur were seriously affected. The severity of September flood was considered to be at par with the floods of 1982.

The vulnerability to floods is enhanced by a high population density especially of the coastal regions, encroachment on the flood plains, poor infrastructure as well as socio-economic conditions and a greater frequency of mud houses. The official website of the government of Orissa identifies 1.40 lakh hectares to be flood prone out of a total geographical area of 15.751 lakh hectares.

Droughts

Like floods, droughts too are common in the state. In fact, many a times both occur simultaneously. The droughts in the State occur with varying magnitude & proportion because of variability of rainfall, sometimes affecting the entire state, sometimes a few regions, and sometimes a few districts. In other words, one or the other region experiences drought every year. Historical data reveals that the first drought of severe nature that struck the State was in 1866 & ever since this till now, drought of moderate to severe nature has been experienced 17 times. This indicates that drought of moderate to severe nature occurs in Orissa once in almost 8 years duration on an average(Ota, 2001). The Subdivisions of Padampur, Bolangir, Titlagarh, Patnagarh, Nuapada, Khariar, Bhwanipatna and Phulbani comprising of 47 blocks have been identified as drought prone zone. Looking at the chronology of drought, it is observed that drought of very severe nature has been experienced by the state on four occasions: 1866, 1919, 1965 & 2000-2001.

Orissa is predominantly an agricultural state with only 35% of the area having irrigation facility and the rest depending on rainfall. The rainfall deficiency in the monsoon season varied from 26 - 36%, seven times during the last 35 years causing severe droughts and crop loss. Droughts in Orissa generally occur during Kharif season and are harmful to paddy crop - the main cereal crop. The impact of drought is mainly felt in the field of agriculture, resulting in loss of production. It also creates problem of irrigation and drinking water, loss of employment, scarcity of essential commodities, migration of farm labourers, rural indebtedness etc. Keeping this in mind, more stress is being given on minor irrigation, crop diversification, soil and water conservation and rainwater harvesting in these regions.

Cyclones

Orissa is more vulnerable to cyclones than any other coastal States of India because it belongs to cyclonic zone. This is what an analysis of cyclonic disturbances recorded in the country during 106 years. In the last century (between 1901 and 2007), There were nearly 323 cyclonic disturbances along the Orissa coast. Of 323 disturbances, 75 per cent are depressions, storms (18 per cent) and severe storms (7 per cent). Orissa is always vulnerable to cyclones in April-May and September-November. The largest number of depressions (7) occurred in 1927, the largest number of storms (4) in 1934 and maximum number of severe storms (3) in 1973. The severe storms of 1909, 1910, 1912, 1914, 1967, 1971, 1973 and 2009 are known to have inflicted terrible damage and devastations on the State (Orissa more vulnerable to cyclones, 2009). Orissa has experienced around 952 small and big cyclones and 451 tornadoes between 1891 and 1970. From 1901 to 1981 there were 380 cyclones, of which 272 resulted from depressions in the Bay of Bengal.

Once every few decades a super cyclone strikes Orissa. The number of cyclonic disturbances has come down from 1980 onwards along the east coast. However, towards the last part of century, the 1999 super cyclone turned out to be an event of the most terrifying magnitude of century. Other Super Cyclones that hit Orissa in the last Century were in 1942 and 1971. The Super Cyclone of 1999 killed about 10,000; affected over 15 million people and 1733000 hectares of total agricultural land. Around 97 blocks, 12 districts, 1846 Gram Panchayats, 14000 villages/wards and 1650086 households were severly affected, claiming as much life and property(Sarangi and Penthoi, 2005).

Orissa State Disaster Management Authority (OSDMA)

Natural disasters can not be averted, only mitigated by capacity building among people. The immediate aftermath of the Super-cyclone in 1999 saw the Orissa State Disaster Mitigation Authority (OSDMA) being set up by the Government of Orissa as an autonomous organization on 28th December 1999. It was registered under the Societies Registration Act, 1860 on 29.12.1999 as a non-profit making and charitable institution for the interest of the people of Orissa, with its headquarters at Bhubaneswar and jurisdiction over the whole State. It came under the Department of Revenue in August 2000. Subsequently, the name of the Authority was changed from Orissa State Disaster Mitigation Authority to Orissa State Disaster Management Authority in September 2008.

The Authority has the mandate to take up the mitigation activities as well as the relief, restoration, reconstruction and other measures in the event of a disaster. These activities cover the entire range of disaster management including preparedness activities like coordinating with the line departments involved in reconstruction, coordinate with bilateral and multi-lateral aid agencies, coordinating with UN Agencies, International, National and State-level NGOs and networking with similar other organizations for disaster management.

CONCLUSION

Orissa is vulnerable to multiple natural disasters like tropical cyclones, storm surges, tsunamis, floods, droughts and even heat waves that damage the crops, cattle, human habitats and urban infrastructure alike. As a leading authority, OSDMA reaches out to people with relief and rehabilitation. It also helps in capacity building among the people for an effective and sustained response to such natural calamities. An efficient system for mitigating natural disasters is the only way out as preventing them is beyond human control.

REFERENCES

"Book on Super Cyclone released (2009)", *The Hindu*, Friday, Oct 30.

India: Transition in Orissa(2006), www.worldbank.org.in/.../0,,contentMDK:21877366~pagePK:1497618~piPK:217854~theSitePK:295584,00.html, Accessed27th December 2009.

Mahapatra, Richard(2006), "Disaster Dossier: The impact of Climate Change on Orissa", *InfoChange News and Features*, March.

Natural Disasters kill 1,300 each year in Orissa: Report, http://www.theindian.com/newsportal/uncategorized/natural-disasters

Ota, Akhil,B.(2001), "Orissa Drought 2001: Its Magnitude and Consequences", Paper presented at the conference *Livelihoods and Poverty Reduction: Lessons From Eastern India*, 25-27 September 2001.

"Orissa more vulnerable to cyclones (2009)", *The Hindu*, Saturday, Oct 31.

Pradhan, N.B.(1979), *Economic Backwardness and Development of Orissa*, unpublished Ph.D. Thesis submitted to Berhampur University, Orissa.

Sarangi, P. and G.C. Penthoi(2005), "Economic Implications of Natural Disasters in Orissa: A Retrospective View", Orissa Review, June: 12-16.

http://www.orienvis.nic.in/disaster.asp

www.orissapanchayat.gov.in/English/SuccessStories.asp

20

Disater Management in Uttar Pradesh

Ms.Lalita Salvia
Dept Of Geography
I.T.College Lucknow

The Indian sub continent due to its unique geographical locational and geological features has the distinction of being one of the most vulnerable areas to natural hazards. Causing colossal losses of life and property. The country is visited by almost all kinds of natural disasters like floods, cyclones, droughts, earthquakes, landslides, avalanches, forest fires and the like . Disasters seem to occur with a strange regularity and multiple disasters striking simultaneously in different parts of the country are not uncommon. While floods might devastate one part of the country another areas might be reeling under drought conditions causing severe economic and social tension.

Introduction

With the tropical climate and unstable lanaforms, coupled with high population density, poverty and illiteracy and lack of adequate infrastrucure, India is one of the most Vulnerable developing countries to suffer very often from various natural disasters, namely, drought flood cyclone, earthquake, landslide, forestfire,hailstorm, volcanic eruption, etc. which strike causing a devastating impact on human life, economy and environment. Though it is almost impossible fully recoup the damage caused by the disasters, it is possible to:

(i) Minimize the potential risks,

(ii) Prepare and develop resilience to such disasters,

(iii) Mobilize resources including communication and telemedical services,

(iv) To help in rehabilitation and post- disaster reconstruction.

Space technology plays a crucial role in efficient mitigation of disasters. While communication satellites help in disaster warning, relief mobilization and tele-medical support, earth observation satellites provide database for pre-preparedness programmes, disaster response, monitoring activities and post disaster damage assessment and reconstruction and rehabilitation.

Various disasters like earthquakes, landslides, volcanic eruptions, fires, flood and cyclones kill thousands of people and destroy billions of dollars of habitat and property each year. The rapid growth of population and its increased concentration, often in hazardous environment has escalated both the frequency and severity of natural disasters.

Asia tops the list of causalities due to natural disasters .Among various natural hazards, earthquakes, landslides, floods and cyclones are the major disasters adversely affecting large areas and population in the Indian sub-continent. These natural disasters are of

(i) Geophysical origin, such as earthquakes, volcanic eruptions, landslides, etc.

(ii) Climatic origin, such as drought, flood, cyclones, forest fires, etc.

Though it may not be feasible to control nature and to stop the development of natural phenomena but the efforts could be made to avoid disasters and alleviate their effects on human lives, infrastructure and property. Rising frequency, amplitude and number of natural disasters and attendant problem coupled with loss of human lives prompted the General Assembly of the United Nations to proclaim 1990s as the International Decade for Natural Disaster Reduction (IDNDR,) through a resolution 44/236 on December 22, 1989 to focus on all issues related to natural disaster reduction.

It is possible to reduce the impact of disasters by adopting suitable disaster mitigation strategies The disaster mitigation works mainly address the potential risks by developing disaster early warning strategies, prepare and implement developmental plans to provide resilience to such disasters, mobilize resources including communication and telemedical services and to help in rehabilitation and post-disaster reduction.

Disaster management on the other hand involves pre—disaster planning, preparedness, monitoring, including relief management capability, prediction, on early warning, damage assessment and relief management.

Scope of Disaster Management

The term 'Disaster Management "encompasses the complete realm of disaster related activities. Traditionally, people tend to think of disaster management only in terms of the post disaster actions taken by relief and reconstruction officials; yet disaster management covers a much broader scope and many modern disaster managers may find themselves far more involved in pre-disaster activities than in post- disaster response. This is because many persons who work in development field or who plan routine economic urban, regional or agricultural development project have disaster management responsibilities eg. housing specialists planning a low income housing project in a disaster prone-area have the opportunity to mitigate the impact of future disaster if the houses incorporate disaster resistant construction technologies. In fact, in dealing with natural hazards, the vast majority of disaster management actions are related to development projects; only a small portion are related to emergency response.

Definition of Disaster Management

'Disaster management 'can be defined as the range of activities designed t maintain control over disaster and emergency situation and to provide a framework for helping at-risk persons to avoid or recovery from the impact of the disaster. Disaster management deals with situations that occur prior to, during, and after the disaster.

Objectives of Disastger Management

(i) To reduce or avoid the human , physical, and economic losses suffered by individuals, by the society and by the country at large.

(ii) To reduce personal sufferings

(iii) To speed recovery

When assisting refugees or displaced persons, a fourth objective is also added, To provide protection to victims or persons whose lives or property are threatened by armed conflict, tribal animosity religious persecutions etc.

Element of Disaster Management

A Disaster Manager must deal with six distinct sets of activities in order to affect successfully the course of events related to disasters. Known as the elements of disaster management, these include:

- Risk management
- Loss management
- Control management of events
- Equity of assistance
- Resource management
- Impact reduction

Risk Management

Consists of identifying threat (hazard likely to occur,), determining their probability of occurrence, estimating the impact on communities at-risk, determining measures that can reduce the risk and taking action to reduce the threat.

Risk management includes:

(1) Hazard mapping

(2) Vulnerability mapping

(3) Estimation of potential losses like physical infrastructure, agricultural losses, economic losses

(4) Development of appropriate disaster prevention and mitigation strategies.

Risk management is accompanied by lessening the effects of the natural hazards or by taking actions in normal development projects that will reduce the risks to an acceptable level, eg. If flooding is determined to be a major risk, the effect can be reduced by physical measures such as dams, flood control, embankments, or channeling of the streams. Risk can also be reduced by moving the flood zone to those that could absorb flood losses (such as, forestry or agriculture).

Loss Management

Loss in disaster include human, structural and economic losses. It addresses each of these through both pre and post disaster actions designed to keep losses to a minimum. The most effective loss management activities prior to disaster and are focused reducing the society vulnerability to the disaster.

Action Includes

(1) Improving the resistance of building and physical structures in the event of disaster

(2) Providing improved safety for the occupants of building settlements situated in hazardous areas.

(3) Increasing and/or diversifying the network of social support mechanisms available to victims and communities in threatened areas.

Post disaster loss management focuses on improving the

response and broadening the range of support given to victims . This includes facilitating relief delivery and stimulating rapid recovery. These are accomplished through emergency preparedness like the estimation of post disaster needs and development of approaches and programmes to speed relief response, warning and evacuation of persons at-risk.

1. The provision of emergency assistance, to help reduce the impact of losses.
2. Reconstruction, to lessen the economic burden of long term recovery.

Control of Events

The critical elements of disaster management is the control of events during and after the emergency. Control is maintained through the fallowing measures:

1. Anticipation of a disaster and the cause and effect relationship generated by each type of event.
2. Mitigation or reduction of the scope of a disaster. It is the most important function in bringing disaster under control.
3. Preparedness by reviewing the anticipated scope of a disaster, managers can plan adequate responses, develop organizational procedures, and prepare to meet the need that are going to arise.
4. Accurate information collection and assessment
5. A balanced response depending on the type of strategy required.
6. Leadership- disaster management should lead rather than follow public action.

Resource Management

Few disaster managers have adequate resources to meet all the competing needs and demands of a post- disaster response. The disaster manager must be familiar with the resources available and make full use of it.

Impact Reduction

Disasters can have an impact far beyond the immediate human physical or economic losses in a very real sense; disasters represent a loss of opportunity not only to individuals but also to entire societies. They can also be serious setback to the country's entire development program. The impact of disaster on individuals and their society should be reduced to a minimum.

Thus, with the development of technology man has been provided with the power to, if not control nature, at least to predict its mood. This is the role of disaster management.

Type of Disasters

Ever since its formation earth has been under going various changes:

both slow and catas trophic. Changes that affect humans adversely are called natural hazards .Some of them are volcanic eruptions, earthquakes, droughts floods cyclones soil erosion, snow avalanches etc. These are caused by natural process occurring in the environment irrespective of human activity.

Sometimes natural hazards are also called natural disasters (French Des meaning 'bad' and aster meaning 'Star 9. in the past these destructive and catastrophic natural changes were considered punishment given by nature for interfering with it.

The World Bank defines disaster ac an extraordinary event of limited duration which causes serious disruption of economy of the country. Disasters can be classified on the basis of their origin as:

1. Meteorological ('hurricanes, cyclones, floods, droughts)
2. Topographical (landslides avalanches)
3. Tectonic (earthquakes volcanoes)
4. Infestic(locust invasion of crops, epidemics)
5. Human ('industrial accidents, nuclear bombs)

The intensity of disasters is governed by the following factors:

1. Historical and social conditions and the level of economic development of a country or a regional affect their vulnerability, in developing countries even potentially modest hazards may prove disastrous. A developed country can tackle disasters easily in comparison to a country with poor economy.
2. The scope of damage that natural hazards may cause depends upon the type of land use. Damage by an earthquake in a desert is less than the damage caused in a densely populated area.
3. The scope of disasters depends upon the geographical position of the country for eg. Coastal areas of Andhra Pradesh and Orissa are prone to cyclones than centrally located Madhya Pradesh.

A natural hazard is an unexpected phenomenon of usual magnitude which occur in proximity and poses a threat to people structures and economic assets caused by biological geological seismic hydrological or meteorological condition or processes in natural environment.

The human induced hazards are caused by human activity such as nuclear explosion, fire, industrial or vehicular accidents etc leading to loss of life property and create serious disruption of human activity.

Types of Disasters

1. Earthquakes: are considered one of the worst natural hazards which often turn into disaster causing wide spread destruction and loss to human lives. The most devastating earthquakes are of tectonic origin 'They are associated with large scale strain in the crust of the earth. There may be earthquakes caused by volcanic eruptions rock bursts subsidence in mines. Damages caused by such earthquakes are confined to small areas.

Magnitude and intensity: are two ways of measuring the strength of an earthquake. The magnitude measured on the Richter scale is a measure of the seismic energy radiated by an earthquake. The intensity is the measure of the damage caused by an earth quake. The Indian Metrological Department has divided the country into 5 zones:

(i) Zone I- No Risk,

(ii) Zone II- Low Risk,

(iii) Zone ill-Moderate Risk,

(iv) Zone IV- High Risk,

(v) Zone V- Very high risk,

From the earthquake point of view, very high risk areas in India are the Himalayan mountains, north eastern India, kachchh west coast around Ratnagiri and Andaman and Nicobar islands. The high risk areas are Ganga plains and western Rajasthan.

Consequences of Earthquake

An earthquake becomes hazard when it hits the populated area. The impact of an earthquake is always disastrous. Passage of surface waves produce fissures through which sometimes water floods out. A marked change can be observed on he drainage system of an area. Rivers sometimes change their courses and use floods. Landslides occur causing destruction. Man made structures are not spared from earthquake hazards. Roads, railways, bridges and telephone lines are destroyed. Earth quakes have worst effect on towns and cities because of high rise buildings and huge agglomeration of human population.

Floods

Floods are major causes of human misery in India every year. Out of a number of natural disasters that the country has experienced, floods are the most important one. India is the most flood affected country in the world next only to Bangladesh. In spite of the fact that floods are a natural disaster, it often turns out to be a social disaster as the people who are severely affected by are generally the poor because they live on the periphery of human habitat the flood affected areas and damages have also increased recently. The reason for this increase in the encroachment of floodplain by the people.

The most flood prone basins in the country are those of the gang-in Uttar Pradesh , Bihar west Bengal the Bramhaputra -in Assam, Baitarni, Brahmani and the Subarnrekha basins in Orissa. Some times floods occur also in Andhra Pradesh Rajasthan Haryana and Gujarat.

Floods occur when a river overflows its banks and spread out over the bordering flood plain. India has a large number of rivers that overflow in certain seasons. The rivers of north and central India are prone to floods during the monsoon seasons, they occur when the surface runoff is high, drainage water Is blocked by landslides or excessive silt is deposited in the river beds. Flash floods in arid areas are associated with cyclones storms. The coastal belts of India get flooded with the occurrence of cyclones.

Flood Control

Floods are not new in India. The practice of building flood protection embankments along the rivers is an ancient one. We had flood protection embankments on the Godavri , Krishna and the Kaveri deltas and the Indo Gangetic plain. The nationwide flood protection programmes began only after independence.

Reducing Impact of Flood

The building of embankments was only the way floods can be controlled in forties. The dams and reservoirs were useful to control runoff and reduce flooding. Severity of flood can be reduced by controlling of deforestation on mountain slopes and in catchment areas. Weather forecast and flood warning system be made a regular feature.

Droughts

Droughts can occur in any area regardless of the amount of rainfall the may receive or irrespective of its scientific and Social advancement. It can occur over a large area, drought can occur at anyplace and time and cause scarcity of water for drinking, irrigation, industry and urban needs. Drought causes deficiency in soil moisture and make the land unproductive. This causes damage to the crops. Droughts are caused by the failure of monsoon or when. it is delayed or arrives early and withdraw without giving rain.

Drought and aridity are closely related and both indicate a shortage of water. Aridity is a permanent condition where drought is. a temporary situation. Arid and semi- arid regions are prone to drought. Drought based on their causes nature and character are classified as:

(i) Metrological drought.' exists when the average annual rainfall is 25% less than usual

(ii) Hydrological drought: is one when the water level in the surface and ground falls.

(iii) Agricultural drought: occurs when the soil moisture goes below the level needed to sustain plant growth.

(iv) Ecological draught: occurs when the productivity of a natural ecosystem fails and causes environmental damage like the death of a large number of cattle, wildlife or trees in the forests.

The main cause of drought is inadequate and uneven distribution of rainfall. West and Central India face an uncertainty of rainfall which they receive in the monsoon season,' the rainfall triggers off hydrological and agricultural drought. About 19% of the total area of India experience drought with 12% of the population being affected by it. There are three types of drought prone areas namely:

(i) Extreme

(ii) Severe

(iii) Moderate

Drought lead to scarcity of food grains (akal) water (jalkal) fodder (tinkal) and often all of these (trikal).

Reducing Impact of Drought

Various devices of remote sensing satellite mapping and GIS

may be used identifying water aquifers. Integrated water harvesting programmes with active participation of people may also be useful. Inter basin transfer of waters from surplus to deficit areas can also mitigate water crisis to some extent e other measures may be building of small dams for collection of water afforestation and use of drought resistant crops.

Landslides

A landslide is the rapid slide of large masses of bed rocks. Landslides are triggered by earth quakes or sudden rock failures. They can also result when the base of a slope is over steepened by excavation or river erosion; severe earthquakes in mountainous regions are a major causes of landslides. A major cause which triggers off the landslides is the weight of the overlying material and the presence of lubricating material like water this is known as solifuction. Freezing and thawing of rocks a mountain slopes cause them to break and roll down the slope causing destruction.

Cyclones

Cyclones of diameter of 600 K.M. or more is destructive and dangerous atmospheric storms on the earth with about 6% of the world wide cyclones; the Indian sub continent is the worst affected areas. The damaging impact of tropical storm is due to winds of hurricane force, hurricane waves and floods caused by heavy showers majority of storms inflict heavy losses because of either strong winds or storm winds.

Reducing Impact

Improved warning system is used construction of cyclone shelters embankments dykes reservoirs and coastal of forestation help immensely.

Forest Fires

Forest fires can be natural .these can be man made either through negligence or mischief. such fires causes loss to vegetation and property great harm to environment and animal life is done. For eg. in Uttaranchal in1995 had one forest fire year affecting 93 7 sq icm (around the year).

In view of the frequency of disaster striking India, there is a need for continued vigil, preparedness and conscious efforts to reduce the occurrence and foe mitigation of impact of natural disasters. Disaster management is a fundamental component of sustainable development because the reduction of disaster loss is equivalent to the increased development. The following suggestion can be offered for an effective disaster management system in India:

1. There should be a proper multi-tier organizational structure, for disaster management in focused and co-ordinated manner. There should be specialized national, state district and village level efforts of various government and non-government agencies.
2. The basic design of disaster management should consist of planned and co-ordinated efforts in all important areas of disaster management:

- Identification and prediction
- Early warning system
- Precautionary measures
- Evacuation
- Relief
- Rescue
- Rehabilitation
- Compensation
- Reconstruction

3. There is need to share the expertise and experience so that states can learn from each other's example. There is also need for training personnel likely to face natural disasters and who deal with relief operations, eg. district-level officers, so that they can perform better in case of natural calamities.

BIBLIOGRAPHY

1. India Physical Environment (NCERT)

2. Resource Management And Environment (TN Dhar)
3. Disaster Managemen(S.L. Goel Ram Kmar)
4. Environment Geography (Sarvindra Singh)
5. Physical Geography (Sarvindra Singh)

INTERNET

Disaster Management (D.P. Rao)

Distribution Of Flood Prone Areas

IrrigationDepartment-Uttar Pradesh

World book: reducing earth quake damage

Causes of drought

Recent development towards earthquake risk reduction in India.

21

Gender Perspectives on Drought Mitigation in Rajasthan

Dr. Neelam Saraswat
Lecturer in Economics
B.S.R. Govt. Arts College, Alwar (Rajasthan)

The problem of drought has become associated with the state of Rajasthan. There is an old saying is relation is famine in the state:

"Teejo kurio, athwon akal"

that is, the state is bound to be hit by *'kuria'* or quasi-famine every third year and by *'akal'* or grave famine every eighth year.

That drought and famine are age-old problems of the state, is also reflected in the following Rajasthani *doha,* describing the districts most affected by it as:

"*Pag poongal, dhad kotde, bahu Barmer,*

Jaye lade Jodhpur, thhavo Jaiselmer."

Which means that feet of famine are in poongal (Bikaner), abdomen in Marwar (including the districts of Churu, Sikar, Jhunjhunu, Pali, Nagaur etc.), arms in Barmer. However, on searching, it can be found also in Jodhpur and that it specially belongs to Jaiselmer.

Furthermore, in the last decades drought has increasingly become more recurrent and unpredictable due to climate changes our earth is facing. Mood of monsoon still continues to be irregular during the current season. In fact, drought mitigation needs long-term strategies of monsoon management, in addition to emergency plan and alternative policies, be it foodgrains' famine (*Annakal*), water famine (*Jalkaal*), animal fodder famine (*Trankal*) and acute famine of all the three (*Trikall*). Such a long term policy is lacking so far.

It is widely observed, researched and documented that women belonging to different social classes, races, ethnic and age groups are more vulnerable than their male counter parts of the same social class/group before, during and after disasters (for example, Ariyabandu and Foenseka 2006; Rohr et al. 2009). However, the needs of women are generally overlooked in the relief and recovery processes and their capacities and skills are not used as a resource in disaster management and planning. This not only results in denial of benefits to women but also worsens their social and economic status. Thus, the need of the hour is to ensure gender-sensitivity in drought alleviation policies and measures in Rajasthan by promoting women to be increasingly involved in roles such as leadership, management and decision making, as well as recognising women's position in their community and the larger society.

Drought Problems for Women in Rajasthan:

In contrast to sudden – onset disasters, such as floods and hurricanes, which often have a dramatic impact on the population, drought is a slow-onset disaster which occurs cyclically (Branco 2000; Winchester 1992). Natural hazards such as droughts cannot be treated as the result of natural and physical forces solely, but as the result of a combination of socio-economic and political forces (Maskrey 1989, Rogge 1992; Wiest et al. 1994).

An accurate effect of the drought phenomenon cannot be ascertained unless consideration is given to the vulnerabilities of all sectors of the society, including women. The vulnerability of women should be understood to be cultural and organisational rather than biological or physiological (Wiest et al. 1994). Women hold a subordinated status within respective communities, leading to gender – based inequalities and vulnerabilities. Thus, women within the vulnerable populations can be categorised as 'vulnerable within the vulnerable' (Ariyabandu, Foensika 2006).

Rajasthan is looked at as a synonym of low status of women, male-dominated society, feudal customs and values, social polarization based on caste, illiteracy and poverty. So impact of drought is different on men and women. In order to understand the role of women in the face of drought in Rajasthan, it is important to understand their vulnerabilities and capabilities.

Work Participation of Women

According to Census of India, 2001, work participation of males is about 50 percent as against only 33.5 percent for females in Rajasthan. Women are mostly engaged in the unorganised sector. In the rural areas, women in the unorganised sector look after the cattle, work in such small scale industries as planting, sowing, knitting, embroidery, handloom and handicrafts at low wages. In the urban area in the unorganised sector women work as small traders and producers. In rural and urban areas women also work as manufacturing labourers.

Alongwith this, women do domestic work for 7-10 hours per day like cooking, collecting the fuel, fodder, arranging for water, bringing up the children. Female work, especially domestic work, is invisible and culturally not considered contributing to household income. Thus, women's work is often under-represented or not reported as work at all, though they affect the economic and social life of the state and the society.

During drought, fetching all water, fuel-wood and fodder for the communities takes 12-14 hours per day of the women. Estimate of their contribution and hardships during drought eludes the policy and planning machinery up to now.

Water Famine

Drought in the new millennium is in fact more of a water famine than 'food famine'. An unprecedented water crisis had surfaced during the drought in 2002. It was a pointer to the shape of things to come as droughts continued to occur with much more frequency and intensity in the state. During the current year (2009-10), pre-monsoon rains have not been adequate in the state. Between 1st June, 2009 to 30th September 2009, 367.62mm rainfall was recorded in the state, which was 33.61mm less than the normal rainfall (552.0 mm). Though Rajasthan accounts for 10.4 per cent of the total area and 5.5 per cent of the total population, its share in surface water is only 1 per cent.

As women arrange for water for domestic purposes, being carers of children and livestock, they suffer more during drought. Moreover, census (2001) data on distribution of workers by economic activity in Rajasthan show that 70.66 per cent of rural female workers in Rajasthan are engaged as cultivators as against 60.91 per cent male workers. Similarly, in urban areas 14.70 per cent women as against 3.96 per cent men are cultivators. Even among agricultural labourers, women workers are in higher proportion (16.84 per cent in rural areas and 6.9 per cent in urban areas) as compared to men (8.87 per cent in rural areas and 1.39 per cent in rural areas). Thus, women contribute more than men in agricultural activities of the state. Hence they face the hardships of drought more than men, even more so in rural areas.

Low Female Literacy Rate

In 2001, literacy rate among females was very low at 43.85 per cent in Rajasthan, the gender-gap in literacy being 31.85 per cent. In rural area, while female literacy rate was lower (37.33 per cent), gender gap was even higher (34.83 per cent). Thus women, particularly in the rural areas, have little opportunities to enable them to leave the agricultural occupation; irrespective of drought conditions.

Health Issues

Some gender-based health factors are also found to put women at higher risk in drought. Women suffer from iron, calcium and other nutrient deficiencies due to low meals, which lead to health problems like anemia, night-blindedness, etc. In addition women face pregnancy care problems. HIV/AIDS rates were found to increase after severe drought conditions.

Domestic Violence Issues

It is observed that alcohol consumption and violent tendencies among men increase in the aftermath of drought, as they adopt these coping mechanism to deal with loss and trauma. Thus, women and children become easy victims of domestic violence, sexual assault and trafficking. Women also face limitations in mobility due to segregation and social restrictions which require women and girls to be accompanied by males if they opt to migrate in search of alternative jobs. The hardships women have to face are compounded for those with new roles as heads of their households due to the drought-related migration of their husbands.

Above analysis of problems discerning impact of drought on women in Rajasthan indicate lack of long term policy of their alleviation. Current efforts mainly include traditional monsoon water techniques, like *johads, baories* and *tanks* and peer sex education programmes, which are being made largely by UN, AUSAID, DFIDW/NGOs.

However, women are not only victims but also agents of change. Example from the world over suggest how women and men, working together, can identify those hazards that threaten their homes and livelihoods and work together to build safer communities.

Linking Vulnerability and Capacity of Women for Drought Mitigation

A right, open-minded approach to gender – related problems is equally closely linked to the actual development of a population. In order to understand the role of women in face of the drought, it is important to understand their vulnerabilities and capacities. Vulnerability refers to the condition determined by the physical, social and environmental factors or processes which increase the susceptibility of an individual or community to the impact of hazards. The concept of vulnerability becomes clearer when consideration is given to capacities (UNISDR 2004). Capacity is a combination of all the strengths and resources available at the individual or community, society and organisational level that can reduce the level of risk or the effects of a disaster. Capacity may include physical, institutional, social or economic means as well as skilled persons and collective attributes such as leadership and management (UNISDR 2004). Women's capacities are, in Rajasthan, undermined due to patriarchal system and their invisibility, in spite of their significant contribution in economic and domestic fruitful activities, as evident from the foregoing analysis of their work participation and other drought issues. The need of the hour is to ensure gender equality in disaster reduction policies and measures by promoting women to be increasingly involved in roles such as leadership, management and decision making, as well as recognising women's position in their community and the larger society.

Women empowerment, in fact, means their direct involvement in all the matters related to the environment where they were born, where they grow up and live together with their families and children (Quagliariello, 2006). Drought is peculiar to the environment of Rajasthan, particularly its rural areas, where majority of the poor women live and work. Thus, the significance of gender-balanced and oriented response to drought risks cannot be undermined. In fact, gender mainstreaming is beginning to be a part of all the latest advanced approaches on disaster management in different parts of the world.

In disaster mitigation and reconstruction, preparedness, response and early recovery constitute the framework of policy and action recommended by UNISDR, 2005. Speaking of struggle against drought, we indirectly speak of water management and water saving, two fields where women could play a strategic role since they are extremely sensitive to all water scarcity related problems. In Rajasthan, probability of drought is very high because it occurs every 2 to 3 years. Treating drought as a social problem apart from being a technical or scientific problem, women and men should be always prepared for water management and water saving for a better use of women's time and energy, and for sanitation security and everyday life, easy access to water is essential, sensitizing women regarding the importance of steps for managing the limited resources of water and adhering to these steps, the same way as they do with their earnings, amount of food, etc., will prepare them better to cope with the risk of drought.

High rates of female illiteracy in Rajasthan demand giving education the place of primary importance in a long time policy of drought response. Education makes women aware of their surrounding environment and the limitation and opportunities such environment is ready to offer. It could alleviate difficulties and improve the capacity to manage scarcity. Knowledge gives the decision power and self-reliance and increases their self-confidence, making them aware of their active role in welfare and safety. Like all development actions, it also results in changing the traditional gender relationships in the society. Women need to be helped in building up their capabilities and skills, they need to be informed and trained because they are not merely the recipients of welfare, but active participants in the development strategy.

Women are housekeepers but we have seen that larger proportion of working women than men are cultivators in Rajasthan. Thus, their training could include not only simple rules for a better and more conscious knowledge of water management, but also competent technical information regarding irrigated agriculture and drought mitigation strategies. This would give them the opportunity to have specific qualification for a problem affecting the reality where the work and the possibility to take part in decision – making processes. Gender – blind interventions for water management not only harm environment, nutrition, health and social life of women, but are also detrimental to agriculture and the economy of the state in general. Also economic value of domestic water use has to be recognised, since women's uses of water are crucial for the survival of rural household (FAO 2002).

In drought situation, women and girls are more likely to reduce their food intake as a coping strategy in favour of their household members. Their malnutrition leads to deficiency of essential nutrients, health problems, malnutrition and morbidity of the children of pregnant and lactating mothers. Hence, effective food security and nutrition strategies require an understanding of the gender dimensions of drought. The participation of women in decisions about how to best implement food security and nutrition programmes is critical to reducing the risks women and girls face in emergency situations (IASC 2005).

Payment made by governments as drought relief are often made to the head of the household which, more often than not, excludes women. This many times results in spending of money on destructive things like and domestic violence. Hence, 'head of household concept' should not be the criteria. Payments should be in joint accounts of married couples or in fixed deposit in the name of a women to avoid misuse. Female officers should also be nominated for disseminating clear information to both literate and illiterate women. Similarly, representation of women at other stages of drought mitigation should be ensured.

Last but not the least, unity and problem sharing among women, partaking the same difficulties and the same willingness to solve them, will surely go a long way in ameliorating the hardships women face during drought. Thus, drought mitigation strategy should include collective approach, rather than the individual one, through organising women into associations which can give them the power to exert much more impact through capacity building. Self help groups of women, reporting considerable success in the area of economic empowerment of women, are also examples of collective strength of local poor women. Such organisation of women and efforts at capacity building would pave the way for equal participation of men and women in drought mitigation.

To conclude, drought in Rajasthan is not an unexpected event and instead of deciding the action on the basis of urgency, prevention through preparedness can prove to be a powerful tool to mitigate it. Women should be active protagonists of this long-term strategy, as excluding them as interest groups bypasses half the population and part from augmenting the risks and hardships of women, it also limits the efficacy of the programmes and policies of drought management.

REFERENCES

Ariyabandu, M.M. and D. Foenseka (2006) : 'Do Disasters Discriminate?' in Duryog Nivaran (ed.), *South Asian Network for Disaster Mitigation : Tackling the Tides and Tremors,* South Asian Disaster Report, 2005, Islamabad.

Brenco, A.M. (2000) : '*Women of the Drought : Struggle and Visibility in Face of a Disaster Situation*', Joao Pessoa : Editora Universitaria.

Budak, B.D. and M. Kantar (2002) : 'Water Resources and Women', in Elkady Mona and Hamdy Atef (ed.) Proceedings of Workshop on *Gender and Water Resources Management in the Mediterranean 2002,* Cairo.

FAO (2002) : 'Women and Water Resources', www.fao.org. Inter-Agency Standing Committee (IASC) (2006) : *'Gender Handbook : Different Needs – Equal Opportunities',* Ochaonline.un.org.

Maskrey, A. (1989) : '*Disaster Mitigation : A Community Based Approach',* Oxford, Oxfam.

Quagliariello, R., Trisorio-Luizzi, and A Hamdy (2002): 'Gender Perspectives in Water Resources Management' in El Kady Mona and Hamdy Atef (ed.) Proceedings of workshop on *Gender and Water Resources Management in the Mediterranean-2002,* Cairo.

Qugliariello, R. (2006). '*Drought Mitigation and Gender Challenge in Social Approach to a Mediterranean Environmental Problem'.* Mediterranean Agronimic Institute of Barj CIHEAM, IAM-B, Italy.

Rogge, J (1992) : *'Research Agenda on Disaster Mitigation'*, Disaster Research Institute, University of Manitaba.

Rohr, Ulrike, Minu Hemmati and Yianna Lambron (2010) : 'Towards Gender Equality in Climate Change Policy : Challenges and Perspectives for the future in Elaine Enarson and P.G. Dhar Chakrabarti (ed.) *Women Gender and Disaster : Global Issues and Initiatives,* Sage, New Delhi.

United Nations Development Fund for Women (UNIFM) (2002-2003) : *Annual Report.*

UNISDR (2004) : *'Living with Risk : A Global Review of Disaster Reduction Initiatives'*, www.unisdr.org.

_____ (2005) : *'Hyogo Framework for Action 2005-2015 : Building the Resilience of Nations and Communities to Disasters'*, www.unisdr.org

Wiest, R.E., J.S.P. Mocellin and D.T. Motsisi (1994): *'The needs of Women in Disasters and Emergencies'*, report prepared for UNDP, www.radixonline.org.

Winchester, P. (1992) : *'Power, Choice and Vulnerability : A Case Study in Disaster Management in South India'*, James and James, London.

22

Natural Disasters in India and in Rajasthan

Dr. Mithlesh Gupta
Sr. Lecturer
BSR Govt. Arts College
Alwar (Raj.)

Diasters are extreme events and claim a large proportion of human and livestock life and cause huge demange to property throughout the world. Any natural hazard become disaster when it came in contact with vulnerals[1] i.e. social setting of human population & human settlements. Structures and centres of economic activity increase the damages caused by disasters. Poverty, population growth and environmental degradtion are the main cause of vulnerability of risk in natural disasters. Disasters be they natural or man made, are the real constraints to development and a threat to our environment.They undermine the developmental efforts and cause loss of life and scarce resources, reductionof productivity and environmental degradation, thus retarding growth. The frequency and severity of local and regional disasters have already reached the crisis level[2]. Environmental hazards may be defined as those extreme events either natural or main induced which exceed the tolerable magnitude with in or beyond certain

1. R.B. Singh ; Disaster management, Rawat publication Jaipur 2000 preface.
2. R.B. Singh , I-bid p. 1

time limit, make adjustment difficult result in catastrophic losses of property, income and lives and because the headlines of different news media at world level[1]. Hazards are generally taken to be the processes, both natural and anthropogenic, which cause an accident / extreme event or danger where as disaster is a sudden adverse an unfortunate extreme beings as well as plants and animals. We also say that environmental hazards are the processes whereas the environmental disasters are the results or responses of environmental hazards. Disasters are always viewed in terms of human being & its intensity is weighed in terms of quantum of damages done to the human society.

DISASTER

What is Disaster?

- It completely disrupts the normal day to day
- It negatively influences the emergency sys.
- Normal needs & processes like food, shelter, health etc. are affected and deteriorate.

Hazardous process always create extreme events but not all the extreme events become disasters. These may become disasters only when they adversely affect human society. For example - a very strong tropical cyclone (typhoon, hurricane or tarnado) becomes only extreme event when it occurs and dies in the midst of an ocean but it becomes disaster when it strikes the inhabited coastal area and inflicts colossal loss to human property and lives.

DISASTER - MAIN FEATURES

- Unpredicatability
- Unfamiliarity
- Speed
- Urgency
- Uncertainty

---

1. Savindra Singh, Environmental Geography ; Prayag Pustak Bhawan, Allahabad 1995. p. 355.

- Threat

Thus in simple terms we can define Disaster as a hazard causing heavy looss of life property and livelihood.

TYPES OF ENVIRONMENTAL HAZARDS AND DISASTERS

Environmental hazards and disasters are normally divided into two broad categories on the basis of main causative factors viz.[1]. NATURAL AND DISASTERS and[2]. MAN-IN-DUCED AND DISASTERS. Natural hazards are further sub divided into two categories as shown in the following charts.

In Short we can classify the two categories of Disaster in to further in the following way :

TYPE OF DISASTER

NAUTRAL DISASTER

MAJOR	*MINOR*
• Flood	• Cold Wave
• Cyclone	• Thunderstorm
• Draught	• Heat Wave
• Earthquake	• Mud slides
	• Storm

MANMADE DISASTER

MAJOR	*MINOR*
• Setting of fires	• Road/Train accident
• Epidemic	• Riots
• Deforestation	• Food Poisoning
• Pollution due to prawan cultivation	• Industrial Disaster/Crisis
• Chemical pollution	• Environmental
• Wars	• Pollution

1. R.B. Singh ; Op Cit P. 308
2. R.B. Singh ; I-bid P. 356

TUBULAR CLASSIFICATION OF ENVIRONMENTALDISASTERS

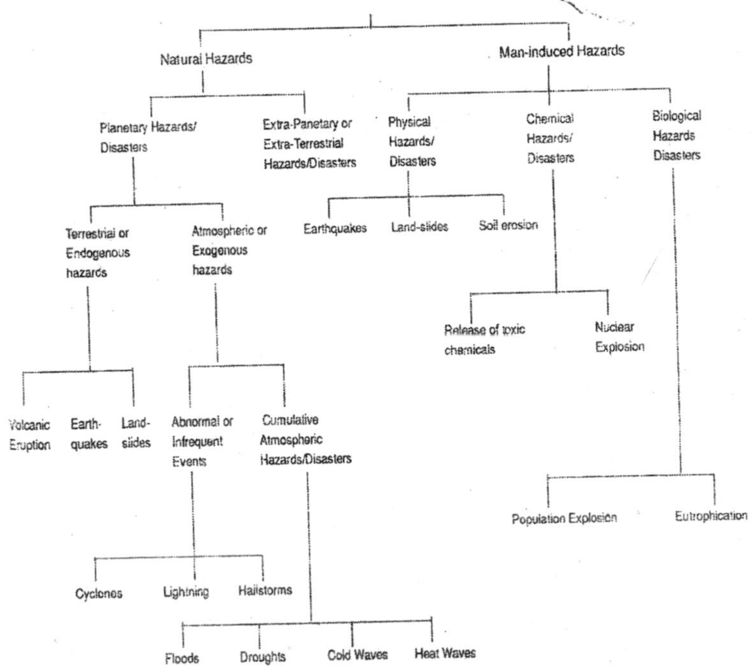

CUMALATIVE ATMOSPHERIC HAZARDS

Cumulative atmospheric hazards are those events which are caused due to cumulative effects of weather events which prolong for longer period of time ranging from a few weeks to several years depending upon the nature of weather events. For example, any hot day may not become disastrous or hazardous but when very hot and dry days prevail for a few weeks in continuation, environmental hazard in the form of heatwaves occurs which affect the environment and human lives, plants and animals. The persistence of exceptionally cold conditions for several days causes severe snowfall. A dry season a year may not be as much disastrous as continued dry season for several years.

1. Savinder Singh, Op Cit p. 357

Floods and Droughts

In Context of India and specially Rajasthan the well known disaster is droughts. Major area of Rajasthan is desert, due to this more than 50% area of Rajasthan is affected by droughts. While since last 5 years the flood is also occurring in several parts of Rajasthan like Jaislmer, Barmer & Jodhpur etc. heavy rainin a short span of time causes floods in desert areas. The villages & town there is no proper drainage system so water remain inside the town & situation becomes serious. Now a days in India general & Rajasthan in Special, highly intensive about earthquake and considered as a highly sensitive zone in Rajasthan like Jaipur, Alwar & Bharatpur. That's why I focussed upon floods drought & earthquake in this chapter.

Floods

Among the natural calamities[1], floods are the most devastating and their impact is too great. Widespread floods are responsible for changing the river course and the silting on the high fertile agricultural lands. Floods cause damage to human lives, properties, livestock and animal husbandry. Floods in the piedmount area are rare, but their frequency is more in the plains. They are more severe and devastating in the plains due to torrential rains, inherent vulnerability of land and deforestation.

India which is one of the disaster prone[2] countries of the world, is one of the best prepared for facing some of the disasters. Response to natural disaster has evolved over time indisaster affected states. The response to the challenge of natural disasters has come to address itself to preparedness to mitigating the impact and reducing the occurence to sustain development. Flood disaster in Haryana result in heavy economic losses apart from the loss of the human life and the hardship inflected on the survivors. Haryana is experiencing floods almost every year causing irreparable damage to life and property.

1. R.B. Singh, Op Cited Page 94
2. R.B. Singh, I bid p 308

Similarly in 2008 district Banswara of state Rajasthan also severaly affected by floods. It intensity was very high. Various villages were likely daminished. Water was lifted by pumps in this area. In this mouth floods affected Haryana, Punjab & Chandigarh where every day routine was disturbed. Flood cause immesne losses and destabilize the state economy, loss of life and property.

Flood simply means inundation of extensive land area with water for several days in continualtion. Generally, floods are considered to be associated with rivers and people conceive floods as the outcome of accumulation of huge volume of water coming out of the rivers through overtopping of river banks during peak discharge period. Infact, flood is an altribute of physical enviornment and thus is a component of hydrological cycle of a drainage basin. It may be pointed out that flood is a natural phenomenon and is response to rainfall but it becomes disaster when it causes colossal loss to human lives and property. It is also important to note that floods are also aggravated by human activities and thus flood hazards is both natural as well as man induced rather man-accentutated phenomenon.Floods are very often associated with alluvial rivers draining extensive alluvial and flood plains.

Causes of Floods

Since the floods of rivers or cloted water are the responses of both natural and anthropogenic factors, the causes of floods at the both types becomes highly complex and their relative importance varies from place to place, which pose a serious threat to human society and necessitate river regulation and flood controll the following causes may be held responsible for devastating floods of alluvial rivers.

1. Heavy rain fall for long period in continuation is the root cause of river floods because immense volume of water either through high intensity rainfall or large scale snow melt is the pre-requisite condition for floods.
2. Heavy spell of rainfall in arid and semi-arid areas where the rainfall is scant, low in infrequent causes flash floods because such areas have poor natural drainage systems and

existing rivers and streams are unable to accomodate enormous volume of water caused due to huge volume of runoff resulting from high intensity rainfall during occasional rain storms.

3. Highly sinuous and meandering courses of the rivers, obstruct the normal discharge of water and thus the velocity is reduced, which delays the passage of water resulting into stagnation of water consequently, the mandering valleys are immediately over flown and meander belts and loops are flooded.
4. Large scale deforestation in the upper catchments is perhaps the most important anthropogenic factors of the causes of the river flood.
5. Increasing urbanization also helps in increasing the surface run off and therefore, dimension and magnitude of floods because extension in the pucca ground cover through the construction of building, courtyards, roads, pavements etc. reduces infiltration of rain water significant and increases surface run off considerably which increases the volume and discharge of storm drains of urban areas (Similar situation in Rajasthan now a days).
6. Blocking of natural flow of the rivers by landsides caused by earthquakes, other natural factors and anthropogeneic factors and clearance of such blockades causes sudden severe flash floods in the downstream section of the rivers.
7. In India valley side slopes of alluvial rivers are ploughed down to the channel transverse to the channel or say transverse to the contours (in order to dry out the moisture accumulated due to alluviation during flood) during rabi season (Winter cropping season) and the farms are never irrigated.

Lastly, it may be pointed out that floods are not always hazards rather these are also booms because these bring rich fertile alluvial soils each time and thus increase agirucltural productivity.

Floods are a great hazard to life. The National Commission on Floods points out that during the period 1953-78 (25 years) on an average about 8.2 million hectares of area were affected by floods every year, of which 3.5 million hectares or about 43 percent were crop lands. During the floods of 1976 to 1978, over 17 million hectares of land per annum were damaged and the trend is that the total area as well as the cropped area ffected, have increased in recent years. There could be several reasons for the increase in the area affected in recent years despite the protection measures undertaken. There is not enough evidence to show any change in the meteorological conditions. There is also no discernible trend in peak discahrge onsites on the Ganga river. The reasons are :

1. Deforestation which has facilitated quicker and increasing run off of river water.
2. Development activities like expansion of rail and road network.
3. Establishment of irrigation system and embankments have aggravated the drainage problem.
4. Breaches in the embankments.
5. Assam, Bihar and Bengal have reported a rise in the beds of some of their rivers.

Floods Cause Havoc in Drought-prone Barmer, Rajasthan

Flood waters had a similar colour this time as well, but that was only initially. Heavy rains diluted the red colour derived from red stones in Jaisalmer, subsequently. Kawas and Maluva were the worst hit by the floods. Houses here are still 15 feet (about 4.5 metres) deep in water.

Ironically, the region's rich gypsum deposits have become a curse for it. The authorities are now discussing option to drain out the floodwater. These include breaking the gypsum layer and boring into the earth. But, environmentalists oppose this option : it will contaminate groundwater and affect reservoirs in the region, they fear. Authorities also have another proposal on their anivl : diverting the water to other areas, either through canals or by pumping it out. Whatever the option, it will take at least a monthy to dran out the floodwater, authorities say.

Barmer has become the focus of attention for scientists, environmentalists and ecologists across the world. And not all of them have bad news. Many environmentalists feel that the terrible costs notwithstanding, the floods could be a boon for the region. Floodwaters might increasethe region's groundwater level in long run, they feel. Oil companies operating in the region aren't too unhappy either. Experts believe when floodwater seeps down, it will force oil to move up.

But that's the future. Despite heavy rains and floods, Barmer is thirsty and will remain so for sometime, say experts.

There's a popular saying in Western Rajasthan : Jannkhiyon laare meh. Loosely translated, it means a good rain always follows dust storms. This summer when Rajasthan's Jaisalmer and Barmer districts witnessed dust storms, people thought it augured relief after six years of drought. The rains did come but the boon fast became a bane. Barmer was deluged with 750mm of rainfall in the last week of August ; five times the district's average annual rainfall. Floods also ravaged arid Gujarat, and neighbouring Maharashtra, while usually-wet Assam reeled under droughts, causing many experts to argue that climate is changing.

"Extreme weather events occur in cycles. But worldwide, the frequency of such extreme events is increasing because of climate change," says environmentalist Anupam Mishra. Similarly, in July 2003, UN's World Meterological Organization had warned of an increase in frequency of extreme weather events becuase of climate change.

The deluge in Rajasthan was cuased by a low perssure zone over the area, itself a result of extreme heat conditions, experts note. Low pressure area in deserts that results from extreme heat is referred to as 'thermal low' in meterological parlance. Such conditions could be caused by global warming, experts reason. "The thermal low caused southwest monsoons to bring rain over Barmer and Jaisalmer," says Rajeevan M Nair, director of National Climate Centre, Pune.

Another school of thought ascribes the exceptional rainfall to Rajasthan's usual weather cycle : a good monsoon usually follows three or four years of drought, but there is excessive rainfall and flooding, once in 75-100 years.

Barmer received 720mm of rainfall in 1990 and in 1994, 600 mm rain fall over the district. But such inordinate rainfall was spread over a year. This time, the downpour was a weeklong affair and was compounded by rainwater flow from neighbouring Jaisalmer. Elderly people in Barmer say that rainwater took the drainage route of rivers that once passed districts Rohali and Nimbala. These now extinct rivers originated in the Jinjhiniali region in Jaisalmer, merged in Luni River before entering Barmer, and finally disappeared into the Rann of Kachchh in Gujarat, they say. Water gushing down the Rohali-Bimbala route drowned Kawas town and village en route, the villagers maintain. Rainwater from Jaisalmer also took the drainage path or the extinct rivers, Leek and Sheepasaria - they add. Water that came along this path caused havoc in Maluva village[1].

Sometimes it is pointed out that floods are a blessing in disguise, as they renew the soil silt and making the soil highly productive. the fallacy in the argument is that while it ignores the colossal loss of life and property, it gives wrong signals as it fails to compare the flood affected area with non-flood affected areas. There is a sense of insecurity caused by the recurrence of floods and farmers do not make long term investments. As a result, agriculture in flood prone areas continues to be backward.

Suggestion, Control measures for flood

1. Wherever feasible, is among the most effective measures for the control of floods. The multipurpose projects on the Damodar, the Mahanadi and the Kosi, which are the most destructive rivers in the country, provide substantial protection from floods in the areas they have been devastating.

---

1. Internet

2. In order to tackle the flood disaster, one should look for the basis causes which lead to these disaster. Very often incessant rain-fall for a number of days lead to flash floods,but watershed management can lead to flood moderation. According to FAO, a dense vegetation canopy provided by a combination of a complete overstorey of mature forest trees and an understorey of mature forest trees and anunderstorey of herbaceous species is capacble of intercepting more than 12 mm of rain from each storm, and soil erosion becomes insignificant. It is recognized that well managed watershed in the basin and sub basin will go a long way in moderating low to medium floods and silt charge.
3. It is an acknowledged fact that reservoirs are time honoured, long term measures for flood moderation and to prolong their life soil conservation measures have to be universally adopted.
4. However, under tropical monsoon conditions, there is a paucity of adequate and refined data on Stream flow and silt discharge as influenced by watershed management, and there is need for intensive hydrological studies in experimental watersheds by the agricultural and forestry research organizations.
5. It should be pointed out that small and large reservoirs along the course of rivers and their tributaries have been universally accepted as an important measure for a long time solution.
6. The National Commission on Agriculture has strongly recommended intensification of soil conservation and watershed management in the catchment of river valley projects and emphasized that all the watershed management plans should be completed without delay.
7. In view of the role of forests in mitigating the floods, a systematic inventory of the forest cover complex is of the highest importance. This will help planning of meaningful

watershed management programme.The step in which geographers can play a vital role is to update mapping of land uses and ocver complexes in the upper catchment of flood prone rivers.

8. At the critical areas should be delineated on the basis of this map for planning of watershed management; a massive programme of afforestation in the catchments should be undertaken in order to provide vegetation cover on marginal and wasteland, and at the same time efforts should be made to declare more forest areas as reserve forests.

Drought : Second Major Disaster

The crop production in India is greatly conditoned by climate variability the occurence of drought episdoe often leads to pantial or complete failure or crops resulting in scarcity or famine conditions. Agriculture remains to be the mainstay of our vast farming community in particular and national economy in general. Hence amongst a few most devastating natural disasters that could be fall our great country is the occurrence of widespread drought[1] in addition each drought episode is unique in its magnitude and metion, and thus its impacts also differ. These uncertainities increase the difficulties for effective drought management and development of appropriate crop management strategies for minimising the severity of the drought impacts.

As the south west monsoon swetp across India with less thanits usual force, many states face a gloomy harvest and a year of food shortages and drought. Punjab, Haryana, Rajasthan, Uttar Pradesh, madhya Pradesh, Chattisgarh and Uttaranchal in the north and Karnataka, Andhra Pradesh and Tamilnadu are facing major crises. Twelve meteorological districts in the country have been hit by poor monsoon this year. Expected to start around mid-June and continue until September, the monsoon has been intermittent, with heavy rains around the north-east resulting in floods in two States

1. Tapeshwar Singh, Drought Disaster and Agricultural Development in India, peopl's publishing house, Preface 1995.

Bihar and Assam, while the north and north west have been relatively dry causing widespread crop damage and economic loss.

Rajasthan is one of the worst affected states. Drought has loomed in all the 32 districts with a deficit rainfall of 53.4%. There are areas where people have not experienced even one proper shower during the whole monsoon period. This is the fifth continuous drought in the state. Approximately 40 million people and 50 million cattle have been affected this year alone. The water table is going down, wells and handpumps have gone dry. Livestock have started dying of hunger and thirst.People have started abandoning their cattle after praying to god for their lives. Migration to cities and other states is up. Social structures in villages have suffered. Weddings have been postponed indefinitely. There is a dreary stillness in the air. Sometimes, it also becomes very difficult for the scientists, politicians, drought planners, and state and central governments to give concise view of drought, because there are significant differences in its preceptions nd social, political and physical implications.

Drought has been a signle major factor affecting economy growht of our country as evidenced by the recent economic history of India. Occurance of drought episode causes a severe setback to economy by seriously hitting agiruclture, which continues to be the main stay of our farming community in particular and national economy in general. The single most difficult task for a representative democracy is to engage in long range planning. In short, government of our type seems doomed to lead in existence that abhors long range planning. The most striking example of this is the drought scenario. Amongst a few most devastating natural hazards that could be fall our beautiful state is a wide spread drought. Perceptions of drought changes with the change of disciplined, for example economist perception of drought is some thing different their the botanist and sreiologist's perception. Drought had different connotations with differing objectives too. The time and space scale of drought limit the stress it can place upon us and the damages it can do. Because India is still a country of agrarian society. Drought are more deadly natural environmental hazards because these are directly related to tone of the three basic requirements of any form of life (such as water, air and food) that is water and are indirectly related to food because crops and other plants and animals exclusively depend upon water. Drought resulting from accumulative effects of water scarcity cause extensive and enormous damage to agriculture and natural vegetation and therefore cause famine and starvation of human and animal population of the regions concerned the meaning and definition of drought are diffciutl propostion[1] because there are much variations in region to another and from are group of people to another. Most people are reasonably well aware when a drought situation exist, but it is very dificult to find an overall acceptable definition of drought. It clearly involve a shortage of water, but can really be defined only in terms of a particular need. The most common view of drought is of rain fall deficiency, but the links between rainfall and the water which becomes available to meet a demands are complex. Therefore, definition of a drought relates not only to water needs but also to the complex set of factors involved to supply that need through the hydrological cycle.[2]

Droughts[3] occurs in hight as well as low rain falls area. It is a condition relative to same long term average condition of balance between rainfall and evaportranspiration in a particular area, a condition always percieved as "normal", yet average rainfall does not provide an adequate statistical measure of rainfall characterstics in a given region, especially in the day areas. According to Hobbs[4] the agriculturist or pastoralist, especially in the differ regions, has assessed the nature of local rain fall and through years of long and same times bitter experience, has learned to adapt his operations to the rain fall characterstics of the area. In other words, drought is related to be failure of the usual rains at a particular time, since,

1. Ibid., Op. Cit preface.
2. Hobbs, J.E., Applied Climatology, Butter worths, Lonon 1980.
3. Tapeshwar Singh ; I-bid Page 3.
4. Hobbs, J.E., Op Cit.

most activities using water will be geared to that whichis normally available.

Definition of Drought

Drought is a "Creeping phenomenan"[1] making an accurate prediction of either its onset or end is a difficult task. To most observers, it seems to start with a delay in the timing (or a failure) of the rains. Other suggest that it can be identified only in restrospect. Scoras of definition of drought are developed by a variety of disciplines, because it affects so many economic and social respects. Generally drought is viewed as of meteorological origin. Drought results from large continued dry weather of lack or in sufficiency of rainfall which causes exhaustation of social moisture, suffering of plants from lack of water, depletion of underground water, supply and reductionand eventual cessation of stream flow. Though, drought has been defined variously, it is generally understood as the period of causing moisture stress to the plant due to lack of rain. Definition of drought might be categoried as either conceptual or operationa with conceputal reffering to those definitions formulated in general terms to identify the boundaries of the concept of drought. The American Heritage dictionary[2] defined drought as "a long period with no rain, especially druing a planting season".

According to Random house dictionary[3] as extended period of dry weather, especially are in Jurious to crops". Operational definitions can also be used to analyse drought frequency, severity and duration for a given historical period as for example daily, monthly or seasonal moisture deficiency or yield departure from normal i.e. expected in order to identify when drought occurred.

---

1. Gillette : H.P., A creeping dorurhgt under way. Water and Sewage Works, March 1950 pp. 104-105.
2. American Heritage Dictionary ; Drught Houghton, Millon, Boston, 1976.
3. Random House Dictionary ; Drought, Random House. 1969.

Meteorological definitions of drought are the most prevalent. They often define drought solely on the basis of the degree of dryness and the duration of the dry period. Thus drought is a rainless situation for an extended period during which some precipitation should have been normally received, depending upon the geographical locations of place and season of the year. In other words period of more than some particular number of days with precipitation less than some specified small amount, socioeconomic drought define[1] it as express features of the socio economic effects of drought can also incorporate features of meteorological agricultural and hydrological drought. They are usually associated with the supply and demand of some economic good.

Thornthwaite[2] has also defined rought as a period of dyness of weather or climate as affects the earth or prevents the growth of plants same other investigators an drought consider thatthe water needs for established human activities in an essential criterion for drought condition.

Impact of Drought

Droughts affect all type of life from in the biospheric ecosystem because both plants and animals directly depend on water. Any shortage of water supply adversely affects them. They the impacts of prolonged droughts include ecological, economic, demographic and political aspects : Prolonged drought conditions in a given region change the biotic component of the nautral ecosystem because , some species of plants and animals perish as they cannot with stand extreme drought conditions. Other if impacts are as follow :

---

1. Kifter, R.S., and H.L. Stewart ; farming hazards in the drought area works progress adminsitration, Monograph XVI, Washington, D.C. 1938.
2. Heathcote, R.L. ; Drought in South Australia in G.P. White, ed. Natural Hazards ; Local, National, Global, Oxford, New York, 1974. p. 129.

Drinking Water

Dry ponds, wells and handpumps are making life miserable for the poor sector of society. About 30% of the handpumps have gone dry. Women have to walk long distances to fetch water. Western Rajasthan is vulnerable in terms of all the scarcities. Water rates have gone up. Tanker tractors are charging extremely high prices. One tanker tractor of 1000 liters costs from Rs. 200 to 500 depending on location and distance. According to Additional Relief Secretary Mr. Karni Singh Rathore, about 26,000 villages will face problems from the drinking water crisis.

PHED has a contingency plant of Rs. 518 crore. Overall 30,000 works of renovating traditional water harvesting structures have been identified under relief works. 3400 new handpumps and 1205 tube wells will also be bored. 1500 tanker tractors are supplying water in 1100 villages. Of the western state districts, the most severely affected is a Pali.

Fodder and Livestock

Most of the reports from District Collectors on the drought situation have prioritized fodder as the main concern. With nearly no agriculture, there is now a situation of fodder deficiency all over the state. Western Rajasthan districts are more affected. Because the drought is regional, neighbouring states like Punjab and Haryana, which used to supply fodder in normal years, are themselves facing similar worries this year. The scarcity in other states is not of great intensity as it is their first or second year of drought and they still have some buffer stocks of fodder, but not to supply other states. There is some fodder in Hanumangarh and Ganganagar districts, which other districts are procuring. There is a steep hike in fodder price - 40 Kg now costs Rs. 180 to 200 and this has led many into debt. Much of the available fodder is contaminated with high levels (upto 25%) of mud.

Due to the non-availability of water and fodder people have started abandoning their unproductive cattle, putting a mark on their foreheads in a last pryaer under open skies. There are reports of animals dying of hunger and thirst. Animal carcasses can be found in the countrysides. Many people have started migrating to other states with their animals. In some instances, neighbouring states are obstructing this migration. Nearly 50% of the livestock could be lost.

The government has plans to open 3000 fodder depots. Many of them have been opened in western districts, but many have no fodder. The government has asked NGOs to open fodder depots and cattle camps but the delay of payments [and in some cases, non-payments] by the governments has demotivated NGOs to open these camps.

Employment

Looking around the daily wage labourers mrkets in the cities, one can easily find people from villages looking for somebody to provide them with work. Around the same time in past years, it has been difficult to find laburers, but now they are in huge numbers quarreling with each other to be hired. These people are migrants from other parts of Rajasthan. The labour wages have gone down sharply (s. 40 per person per day), whereas according to Government regulations the minimum wage for a person per day is Rs. 60 Nearly 10 million families in Rajasthan are affected because of drought this year. The worst affected are landless agricultural labourers for whom relief works are the only hope.

Consequence of Droughts

1 Some species of plants and animals perish as they cannot withstand extreme drought conditions.

2. Some animals migrate to other places and hence there is marked decrease in the population of certain animal species.

3. Some aniamls die of hugner and starvation.

4. There is stiff competition for food due to scare, city created by drought among the animals which results in the elimination of weeker animals.

Other consequences of the droughts are -

1. *Desertification* -Continuous increasing the area of

Rajasthan generally in whole world & nation & particularly in the Rajasthan.

2. *Deforestation* - Continuously shinking area of forest affect the number of plants & thus reduced the size of forest.
3. *Green house effect* - Due to the increase of temperature which directly affect the earth atmosphere which constantly going on warming. Bryson suggested that increasing atmospheric turbidity and green house warming both of which are probably attributed toman, might be implicated as cause of many drought. Both these effects tend to cause the zone of sub tropical high pressure (anticyclone) to move equaterward

Suggestion for Drought Control

1. To increase the amount of precipitation, to increase the rate of infiltration of rain water.
2. To introduce the dry farming techniques to reduce the dpeendence of farming on rain water.
3. Checking of desertification or desert spread.
4. Introduction of water conservation schemes.
5. Development of horticulare and pastures, ravitalization of drought prone area programmes (DPAP).
6. Construction of water drainage, reservoirs, digging of wall etc.

Earthquakes : Third Major Disaster

Earthquakes have an odd position in the file of disaster studies. They are deadliest disaster inthe 1970's[1]. They killed 38,970 people per year, earthquakes are result from movement of one rock mass past, another in response to tectonic forces. Rock is elastic and can accumulate strain where adjacent area of rock are subjected to forces pushing or pulling them. When the stress exceeds the

---

1. L.R. Reddy, The pain and horror Gujrat Earthquke A.P.H. Publication.

strength of the rock, the rock breaks along a pre existing or new fracture plane called a fault. The rupture extends outwards along the fault plane from its point of origin or focus.

Earthquakes occurs[1] when the plates of the earth's crust run into each other or slide past each other, most earthquakes occur along the edge of the occanic and continental plates. When the tectonic plates below the earth's surface shift on earthquake occurs. When the shift happens it causes a tremor on the surface.

An earthquake is a major demonstration of the power of the tectonic forces caused by endogenetic thermal conditions of the interior of the earth. 'Definition - An E.Q. is a motion of the ground surface, ranging from a faint tremor to a wild motion capable of shaking buildings apart and causing gaping fissures to open in the ground[2].

In other words the E.Q. is a form of energy of ware motion transmitted through the surface buyer of the earth in widening circles from a point of sudden energy release the focus[3] earthquakes are caused due to rapid movement of tectonic plates. Tectonic plates always keeps moving when movement is noticeable, it is called earthquake.

The earth's eraist is made upto 2 separate tectonic plates. These plates move more and drift at very slow rates of just a couple of inches a year. As the plates move, they grind the scrape against each other, causing earth quakes that can range from mild tremors to major quakes. The magnitude or intensity of energy released by an earthquake is measured by RICHTER SCALE devised by Charles F. Richter in 1935. The number indicating magnitude or intensity (M) or Richter scale ranges between 0 and 9 but infect the scale has no upper limit of number because it as a logarithmic scale.

The seismic is emitted from the rupture as seismic waves. The fastest are the primary (or P) waves, also called compressional

1. Internet
2. Savinder Singh P. 360
3. A.N. Strahler and A.H. Strahler 1976.

waves, which one compression adiation waves and travel in average crystal rocks at a about 5 km per second. The secondary or(S) waves, which are slower, are shear waves with a speed in the crust of about 3 km per second. The slowest waves are surface waves called Rayleigh and love waves whose depths of penetration are dependent an their wave lengths. The severity of ground shaking increases as magnitude increases and decreases as distance from the epicentre increases. Building vibrate as a consequence of the ground shaking ; damage takes place if the building cannot with stand these vibrations. Compress ional Waves (P Waves) and Shear waves (S Waves) mainly cause high frequency vibrations (greater than 1 hertz) which are more efficient then low frequency waves in causing, low building to vibrate.

Effects of Earthquqkes

The effect may be restated that the intensity of the earthquakes and their hazardous impacts are determined not on the basis of the magnitude of seismic intensity as determined by Richter or MERCALLI scales but are decided on the basis of quantum of damage done by a specific earthquake to human lives & property. Major effects are as follow :

1. Slope instability and failures and land slide.
2. Damages to human structure
3. Damages to the towns & cities.
4. Loss of human lives and property.

Furthermore, when a catastrophe is due to a combination of various natural forces and elements, one event may not only 'open the door' to the following, but may make the latter more destructive.

Examples of the most common chains of disastrous events triggered by an earthquake are as follows :

Earthquake	landslide	flood;
Earthquake	fire	conflagration
Earthquake	contamination of potable water	disease epidemics;
Earthquake	tsunami	floods on distant coasts

Suggestions to Prevent the Earthqukes

Earthquake damage varies not only with the magnitude, location and depth of the shock but also, amongst other things, with the type of construction and the various actions taken or foregone by the affected people. For the purpose of social analysis, the treatment of earthquakes as hazard, rather than simply as a natural prevent, has a particularly important implication. Preventive tool against earthquake are as follows :

1. To decrease the level of potential risk.
2. To mitigate the consequences of destructive events.
3. To mitigate or prevent the development of a chain of disastrous events.
4. To facilitate and to hasten rehabilitation and reconstruction.
5. To localize and limit the scope of catastrophes.
6. To avoid the concentration of population and of economic activities in one or in very few sports.
7. Location of new cities and towns in areas of lowest possible risk (zones of lower earthquake probability).
8. Limitation of the expansion of existing settlements located in high risk zones.

To avoid of the location of new manufacturing plants and water houses in high risk zones.

REFERENCES

1. Singh R.B., Disaster Management, Rawat Publication, Jaipur 2000.
2. Singh Savinder, Environment Geography ; Prayag Pustak Bhawan, Allahabad, 1995.
3. Singh, Tapeshwar, Drought disaster and agricultural development in India, people's publishing house, Preface.
4. Hobbs J.F., Applied Climatology, Butter Worths, London, 1980.
5. Gillette ; H.P. ; A Creeping drought underway. Water and Sewage Work, March 1950.

6. American Heritage Dictionary.
7. Random House Dictionary
8. Kifter R.S. ; and Stewar, H.L ; farming hazards in the drought area works progress administration, Monograph XVI, Washington D.C. 1938.
9. Heathcote; R.L. ; Drought in South Australia in G.P. White ed. Natural Hazards ; Local National, Global, Oxford, New York, 1974.
10. Reddy, L.R., the pain and Horror, 'Gujrat Earth Quake' A.P.H. Publishing Corporation, Delhi 2001.
11. Strahler, A.H., Arid Strahler A.H. : 1976.